The Sustainability Mirage

The Sustainability Mirage

Illusion and Reality in the Coming War on Climate Change

John Foster

publishing for a sustainable future

London • Sterling, VA

First published by Earthscan in the UK and USA in 2008

ISBN 978-1-84407-534-8 hardback
    978-1-84407-535-5 paperback

Typeset by Domex e-Data, India
Printed and bound in the UK by TJ International, Padstow
Cover design by Rob Watts

For a full list of publications please contact:

Earthscan
Dunstan House
14a St Cross Street
London EC1N 8XA, UK
Tel: +44 (0)20 7841 1930
Fax: +44 (0)20 7242 1474
Email: earthinfo@earthscan.co.uk
Web: **www.earthscan.co.uk**

22883 Quicksilver Drive, Sterling, VA 20166-2012, USA

Earthscan publishes in association with the International Institute
for Environment and Development

A catalogue record for this book is available from the British Library

Library of Congress Cataloging-in-Publication Data

Foster, John (John Michael), 1949–
  The sustainability mirage : illusion and reality in the coming war on climate change /
John Foster
    p. cm.
  Includes bibliographical references.
  ISBN 978-1-84407-534-8 (hbk.) -- ISBN 978-1-84407-535-5 (pbk.) 1. Sustainable
development. I. Title.
  HC79.E5F675 2008
  338.9'27--dc22
                              2008028487

The paper used for this book is FSC-certified.
FSC (the Forest Stewardship Council) is an
international network to promote responsible
management of the world's forests.

Mixed Sources
Product group from well-managed
forests and other controlled sources
www.fsc.org Cert no. SGS-COC-2482
© 1996 Forest Stewardship Council

Contents

Acknowledgements

As will be clear from the Preface, this is not meant to be an academic book. But it couldn't have been written without the academy – in particular, without the Centre for the Study of Environmental Change at Lancaster University, of which I was privileged to be a member between 1992 and 2001. I owe a great deal to all my colleagues there during that period, most notably to Bron Szerszynski, Brian Wynne and – especially – Robin Grove-White.

Some of our research involved collaboration with the Lancaster Philosophy department, through which I learnt much from Alan Holland and John O'Neill, among others. I was also lucky enough to find my way into contact with the Centre for Research in Education and the Environment at the University of Bath, where the work of Steve Gough and Bill Scott has provided me with a continuing stimulus.

Universities are of course academic institutions in more than one sense, and I should also record my debt to the committee of senior managers at Lancaster who decided that, after a year of sweating blood to create a merger which saved the Centre and Philosophy Department from extinction, I had carelessly reorganized myself out of a job. Without this wholly unexpected gift of leisure, I should probably never have made a start on the book. Thanks of a different order are due to successive Heads of the merged Institute, and later of the preserved Philosophy Department – particularly David Archard and Mairi Levitt – for encouraging me to stay associated as a freelance. Enjoying many of the advantages while avoiding all of the drawbacks of affiliation to a modern university has been invaluable for this kind of writing.

Thanks in this connection to my daughter Clare, for prompting me to reinvent myself as a freelance philosophy teacher, and to Myfanwy Williams for much aid and comradeship in the process.

I have had helpful comments on various drafts at various stages from Andrew Dobson, Robin Grove-White, Alan Rayner, Bill Scott, Stephen Sterling, Garrath Williams, Myfanwy Williams and two anonymous reviewers for Earthscan. None of them is responsible for the many deficiencies which remain.

At Earthscan itself, I must thank my editor Rob West, for commissioning the book and for his tactful professionalism in helping me learn (however partially) how to write it. I also owe him the suggestion for the main title, which suddenly made so much of what I was on about clear to me.

A good many of my chapter drafts were roughed out by candlelight in a remote Welsh cottage – a marvellously peaceful place in which to think and write, but lacking electricity, mains water and indoor sanitation. Luckily, these are *not* the conditions to which we must all resign ourselves if we are to take the climate war seriously, but it does help sometimes to experience them. Thanks to Fiona McLeod for long friendship, wisdom and the frequent loan of this saving retreat.

And above all, thanks to my family – to my mother and the memory of my father, for crucial help at crucial times; and to my sons Paul and Richard, as well as their sister, for tolerating a parent too preoccupied for too long.

The dedication to my wife Rose records a debt too deep to put into words – though the whole book is one way of trying.

A Note on Notes

Although indulging myself in the very occasional footnote, I have not included references in the body of the text. The practice of breaking up continuous prose with bracketed citations or lots of little superscript numbers has always seemed to me a nuisance. Do you check the bibliography, or look up the note, or not – or later? Even pausing momentarily to think about it distracts you from the flow of the argument. You are often being put in this position merely by the author's nervousness of venturing anything substantive, anything personal by way of emphasis or interpretation, without covering his or her back. But this is a very bad habit for writers to acquire, as well as an annoyance to readers. Books should stand up for, and by, themselves.

This is not, of course, to deny – still less attempt to conceal – my own large indebtedness to other people who have written on these issues. Where I have quoted or referred to somebody, or have consciously drawn on somebody else's work, there will be found by those interested a bibliographical or contextual note at the end of the book. These notes are identified to the chapters, and within these to the pages and parts of the text to which they relate.

Preface

Sustainability, Mirage and Reality

A mirage is a twist in the light. We see what is real, but we see it in a misleading place and perspective. This is a very particular kind of illusion. It is neither hallucination, an appearance which corresponds to nothing objective at all, nor a distorted image of some object which, if we saw it undistorted, would look different in itself. The classic case of mirage is the desert landscape across which we see the sky – but with the refractive effect of hot desert air locating part of the image below rather than above the far horizon. Naturally enough, since seeing is always interpreting, the observer will take this for distant water reflecting the sky. If thirsty travellers fail to recognize the phenomenon, the appearance of water may draw them out of their way – and, receding before them as they advance, betray them to a barren reckoning.

What has this to do with sustainability? It is an image for a radical mistake which we are now, as a society, in danger of making over that vitally important idea.

But this is, in turn, a very particular kind of mistake, and I want to be clear at the outset about what I am *not* saying. I am certainly not denying the importance of sustainability. It is, indeed, literally vital. Recognizing the ecological, and therefore the social and economic, unsustainability of our current way of life – not just in the advanced post-industrial societies, but worldwide – has been by far the most significant achievement of political thought over the last half-century. Correspondingly, the need to find alternative ways of providing for ourselves which do not jeopardize human and other life on Earth is unavoidable, and now extremely pressing.

Nothing that I argue in this book is intended to impugn the force of those claims or diminish their urgency. I do not contend that they are either scientifically unfounded or ideologically suspect. Nor, it should probably be added up front, am I being paid by any consortium, firm, lobby, stakeholder or interest group – or indeed by anyone at all – to make my case. This is emphatically not one more contrarian attempt to dismiss the sustainability agenda as wildly over-hyped, something we need not really worry about which has been foisted on us by hysterical environmentalists or covert enemies of our capitalist freedoms. Consider the increasingly dominant, indeed overriding, issue of climate change. The scientific consensus is now telling us with more-or-less one voice that unless atmospheric CO_2 equivalent is kept from rising above something between 450 and

550 parts per million by around the year 2050, we will be unable to hold the now-inevitable increase in background global average temperature within the 2°C which is regarded as just about manageable for human civilization in anything like its present form. Should the increase exceed that level, the chances of a runaway further increase driven by positive feedback effects rise dramatically. And at only a few degrees higher in average terms, the consequences for the environment, and thus for humanity, would be disastrous: flooding, drought, disease and famine on a worldwide scale hitherto unknown and barely imaginable. There could be no more urgent sustainability concern than this.

I am so far from dismissing these horrors, indeed, that I have called our active engagement in preventing them 'the climate war'. This comparison, uncomfortable as many will find it, seems apt as no other could be to the challenge and the response from all of us for which it calls. The worldwide effects of global warming have been authoritatively likened to a slow-motion nuclear holocaust. Resisting this order of threat, if it were posed by some rogue regime or (in the classic sci-fi scenario) by malevolent aliens circling our planet, would certainly justify war. But neither even of those analogies is adequate, since this is a war of a quite unprecedented kind: the enemy being not external and elsewhere, but ourselves.

Put like that, the situation can sound terribly daunting. Human beings have never faced a requirement of remotely this order – to use their foresight and their capacities for cooperation, across the whole globe, in a process of common action through which wisdom and responsibility triumph over ignorance, passion and selfishness. On the other hand, one has to go on believing that there are grounds for refusing to be daunted. The reach and vividness of modern global communication is also staggeringly unprecedented. Unfolding events and prospects can be brought home to people worldwide, through their televisions and computers, with a compelling immediacy and a strength of supporting analysis never before achievable. Moreover, although one can forget the fact in frustration at the multiple present problems, the means and agencies of global common action are also, in historical terms, such as humanity has never previously possessed. Providing enough people wake up to it in time, the climate war which is now declaring itself is perilous, but not utterly hopeless.

But what do people have to wake up to feeling and doing? How is society to respond to the information that carbon emissions must be urgently and dramatically cut, and that there remain about fifteen years, at best twenty, in which to do it? What *kind* of motivation to what *form* of action is at issue? These are the questions which I am intent on raising in this book.

The sustainability imperative, like what is mislocated in any mirage, is firmly real. But that is just the point: although it is real, we are in danger of mistaking *where* and *how* it is real. This danger stems from the way in which a particular model of the issues and how to deal with them has risen with such startling rapidity to dominate thinking about them worldwide. This is the model or paradigm of *sustainable development*.

The swiftness with which this model has come (in historical terms) out of nowhere is actually quite easy to forget. I try to keep myself reminded of it by recalling, now and then, an incident from the early 1980s. I was a parliamentary candidate for the Ecology Party, as Britain's Greens then quaintly called themselves, in a suburban London constituency, and we had arranged to hold the adoption meeting in the municipal library. Turning up on the appointed evening (we were too innocent, as well as too overstretched, to have checked out the venue beforehand), we found that we had been allocated the library's junior section. Though easily large enough for our expected audience, it was also festooned with big cardboard cut-outs of interesting birds and beasts, dangling cheerfully at adult head-height from strings criss-crossing the room. I tackled the caretaker: might these decorations possibly be removed for the occasion? He gave me a look in which I could not detect the gleam of irony, and said, 'But that's what you lot are all about, isn't it – furry animals?'

He couldn't have said that now. Greens have been elected, in the intervening quarter-century, to a wide range of local, national and international bodies – and the influence of their ideas has far outrun the numbers of these representatives. Established parties have taken many of their themes on board, national strategies proliferate, the European Union has been trying to put meaningful regulatory regimes in place and world leaders assemble periodically to discuss further progress. And all this advance from the margins into the mainstream, in a mere quarter-century, has been achieved under the banner of 'sustainable development', essentially as defined by the Brundtland Commission: that is, the idea that the pursuit of economic wellbeing in the present shouldn't compromise the conditions for its continuing pursuit in the future.

I trace the history of this process, though in only a bit more detail, in Chapter 1. But what could be the objection to it? What could be wrong with this approach, and what more promising alternative could there be?

That is what the book is all about, and it would be idle to try summarizing the whole case here. But I owe the intending reader at least a pointer. Helpfully to hand comes a recent newspaper piece by the distinguished environmental economist Paul Ekins. In this article, Ekins scorchingly exposes what he calls the 'Alice-in-Wonderland economics' informing government cost–benefit calculations around the proposed airport expansion at London's Heathrow. These calculations purport to show the expansion yielding a net annual benefit of nearly £6 billion – but they only do so because of how the costs of emitting 180 million extra tons of CO_2 between 2020 and 2080 are arrived at. These costs are calculated using a 'shadow price of carbon' – the estimated costs of damage from the associated climate change – of £15.50 per ton of CO_2. But that damage-cost estimate in its turn depends on the assumption that the world will be able to hold its atmospheric CO_2 concentration to a pretty challenging 550 parts per million (which will need emissions across the whole globe to stabilize in the next ten years, and then reduce, with countries like Britain having to achieve cuts of 60 per cent, at a minimum, to play their part). The Treasury and the Environment Department, which are pushing the Heathrow project, help themselves to these figures *merely because the government has announced a policy commitment to them*, and then use them to justify a major expansion in air traffic which will unquestionably make them massively more difficult to deliver. This, says Ekins very justly, is 'a cake-having-and-eating strategy if ever there was one, intended to permit the government both to claim to be committed to climate change mitigation and to have all the aviation expansion it wants'.

Put bluntly, the critical part of my argument in this book is that this kind of doublethink is not, actually, a *perversion* of the sustainable development model – not something which we can guard against and from which we can preserve sustainable development policy if we take sufficient care. Rather, the fact that sustainable development policy gets used in that way to subvert itself is deeply *inherent in the conceptual structure* of the idea. Its lending itself so readily to that sort of bad faith is not an unhappy accident of one particular pattern of calculation. Nor is it chargeable merely to one particular pusillanimous government. It is built into the model itself.

Why? Central to the problem here is the way in which we habitually construe sustainability concern for the future on an *ethical* model, as a concern to deal *justly* with future people in matters of ecological resources, benefits and values. And closely associated with this ethical model is a conception of the relevant science. This is taken to be capable of predicting the quantified consequences of our present actions and refrainings accurately enough for us to have a good practical idea of what such fair dealing with the future would actually consist of. It is recognizing that imperative of fairness to the longer term which must be what drives us to make any really significant changes in current habits and lifestyle patterns (since prudential fears about what climate instability might mean in our own lifetimes will at best motivate us only to incremental measures of mitigation or adaptation).

This model of change, which is on its way to becoming political second nature, is what I call the mirage. Paradoxically, since it seems to embody such commitment and clarity of purpose, it threatens to turn sustainability into something which will in practice recede from us and eventually elude us even as we pursue it. The reasons for this are embedded in the structure of ethical motivation, scientific foreknowledge and political behaviour as these combine in a scientifically informed democracy. In the first part of the book, Chapters 2 and 3 try to show in detail how and why that is the case.

But we don't *have* to proceed on this model. As with an actual mirage, there is a different way of taking it. We can see in the image confronting us not distant water, towards which we need to plot our path, but an indication that the desert air is already very hot, so that we should be careful with our existing water supplies, and meanwhile look around for a genuine chance to replenish them. By analogy, there is a different way to respond to the news that our present socio-economic trajectory seems to be a very long way off producing a humanly habitable longer-term situation. We can acknowledge the urgency of that position by recognizing the extent of our present need to change, without supposing that we can yet know which changes will take us where, or assuming that we can programme the consequences of change across anything but the very short term. We can read the gap between likely and desired long-term outcomes as indicating not a path *ahead* which we have to follow, but just how *deep* our difficulties currently go. This doesn't mean that we don't still try hard to find quantified solutions for the problems. But as is very often the case in life, acknowledging how deep the problems go can also be a way of letting solutions find us. It may open us up to a new flexibility and readiness to explore – something which is frequently inhibited by the determination to plan our way out and the illusion that this maintains us in control.

So far, of course, this is little more than analogy. The third part of the book – Chapters 6 and onwards – puts the suggestion to active work. It explores, in an inevitably fairly outline way, how we might re-imagine our expectations, priorities and systems to build this kind of genuinely sustainable capacity across the broad fields of energy use, enterprise, education and social decision-making. And this is a crucial part of the reason for canvassing an alternative conceptual model or paradigm at all. Instead of stunting and chilling imagination into the forms of strained prediction and cost–benefit bargaining which go with the now-dominant sustainable development idea, we might hope to liberate it for open and creative exploration.

All this, however, turns on the crucial issue of *motivation*. This lurks beneath all our attention to the climate issues. Former US Vice-President Al Gore, for instance, ends his sombre and powerful documentary film *An Inconvenient Truth* thus: 'Future generations may well have occasion to ask themselves, "What were our parents thinking? Why didn't they wake up when they had a chance?". We have to hear those questions from them, now.' Appeal to the tribunal of our successors is a familiar turn of green argument, and forceful enough in context, voiced with Gore's measured impressiveness over the film's closing shot of a river flowing slowly on. But for all that, his closing trope just transposes the mirage effect into the modality of hearing. To be awakened to our ecological responsibilities, we must put the uncomfortable questions *to ourselves on behalf of the future*, as well as answering them on our own account. But then it is an illusion that we hear from the future – all we ever really hear is ourselves. The scope which this gives us for playing false with both challenge and response is crucial in enabling us to begin fudging these responsibilities even as we acknowledge them.

Chapters 4 and 5 link the critical and constructive parts of the book by addressing this pivotal issue. What could make the sustainability imperative powerful enough to keep us creatively exploring – with enough vigour and commitment to save the world, which is what is at stake – if we abandon the idea that considerations of ethical obligation can combine with scientific prediction to give us a mandate from the future for a sufficiently urgent long-term programme? Where else could we possibly find the need and drive to change?

Again, I can only invite the reader to consider and assess my detailed answer. Its spirit is this: our true ecological responsibility, to both the future and the past, is to make human sense of our own lives – to live them meaningfully in the present, the only time we really have, as the kind of creatures we really are. How we attend to the future which these lives look like bringing about forms a vital part of that meaningfulness, in ways which I break new ground by analysing. We hear this future not in the imagined voices of its unborn inhabitants mandating or reproaching us, but in the tenor of our own self-questioning as we try to understand and grapple with what we are presently doing in the world. And the force of that real questioning is actually much harder to evade.

* * *

This book is not trying to persuade people to wake up to the climate war. Yet unless millions of people so far unpersuaded do wake up – in the first place, in countries like Britain, which must carry the burden of global leadership on this issue – the war will be lost. So why read the book?

It is true that millions more must come – and very soon – to the point of saying 'we just can't go on as we are'. If they don't, the biosphere (and so human civilization) won't be saved. But that doesn't mean that if they *do*, it *will* be. What is absolutely critical here, and what I am concerned with, is how we conceptualize what must be involved when people – ourselves, of course, included, whoever 'we' are – come to be persuaded that we must change.

Most books about this whole topic focus, by contrast and very understandably, on actual changes which we urgently need to make to our lifestyles, systems and institutions. It is increasingly taken for granted right across the board that we know well enough by now what sustainability is and why it matters. An attempt to reopen this question therefore risks being treated with some impatience. It may be true, as Hegel claimed, that once the realm of concepts is revolutionized, reality cannot hold out against it. But if so, the work of conceptual revolution in this arena is widely held to have been done. The real business, surely, is to keep prodding the reality along.

But there is another side to Hegel's point. We can do a lot of things which seem to make much practical sense on the ground, and they may for a while seem to be moving us forward, but if there are more than minor problems with the framework within which we understand and represent to ourselves what we are doing, the realm of concepts will quickly begin to hold out against reality. It will impede, distort and misdirect what we are trying to do, undermining and vitiating our best efforts. That is the process which I believe is beginning to happen with sustainability conceived hegemonically as sustainable development. And it is not just a process of stunting imagination. It is, even more alarmingly, a process for which we simply haven't time. We have left ourselves, at best, the margin for *one* serious go at saving civilization. Revisiting the conceptual discussion while there is still the chance, and asking whether the necessary revolution is yet complete, is therefore essential work.

To anyone still inclined to impatience, all I can say is that I have tried very hard to do this work directly, and not in terms of what X has written about Y's critique of Z and so forth. Indeed I have tried as far as I could to avoid discussing academic philosophy, social or political theory at all – and where this has not been wholly possible, to avoid assuming any prior familiarity with it on the reader's part. Having some experience of the academy, I believe passionately that there must be hope of exploring complex thoughts beyond its limits if there is to be any hope at all. I have done my best, in fact, to write at first hand for the informed general reader who is not afraid to think. My best may still not be very good, the academic mindset being insidiously hard to escape – but the attempt is at any rate made in that spirit.

My approach also expresses a particular conception of what is now sometimes called 'applied philosophy' – conceptual work addressed to areas of contemporary practical concern. I believe that the writer's job here is emphatically not just to be a kind of neutral consultant, framing particular issues in terms of how the different established traditions of thought might analyse them, and then drawing out practical implications and recommendations from those analyses. That can obviously be a helpful thing to do, but for the issues with which I am dealing, it is far too bloodless. The real challenge is to get as clear as one can, for oneself and any others who may be interested, about one's own understanding of these issues, from the life-perspective of one's own engagement. That is what I try to do in this book. Of course, one runs thereby far more risk than do the neutral consultants of falling flat on one's face. But taking such risks is what writers are for.

PART I

WHAT'S WRONG WITH SUSTAINABLE DEVELOPMENT?

If one is to rule, and to continue ruling, one must be able to dislocate the sense of reality. – George Orwell

1

The Sustainability Horizon

With the publication of the Stern Report in 2006, we entered stirring times for sustainability. Any set of policy recommendations which manages to unite Shell UK, the TUC, Friends of the Earth and the Treasury in its favour must have a very great deal going for it. And indeed, there does seem to have been a sudden surge of interest in and concern about these issues – at least as far as they are represented by the need to mitigate or adapt to climate change. Probably now for the first time, there is the chance of real public recognition of global warming as an urgent problem, and of hard-nosed political work to address it. It helps, of course, that it is a Treasury economist who is now recommending action, rather than the merely academic and 'green' economists who have been recommending it for about two decades. The Report's establishment pedigree, in fact, will surely give a major impetus to what has now become the standard prescription on climate change.

Just to summarize that prescription: governments rely on scientific prediction to steer their economies towards a low-carbon future, more or less directively depending on the particular national and sectoral circumstances. To this end they use a complex mixture of taxation, regulation and public investment in pursuit of a wide range of specific sustainability standards and targets. Corporations meanwhile recognize the business case for responding positively, raise their sights (with some government support) to the longer term and shift profitably into the new range of opportunities available. In the stark new light of realism both about climate trends and about the inevitably global-capitalist context for action, what else could we do? How could that possibly *not* be the way we must now go?

That kind of question is a warning sign that we may be in thrall to one particular way of looking at things. It is always a public service to try and think the unthinkable, even if all it achieves is to bring the grounds of our assumptions into view so that we can re-endorse them. But, of course, it sometimes achieves more than that – a kind of mental liberation, which can take us onwards in unforeseen directions. And thinking the unthinkable is an especially important public service to perform in this particular context. If the standard prescription for combating global warming were indeed workable, we might still just have time to implement it before things start to run potentially devastatingly out of control. But what we certainly don't have time for is to find out ten or fifteen years down the line that it was never *going* to work.

I want to argue in this book that unless we change our approach there is a very real chance of our finding out precisely that. Our standard model of sustainability, cashed out for policy purposes as *sustainable development*, is so far from being the unchallengeable way forward that it could now be about to mislead us dangerously, if not terminally.

The dominance of sustainable development

That said, the fact that we are where we are is a triumph for the environmental movement, from its more-or-less standing start forty years ago, and the sustainable development idea has been a centrally important aspect of this achievement. The mainstreaming of ecological awareness and concern has been achieved in an extraordinarily short time for such a huge shift in the conventional wisdom. Significant changes in the overall sense that societies make of themselves have tended in the past to occur very slowly and patchily, with the transition from a few isolated voices to a common consensus taking centuries. Certainly, with improving communications and growing economic integration, the pace of cultural and conceptual change has been speeding up, as we can see if we think in turn, for instance, of the Christianization of Europe, the Renaissance, and then the French, Industrial and scientific revolutions. But it is still very striking how swiftly – indeed, in historical terms, how precipitately – the 'green turn' has been promoted from the fringes to the centre of human affairs, and how readily an accommodating discourse has been found for it. The emergence of sustainable development thinking in response to the environmental crisis has been a phenomenon of utterly unprecedented rapidity.

There is no need here for a full historical account of the process by which this idea has established itself; but it is worth noting the principal milestones, if only to register the speed of our passage. Awareness of how attitudes and behaviour towards the non-human natural world shape our humanity is indeed a Western cultural inheritance going back to the Romantic movement and beyond. Influential traditions of thought about the way our relations to nature bore on our economic life (represented classically by Ruskin and Morris in England and Thoreau in America) then flowed on through the nineteenth and early twentieth centuries. As a consequence of this pre-history, when the conceptual seeds of sustainability discourse were sown by the early scientific environmentalism of Carson, Commoner and others in the 1960s and 1970s, they found a fertile soil principally in the US and Western Europe. As the evidence mounted that human impacts on the rest of the biosphere were causing trouble, these seeds began to sprout across the globe. Organizations like the United Nations took an interest, with a particular growth spurt coming from the UN Stockholm Conference on the Human Environment in 1972. The term 'sustainable development' itself, as a policy idea for putting our newly perceived ecological responsibilities into practice, first achieved prominence in the World Conservation Strategy published by the International Union for the Conservation of Nature in 1980. It then moved to centre stage in 1987 with *Our Common Future*, the report of the UN-sponsored Brundtland Commission, whence it served as the organizing principle of a further UN conference, this time on 'Environment and Development', held in Rio de Janeiro in 1992. As central to the agreements signed there (in particular, the Agenda 21 action programme), the sustainable development idea has since informed a huge and burgeoning volume of activity by central and local governments, non-governmental organizations, development agencies, community groups, business firms – and, of course, academics.

There are a range of definitions of the idea which has thus more-or-less burst upon the world, but what matters here is less definition than the broad topography of the sustainable development concept. The main features of this are twofold. In the first place there is recognition of a duty to strike some sort of balance between the present and future availability of natural resources for the human project. In the second place, there is the assumption that we can find ways of measuring our success or failure in striking that balance, such that policymaking can be designed to ensure the discharge of our future-respecting duty across society as a whole.

Thus, accepting a sustainability constraint on (especially) our economic activities means trying to work within the requirement that henceforth they must not derogate from the powers of the biosphere to regenerate resources and support for their continuance at an equivalent level, or for that of acceptable successor activities. The harvesting of a renewable natural resource, such as a fishery, for instance, will be conducted sustainably in the sense of this constraint when the annual catch leaves a sufficiently numerous breeding population in the sea for the stock to regenerate itself so that it can support the same level of take in the following season, and so on indefinitely. The activity of using a non-renewable resource, such as a fossil fuel, obviously cannot itself be sustainable in precisely the same way; but it can still be part of a sustainable energy economy, provided that we do not simply use up the coal or oil regardlessly, but invest enough of the revenues to build up alternative, renewable energy sources which can be phased in as the fossil fuels phase out in order to meet an agreed level of continuing energy demand indefinitely. (This is part of the point of the clause about 'acceptable successor activities'.) Similar considerations apply where the resource on which an activity draws is the capacity of natural systems to absorb its associated discharges, for example of nitrates or greenhouse gases to water or the atmosphere respectively. Such activities are sustainable when they are structured to operate on a permanent basis within these naturally self-regenerating absorptive capacities (which will often, because of ecosystemic interdependence, mean those of a very wide range of interconnected environmental media).

Within the sustainable development framework this sustainability constraint is formulated as applying specifically to our pursuit of 'development' – that is, to collective actions and policies designed to achieve present or short- to medium-term improvements in human welfare. In perhaps the best-known version of this, due to the Brundtland Report, we are to go on trying to meet present needs, but only in ways which do not jeopardize the ability of future human generations to meet their own needs. Historically, this formulation, from a large UN Commission, represented a compromise between its members from the poorer South, who didn't want the roll-out of economic development abandoned, and those from the rich North who had the luxury of beginning to appreciate its downsides. The terms of this compromise were expressed, however, as the recognition of a constraint from the future. Overtly, this rests on what looks like a straightforward requirement of fairness. The needs of future peoples will be no less *needs* than ours are, so how could the mere fact that we are around now, and they are not, justify our behaving in ways which have the effect of privileging ours over theirs? More basically, though, some such constraint seems to be implicit in the idea of *development* itself. Once our most pressing survival needs are met, the aspiration to improve the human condition seems peculiarly empty unless the improvements are such as we can be confident of handing on to our children, and can hope that they will be able to hand on in turn to theirs.

The intended practicality of the constraint is the other crucial aspect of the framework. A requirement of fairness to futurity is merely aspirational unless we can derive from it some kind of criterion, or set of criteria, for adjusting the scope and methods of present development in the light of its anticipated ecological as well as its economic and social consequences.

Thus, for example, the Sustainable Development Strategy of the UK Government, *Securing the Future*, expresses these criteria in terms of two broad objectives or directing principles, neither of which is supposed to be sacrificed to the other in the framing of particular policies, plans and programmes. These objectives are, respectively, 'living within environmental limits' and 'ensuring a strong, healthy and just society'. The former requires us to identify and respect those limits to present activity implicit in preserving natural resources and ecosystem functions unimpaired for ourselves and future generations; the latter links this process to the meeting of present and future human needs for wellbeing, equality of opportunity and social cohesion. The strategy is informed by the confident expectation that sustainability criteria cashed out in these terms and conforming to these broad objectives can be operationalized through the kind of economic and social management machinery available to modern democratic governments. It endorses three further, contributory principles for the use of this machinery: achieving a sustainable economy (combining prosperity and environmental efficiency), promoting good governance through public engagement and participation, and using sound science in a responsibly precautionary way.

The assumption in all this is that policies, laws and regulations carrying broad popular endorsement and steered by normal bureaucratic regimes, increasingly through the use of agreed measures and indicators scientifically grounded and objectively applied, can address the problems of adjustment now recognized. The construction of such a legal and regulatory framework is now a major concern of both local and national policymakers, its implementation a growing task of bureaucracies, and working within it an increasingly important feature in the calculations of business – especially, but by no means exclusively, in the West and North of the world. Meanwhile, vigorous agitation around the multiple pressure points for change provided by this emerging framework is carried on by a whole new layer of non-governmental agencies, citizen and voluntary activity worldwide.

In summary, therefore: over the course of the past half-century, we have seen the discourse of sustainable development achieve worldwide recognition and claim a growing moral and political authority. Although this process had been prepared for by deep cultural shifts in the post-Darwinian period – away from transcendental religious accounts of the world and towards a naturalistic view of humanity and a general outlook thoroughly informed by science – it has nevertheless achieved itself with historically startling swiftness. Sustainable development now defines the sustainability horizon, the framing for collective concern about the longer-term global future. It shapes both the arena and the direction of aspiration – a trajectory into the distance which humanity must now deliberately pursue if it wants to avoid the dangers of resource depletion, ecosystem damage and, especially, climate change.

This has been, by any standards, a major achievement of political resourcefulness and international collaboration – perhaps the greatest since the establishment of the UN itself, and not even (as in that case) driven by the direct stress of world war. It is also in itself challengingly unprecedented. Never before have we been faced with having to devise a global regime for patterns of human life and work reflecting the real biogeophysical constraints under which we have now to operate as a natural species. Never before have we had to *think* of ourselves in that way, as a specific form of life with a global habitat and a mind-boggling technical reach. And yet we seem to be rising to the challenge. So the coming of sustainable development might seem to give grounds for real optimism. It ought surely to be encouraging that, even at this global level, we can recognize a common danger and move so comparatively swiftly to address it.

But – and it is a huge 'but' – such optimism is only well founded if the response really addresses the danger. If the sustainable development picture of what sustainability is about and how we should pursue it actually offers a deeply misleading model of our motivations and our understanding of the relations between present and future, the prospect is very much less reassuring. The argument I am going to develop through the book is that this is indeed the case. The sustainable development model provided a compelling in-principle picture of what was going wrong with the unbridled drive for technological progress. But because of its flawed structure, that model has an inherent liability to undercut and undermine itself when translated into a framework for practical action. Policy efforts deployed within this framework to address the now-recognized urgent problems of climate change (above all) could well therefore be frustrated by the inherent defects of the model on which they are being understood and defended.

Why, though, should we suspect sustainable development in that way? Why should we even incline to think of it as a *structurally* deficient policy model? One can dislike its economistic picture of the issues, and many people with green concerns have done so. Such concerns can spring from a love of the natural world and a shame at humans' treatment of it which seem far away from the sustainable development language of resource usage and the management of natural capital – although undoubtedly having learnt that language was what got Greens listened to in the mainstream. But structural deficiency is much more than just the fact of an alienating discourse. What might prompt us to allege it?

I want to start from two major areas of concern which even people firmly committed to the sustainable development project will readily acknowledge. These are, firstly, the yawning gap between words and actions, between rhetoric and practice, in the field of sustainability politics; and secondly, the problematic compatibility of sustainable economies with a globally triumphant capitalism. I shall suggest that both these concerns, taken seriously, push us towards radically questioning the standard model.

The reality gap

The gap which has already opened up between the mainstream political rhetoric of sustainable development and the reality of change on the ground is very wide. It is indeed scandalously wide, if we recall what is at stake and how much warning people and governments have now had. After all, the Stern Report, while the most authoritative, is by no means the first set of injunctions from official sources about the need to alter collective and individual behaviour if lethal environmental damage is to be averted. UK governments since the later 1980s have actually been getting quite good at producing such injunctions. The quickest way to indicate the extent of the reality gap, in fact, is to look at what *Securing the Future*, the official UK Sustainable Development Strategy last updated in 2005, would actually commit us to if taken seriously, and compare it with what is happening – or, very much more typically, not happening – in practice.

This UK Strategy is a fair test case. It is the upshot of a development process led by governments of two (somewhat) different political complexions, extending over ten years or more and in its latter phases supported by extensive public consultation. In itself it is a comprehensive and well-argued document. Stripped to their essentials, the four 'priorities for UK action' identified by the Strategy are:

1 *Sustainable consumption and production.* The key here is 'to break the link between economic growth and environmental degradation'.

2   *Climate change and energy.* 'A profound change in the way we generate and use energy, and in other activities that release [greenhouse] gases' is recognized as necessary under this heading.
3   *Natural resource protection and environmental enhancement.* Acknowledging that natural resources are vital to our existence, the aim is simply 'to ensure a decent environment for everyone'.
4   *Sustainable communities.* Embedding the principles of sustainable development at all levels will require communities to have 'more power and say in decisions that affect them'.

No-one involved in pushing sustainability slowly towards political credibility over the last quarter-century could deny that having these things on the national agenda at least represents an offer to take the issues seriously.

The four priorities are of course closely interconnected. Consumption and production will be sustainable only to the extent that they minimize greenhouse gas emissions and environmental degradation, and only if communities have appropriate economic and social arrangements in place will such sustainable consumption and production be possible. So, taking all that interlinkage as read, what *order* of action (that is, broadly governmental action, though premised on appropriate changes in the corporate sector, in the institutions of civil society and by people at large) would genuinely answer to the announced intention in each case?

One does not have to be a fanatical green activist, but only someone alive to the real size of the problems, to see that, as regards sustainable consumption and production in general, 'breaking the link between economic growth and environmental degradation' would require not just increasing the ecological efficiency of products and services across their whole lifespan, but confronting consumption choices in key areas (personal travel, food sourcing and domestic energy supply) with their full environmental costs, and investing seriously in more sustainable forms of provision in all these areas. Specifically in relation to climate change and energy, a change 'profound' enough to meet the case would mean not just investing massively in renewables and supporting energy efficiency – we would also need to be heavily taxing aviation fuel, creating an integrated public transport system through significant new investment, rolling out mandatory congestion charging to all major cities, and using a whole raft of other incentives and penalties to encourage a shift away from private car usage. Protecting natural resources genuinely recognized as 'vital to our existence' would require no new green-field housing developments, no new airports or runways, and no more road-building beyond present commitments. Nor would the sustainable communities required to support these changes be possible without fiscal incentives to decentralize workplaces, promote genuinely local production for local needs and transfer significant revenue-raising powers from central to local government.

Another way of putting all this would be to say that there is no hope whatever of a set of technical fixes allowing us to escape the need for major change. Consider, for instance, what would be involved in a real attempt to 'break the link between economic growth and environmental degradation'. The Strategy talks hopefully and almost exclusively in this connection about increasing the ecological efficiency of products and services across their whole lifespan – that is, reducing the ecological impact of unit production. To remind ourselves of quite how hopeful this sort of aspiration is, recall the 'Ehrlich equation':

$$I = PCT$$

where I is total environmental impact, P is level of population, C is per capita consumption and T (the technology variable) stands for the environmental intensity of consumption (as what is called ecological efficiency or resource productivity increases, so that each unit of consumption uses up less environment, the value of T decreases). What the equation formalizes is the essential structure of the environmental crisis: it says that the more of us there are, consuming the more *stuff* requiring the more biospheric resources to produce, distribute and eventually dispose of it, the worse the ecological overload gets. This is a no-brainer, but the formalized version allows us to highlight some points with helpful starkness. Thus Paul Ekins has used it to emphasize what would actually be involved in reducing environmental impact by 50 per cent over the period 2000–2050 (a target given credence by officially sanctioned aspirations to reduce greenhouse gas emissions, for example, by 60 per cent on 1990 levels by mid-century). Assuming a world population increase from around 6 billion to around 9 billion (probably an underestimate) and an economic growth rate of 2–3 per cent (modest in conventional terms, but actually yielding a quadrupling of notional per capita consumption over fifty years), some very simple arithmetic shows that meeting this target would require the environmental intensity of production, T, to decline by a factor of about twelve, or in other words the environmental efficiency of unit production to rise by more than 90 per cent over this fifty-year period.

Now, although some genuine progress has been made over the last decade or so in improving resource productivity, this sort of target just looks unachievable – whether we are looking at either its technological or its political feasibility. As the Sustainable Development Commission observed in a recent authoritative report:

> ... the overwhelming consensus amongst academics, think-tanks and NGOs is that resource productivity will not, on its own, deliver the desired reconciliation between the pursuit of economic growth and the non-negotiable imperative of learning to live within the Earth's biophysical constraints.

A real commitment to decoupling current production and consumption patterns from environmental degradation would involve, inescapably, some effective intervention in the value of the *consumption* variable *C*. Genuinely sustainable consumption, that is, must involve both consuming differently and (at least in the West) consuming *less*. It means consumption which satisfies need but does not cater to greed, is not constrained by current environmentally damaging patterns of international trade, does not depend on using up irreplaceable raw materials and ecological resources, does not generate unassimilable wastes, and is not artificially boosted by an advertising industry devoted to making invention the mother of necessity.

Of course, nothing remotely like this is happening, either here or in response to any of the four priorities identified. Nor, in fairness (whatever one might sometimes feel in exasperation), can this be blamed on government. Only an exceptionally brave democratic government will get out very far ahead of its electorate in any new direction of thinking or behaviour, and the public at large does seem to exhibit pretty much the same order of disjunction between rhetoric and reality on the sustainability issue. A UK government public attitudes survey in the early 1990s, for instance, indicated that, while 80 per cent of people believed there is too much traffic, only 25 per cent had actually tried taking up alternatives to the private car. And nothing much has changed since, in actual practice. DEFRA's 2007 survey of public attitudes and behaviour towards the environment showed three-quarters of the population believing that reduced car usage and air travel would have a significant impact on the UK's carbon emissions – but more than 50 per cent of people who take short-haul flights declining to feel guilty about it. Not walking the talk on sustainable development is, it seems, a very general failing.

This reality gap is certainly an important datum. The question is, what does it tell us? Many who endorse the sustainable development paradigm regard it as frustrating, certainly, but not fatal to their hopes. They would say it shows merely that we have not yet tried very hard to go beyond the rhetoric, to translate welcome theoretical endorsement, and perhaps a general shift of perception, into change on the ground. There are various explanations for why not, pointing to quite genuine problems of engrained habit, fear of the new, institutional inertia and the disincentives confronting individuals who might try to act on their own.

There is also a more general argument. The period from the 1972 Stockholm Conference until comparatively recently saw considerable progress, at least in the OECD countries, on what the former environmental campaigner and senior government adviser Tom Burke calls 'the easy politics of the environment'. This agenda comprises broadly the issues of air and water quality, recycling, chemical and radioactive pollution, and endangered species. Remedial action in all these areas, as Burke notes, has tended to receive broad public support once the issues are understood. Such action offers solutions which can cut costs in the medium term and which can typically be seen to produce a lot more winners than losers. It can also be seen as addressing itself to matters of fairly minor political significance – things on which everyone could hope to agree, after a little rational consideration, since crucial questions of ownership, power and deep-seated expectations have not yet been raised.

But while such progress is welcome, the easy politics is not, as the label suggests, really the problem. What has been looming more and more threateningly since the Rio de Janeiro 'Earth Summit' in 1992, by contrast, is the *hard* politics of the environment: climate change, soil loss, deforestation, the state of the oceans and the threats to biodiversity at large. At stake in each of these arenas is not just the condition of one or more of the Earth's major ecological systems, but also established patterns of global economic and cultural hegemony. In these problem areas, the issues are often powerfully contested – not just politically and culturally, but scientifically too – and any real attempt to tackle them is likely to yield, in the short to medium term at any rate, more losers than winners. (It certainly threatens to make losers of societies and groups who, however the actual numbers stack up, wield far more global power than the potential winners).

The advanced societies have therefore, by and large, been shirking the plunge. The hard politics is now imminent and inescapable. Unsurprisingly, however, a rhetoric expressing the steadily accumulating rational persuasiveness of the environmental case has hitherto largely outstripped the reality of what has been attempted in practice. But this problem (it is claimed) is not insuperable once the collective will is there, and as such the current reality gap is one which emergent events like Hurricane Katrina and the Stern Report will now begin to push us across.

But what if they don't? How long can we wait to see? And what if the reason why they don't is that what I have called the reality gap is after all not a temporary phenomenon, an unavoidable phase in the process of mainstreaming sustainability, but a structural feature of the sustainable development model itself? What if it reflects a mirage-nature in sustainability goals themselves – a characteristic trick of constantly receding as we try to approach them – and does so because that is the underlying truth of our relation to them? In that case, we might well wait until it is far too late for action to make enough difference before this truth became so plain as to be unignorable.

The stakes are just too high, in other words, not to give some real attention at this stage to what a critique of the standard model in these terms might have to say for itself.

Working with the grain of capitalism

Such attention must, however, recognize the context for any plausible critique. That is that the capitalist system is now a given.

For a long time many people thought, or hoped, that proper attention to our environmental responsibilities would have to mean an end to this system, which had so plainly generated ecological crisis. This has been the implicit, and often explicit, political rationale of a great deal of vigorous environmental campaigning over the past thirty years. But the overthrow or voluntary abdication of capitalism on environmental grounds was never remotely likely – and now, given the political and economic history of the last twenty years, such a prospect looks merely risible. Concerned people of all shades of green simply need to face this fact. It is certainly a premise of this book, and one for which I shall not spend any time arguing. For good or ill, the global market economy is where we have to operate to save the planet: it's there, or nowhere.

This is not in any sense to *exculpate* capitalism. There is no denying that certain features of the major capitalist societies of the past century, associated with a peculiarly blind form of short-term thinking, have been heavily responsible for the present ecological crisis. Principal among these features has been the consumerist materialism which these societies have encouraged, with its artificial creation of new wants not emerging spontaneously through the natural co-evolution of culture and material circumstance, but deliberately manufactured by hectic advertising in order to inflate the levels of profitability at which the whole system operates. As better communications and geopolitical change have spread emulation of this socio-economic form more and more widely around the world, demands on raw materials and ecosystem resources and services have increased exponentially (to the extent that the annual global production of a century ago is now achieved every fortnight)*, and the biosphere's resilience has been stretched towards, and in some cases beyond, breaking point. Indeed, environmental limits are not (as they are often represented) something which we will be running up against at some point over the next few decades unless we change our ways. The shortness of time before predicted collapse measures also the extent to which the tensions straining towards collapse now pervade the system. We have in effect already reached the limits – they press on us in the form of systemic volatility and instability across a whole range of circumstances under which business and society increasingly have to operate.

In bringing us to this pass, capitalism has responded to, and in turn has helped to widen, the post-religious gap in the human soul which the modern world has tried to fill with more and more *things* – with material possessions and (imagined) security as a substitute for life-meaning and real human purpose. That gap, or void, is of its nature unfillable by such means – something we all know, deep down, even as we succumb to the latest seduction. Its characteristic ever-craving emptiness has thus itself become a powerful driver for the hypertrophied version

---

* I cannot now recall where I came across this comparison, which has, however, stuck in my mind as such statistical nuggets will. Anyone who can't accept it without a reference is free to discard it – the general line of argument remains unaffected.

of capitalism which currently dominates the world. This capitalism, powered by self-deception, depends on a hysterical refusal to see what it is doing and to face the consequences for the biosystems in which it is embedded.

But none of this alters the fact that it is still capitalism which must mend itself and clear up its own mess. There is no other help to call on. The capitalist nexus has now been assimilated into the human ecology of the world. Increasing recognition of these realities informs the work of respected figures like Paul Hawken and the Lovinses in the US, and in the UK of key thinkers associated in particular with Forum for the Future. Books such as Paul Ekins's *Economic Growth and Environmental Sustainability* and, more recently, Jonathon Porritt's magisterial *Capitalism as if the World Matters* argue in detail that we now have to create the conditions for what might be called 'sustainability capitalism' if there is to be any hope of tackling the world's steadily worsening environmental situation.

If sustainable development is to be our paradigm of action in pursuit of sustainability, therefore, that requires at minimum that sustainable development run *with* the deep grain of capitalism, rather than actually *against* it. But does it? Is it actually compatible with the dynamic strengths and forces within this system, through which any future at all will have to be realized?

Those who have so far pushed the case for a new 'sustainability capitalism' certainly seem to think so. For them, the necessary transition has two principal and complementary tracks. The first involves governments in setting a new framework of taxation and regulation capable of tilting the operations of the market towards the delivery of sustainable outcomes. The second involves corporations themselves adopting criteria of business excellence which result in sustainable products, processes and sourcing patterns. Action along both tracks is seen as a matter of deliberately bringing in the longer-term perspective as a corrective to short-termism. The perverse imperatives of the currently dominant business model are tamed by building in structural features representing the longer-term requirements of climate and ecosystem stability, maintenance of natural resource levels, and the associated shifts towards more equitable patterns of distribution.

At the heart of this 'business case' approach is the good sense it is supposed to make for firms to keep ahead of the curve and the competition by anticipating change. Forward-looking businesses see ecological and resource pressures coming, and improve the eco-efficiency of their sourcing, production and distribution processes in advance. Similarly, they see pro-sustainability tax and regulatory changes coming, and reconfigure their operations to facilitate easier compliance. In both these ways they boost the bottom line by reducing or avoiding costs. At the same time, such behaviour will strengthen a firm's reputation with the growing proportion of its customers and other stakeholders who are persuaded by the sustainable development case, thus helping to build product loyalty and also to recruit and retain committed staff. Most importantly, firms on the lookout for sustainability-enhancing innovation in processes, products and services will gain powerful first-mover advantages in increasingly volatile markets. All this, it is argued, means that the pursuit of sustainability, far from crippling competitiveness, delivers increased shareholder value.

This argument is seeking to make an absolutely vital linkage. But crucially, it only seems to achieve it by taking for granted the feasibility of some assumptions about future developments which have to be extremely robust in the accounting sense. To treat costs avoided (which may of course entail significant costs *of* avoidance) responsibly and persuasively as savings in a company reporting context, for example, you need much more than a guesstimate of their order of magnitude. To invest responsibly in specific sustainability-relevant innovation, when such investment may hazard alternative profiles of profitability, you need more than vague ideas or pious hopes about the actual sustainability value of particular new products and services. The business case and the governmental framework-setting case in effect mirror and reinforce one another in their dependence on the fundamental idea of the standard sustainable development paradigm: *that we can get real leverage on the short term through sufficiently reliable prediction of the longer term.* The government or firm which is most responsible about sustainability is the government or firm which responds most alertly and sensitively to the signals that bounce back to it from the future.

The trouble with all this is twofold. First, there *are* no signals back from the future – only signals which the present sends itself about what it thinks will happen in the future; and beyond the very short term, such signals are inherently unreliable, a point which I will develop in much more detail in the next chapter. Second, and crucially, the whole point of capitalism – the reason why it has been responsible for such an unprecedented explosion of human welfare, all told, over a mere couple of centuries – is precisely that it trades on this reality of the human condition.

Historically, capitalism brought together newly won liberties of individual action, slowly accumulated surplus value and some key technological breakthroughs in a spontaneously created system for dynamic response to the inevitably short-term nature of our knowledge. It thus became the most powerful material form yet to have emerged of the exploratory open-ended learning and adaptation which is our species' natural way of dealing with its epistemic relation to the future. The source of creative energy in this system is its generation of competitive diversity in response to widely distributed and largely tacit knowledge of immediate drivers and constraints. Its essential strength is the flexibility through which this multiplicity resolves itself iteratively forwards in renewed multiplicity at (normally) higher levels of material satisfaction. Products and services, all making a slightly different bet on what will run, on what the near future will endorse, turn out to reward some producers and squeeze the margins of others; these outcomes reorient the next round of production towards reflecting emergent patterns of behaviour and satisfying emergent patterns of need, patterns which were strictly unpredictable at the earlier stage because their emergence itself depended on how things actually panned out. And it is because we all know (in practice, as the common basis of our daily lives) just how little we can really second-guess the future that this constant efflorescence of dynamic diversity goes on reproducing itself.

Its focus on the short term, in other words, is not a curable bad habit but the natural, proper and inevitable *habitat* of capitalism. Entrepreneurs succeed by addressing themselves to a moving horizon of comparatively short-term opportunity – a horizon which as it moves, but only as it moves, carries us into an indeterminable future with which the whole social enterprise is always learning just in time to cope. It is surely clear that only by working with the grain of these very deeply embedded system characteristics can we hope to effect the key linkage of increased shareholder value and improved resource productivity in successive presents, on which the possibility of any genuinely sustainable capitalism must depend. But the currently standard sustainable development model of getting leverage on the short term by pursuing longer-term obligations and targets seems to run directly across that grain.

So here are two substantial straw-bales on the wind. Both the reality gap and the poor fit with the deep structure of capitalism suggest that the sustainable development model may be more than just rather ineffectual so far. It is at least plausible that the problem may be something much deeper. We must now turn to exploring what that problem might be.

Pursuing the Mirage

There is a famous photograph taken from the Apollo 17 moon-shot in 1972. The Earth hangs full in space – the green and ochre of the land-masses, the vivid blues of the inshore waters and deep oceans, the brilliant snows of Antarctica, all clearly visible under delicately etched swirls of white cloud. It is an image of beauty and grave majesty, and also of a startling vulnerability. Looking closely, you can just make out the fine margin of the atmosphere, curving a fraction above the horizon of the African land-mass; and for a moment, the whole globe seems to float with the delicacy and iridescence of a bubble. A particular awareness of the human condition begins to crystallize as one contemplates this image: we are one species among the myriad which the Earth's green mantle of life has brought into existence – and yet the only one with the power to see and respect, or to damage and degrade, the planet as a whole.

The photographs produced by the Apollo missions gave this awareness irresistible form. As the astronomer Fred Hoyle very presciently remarked, well before any of these images had actually appeared: 'Once a photograph of the Earth, taken from outside, is available ... a new idea as powerful as any other in history will be let loose.' The new idea is that of *ecological responsibility* – a whole emerging frame of mind, constituting what we could also call the later twentieth-century 'green turn' in human affairs.

The claims of this new responsibility arise in part from a new scientifically informed understanding of the biosphere and our place within it. What humans do collectively (as societies or economies) now has to be understood within an ecological framework. Increasingly, our chosen courses of action and patterns of living have consequences which are not simply immediate and visible, nor even just short term and relatively predictable, but long term, ecosystemic and almost unimaginably complex. We have become familiar with the ideas of interrelationship, food-chains, feedback loops, the cybernetics of homeostasis and cyclical self-renewal, and the systemic importance of biodiversity. We have learnt, too, from evolutionary biology how human beings inched upright from among our primate kin on the African plains prominent in that Apollo photograph, and how humans are both physiologically and psychologically a product of the whole Earth-system. And we have come to understand much more than we did about the biospheric effects of our vast and various technological armoury. We know that our present form of economic life, taking the world as a whole but powerfully driven by the economies of the West and North, is now, through these ecological interconnections, causing multiple forms of damage – to the life-supporting functions of the biosphere, to its natural richness and diversity, and to its beauty and amenity. It is clear that we must treat all this amazing web of interconnection with a great deal more humility and care than we have been used to doing. New understanding passes seamlessly here into new attitudes and values. We respect the great blue-green presence, as it confronts us in the Apollo image, in the way we are advisedly respectful towards anything huge and powerful which we only partially understand and which (we can see) retains enormous potential to surprise us. We also, increasingly, find ourselves valuing the natural world as such: it seems just too obviously discordant to recognize humans, on the one hand, as a naturally evolved part of this intricately interdependent and beautiful whole, and yet on the other hand to consider them the sole kind of thing which confronts us with value-in-itself.

These new forms of understanding and value mean that how we respond to the unprecedented human impact on global ecological systems must itself, as it were, be ecologically framed. Humans clearly enjoy a unique position among terrestrial species, but we can no longer see that uniqueness as constituted by our being somehow the point or goal of it all. Rather we must pursue a kind of harmonious adjustment of which the model is the self-balancing of ecosystems and the interdependence of the living world. Even as an overwhelmingly dominant part of the whole, we are still dependent on its overall integrity, and that dependence must thoroughly inform the sense we now make of ourselves in ecologically responsible thought and action.

Sustainability considerations are thus not by any means the whole of what ecological responsibility involves, but appeal to that aspect of it which calls for humanity to be a *going concern* across time. At the heart of the green or ecologically responsible turn of mind is a commitment to human being as radically *terrestrial*. Acknowledging that we are an integral part of the whole Earth-system and have a unique responsibility to look after it, comes to be seen as a condition of any meaningfulness we might find in our existence. And a key part of that recognition is a widening and ever-growing sense that it is intolerable for us now to be acting (whether collectively as societies, through our institutions and businesses, or individually) in ways which are liable to build up into catastrophic consequences for our own and many other forms of life on this beautiful planet.

The trouble is that we have tried to capture that very genuine but richly embedded sense on an *ethico-scientistic* model which basically expresses it as a concern to behave *justly* towards future people, through ensuring that they are no worse placed in respect of the ecological resources required to meet their needs than we present people are in respect of meeting ours. Ecological responsibility is thus represented as responsibility *to* future people *for* the state of the Earth which they inherit ('leaving the planet as we'd like to find it'). This is evidently an essentially ethical model, premised on a relationship of obligation between present and future people – 'doing right by them', 'not cheating on our children', or however this is phrased. It aspires to be scientific, because we rely on science to help us recognize what resources need handing on as critical natural capital and to tell us how to go about maintaining them. But it is actually *scientistic*, I shall argue – that is, it lays false claim to scientific rigour and authority – because of the character of that reliance.

This ethico-scientistic paradigm of our active relation to the future is at the core of sustainable development, as that idea has come to prominence through the history sketched in Chapter 1. Redescribing it in these terms, however, brings out specific structural features which otherwise – sustainable development being now, as I noted, so firmly established in mainstream thinking – we might simply take for granted as the *inevitable* way to cash out our sense of ecological responsibility. It might also make it easier to see the fundamental things that I want to claim are wrong with it. These are, in the order in which I shall discuss them:

1   That long-term scientific prediction of the behaviour of ecological systems is inherently uncertain – and, if offered as anything other than inherently uncertain, dangerously hubristic;
2   That we all really know this, and rely on knowing it to 'float' the standards (expressed as targets and indicators) which are supposed to be benchmarking our remedial action; and
3   That we are drawn, in turn, to do this by our tacit recognition that the underlying 'stewardship' model of ethical obligation is really only pseudo-ethical.

All this amounts to the anatomy of a mirage effect – a deluding goal which always and necessarily recedes as we strive towards it.

If sustainable development were both an inevitable paradigm for ecological responsibility and structurally flawed in this kind of way as a framework for exercising that responsibility, we should be in very serious trouble. Indeed, with the stakes as high as they are, we should be in probably terminal trouble. But seeing what is wrong with the sustainable development approach can also help us towards seeing why that approach is actually not inevitable at all.

UNCERTAIN SCIENCE

Planning ahead

The following is from a recent report by the Sustainable Development Commission on *The Role of Nuclear Power in a Low Carbon Economy*:

The 2003 Energy White Paper was a watershed in energy policy and was unique internationally for committing the UK to a 60 per cent cut in CO₂ emissions by 2050. Although it is now possible that this target will need to be increased, in order to meet the international obligation to avoid dangerous climate change, the EWP contained a bold vision for future energy supply and demand. The four primary goals were:

- *Putting the UK on a path to cut CO₂ emissions by 60 per cent by 2050, with real progress by 2020;*
- *To maintain the reliability of energy supplies;*
- *To promote competitive markets in the UK and beyond; and*
- *To ensure that every home is adequately and affordably heated.*

Since then, there has been mixed success with the policy measures put in place to deliver these goals.

It is worth asking oneself, as I have asked a number of lecture and seminar audiences, what is most startling about the Energy White Paper on this account. Is it, for example, the commitment (like a sudden guest appearance by the ghost of Nye Bevan) to adequate and affordable heating for every home? Is it the vigorous support for renewables and microgeneration? Or perhaps the aspiration to international leadership on climate change issues, once a major New Labour selling point though now increasingly a matter of tongue-tied embarrassment?

Actually, the really startling – indeed staggering – aspect of the passage is surely its completely unquestioned assumption that adopting a planning horizon of forty-seven, or even of seventeen, years could be an act of sober and responsible administrative realism, rather than a piece of self-delusion. It has always been a feature of the actual human situation, to which one accommodates oneself more or less painfully as one matures, that the best-laid plans are liable to go pear-shaped and one never really knows what's going to happen next week, never mind next year.* The idea, so embedded in the formation of sustainable development, that, at the collective level, 'rational', science-based planning could somehow transcend these inherent conditions on our knowledge and agency, can fairly be called a gross exaggeration of our natural capacities.

I have found that few people come out with this straight off. But it is not that the passage doesn't expose one to the full force of what is being taken for granted here. The Energy White Paper is clearly not being commended for just sketching out, in a loosely indicative way, the kind of world we need to be moving towards during the remaining lifetime of someone now (say) in his or her mid-thirties. As the concluding reference to policy measures makes plain, the whole apparatus of

---

* As the saying goes: if you want to make God laugh, tell him your plans.

sustainable development is geared to the justification and licensing of quite specific regulations, incentives and prohibitions *now*, on the basis of trajectories (as in this case for CO_2 emissions) predictively quantified over these timescales. That the assumption about the plausibility of such a long-term planning horizon doesn't leap out at more people can only be because it is such an unquestioned element in the new sustainable development consensus. It demonstrates very plainly how the pedigree of that model for environmentally responsible action can be traced back to a formation in the 1970s, when governments still strove to plan the economy in detail, or the early 1980s, when the belief that they might yet do so again offered an increasingly dilapidated refuge from Thatcher–Reagan neo-liberalism. Sustainability thinking, one might indeed argue, was where this mindset then went into internal political exile, to re-emerge – refashioned but not essentially transformed – in the growing respectability of the sustainable development model from the mid-1990s onwards.

But do we really want it back? We are surely now a good deal more sophisticated about prediction, and we have heard of chaos theory. We are much less ready to see our advance into the technologically altered future as anything like following a map, even a map with large areas still left blank – and much more prepared to see it, in the words of my Lancaster colleague John Urry, as like 'walking through a maze whose walls rearrange themselves as one walks through: new footsteps have to be taken in order to adjust to the walls of the maze that are adapting to each movement made through the maze'. Predictive modelling under such circumstances very rapidly encounters ineliminable uncertainty. Some of this uncertainty – reflecting the sheer multiplicity of causal interconnections and feedback loops in the movement of materials around ecosystems, for instance – consists simply in our not knowing things which we might come, through progress in the relevant sciences, to know. Some of it is a matter of our having only fairly well-defined probabilities to go on. But the domain of such 'positive uncertainty' is surrounded by a much wider domain of indeterminacy, arising from two distinct but importantly related sources. These are, first, the enormous dynamic complexity and capacity for emergence inherent in the interactivity of living systems and, second, the socially contingent nature of the scientific knowledge with which we try to model and predict such interactions.

The dynamic complexity we can take for the moment as read – I will return to it shortly. But what does the latter claim mean?

The social contingency of science

The socially shaped character of scientific knowledge has been increasingly recognized in recent years, building on early insights by Kuhn and his successors in the history and sociology of science. This involves a shift in perspective which challenges the positivistic Baconian picture of science as systematically unlocking the objective secrets of nature through steady empirical enquiry and the accumulation of knowledge. Instead, science comes to be seen as a powerful human construct, the directions, preoccupations and overall substance of which are shaped, generally invisibly, at any particular stage by the human life in which it is embedded. This is not to impugn its objectivity, just to point to the fact that it remains always a human activity conducted in a social, cultural and practical context. It can only be objective at all (that is, it can only attend scrupulously to the phenomena confronting it) within framing assumptions more-or-less tacitly supplied by that context. But then, even the most precisely expressed scientific knowledge inherits the contingency of the human activities from which such frameworks emerge; and given the scope and complexity of human–environmental relations, such contingency will be pervasive.

That recognition has recently played a significant role in public debates over environmental policy. The Baconian model, which still underpins the political authority claimed for 'sound science' by governments like the UK's, has increasingly been challenged as inappropriate in the policy arena. A succession of science-related environmental controversies in the 1980s and 1990s – for example nuclear waste management, CFCs and the ozone layer, Brent Spar and marine science, agricultural practices and BSE/CJD, and disputes about the safety or otherwise of GM crops – have brought home just how socio-politically shaped the state of scientific understanding of any of these issues will tend to be at any particular historical moment. This has prompted searching questions about the degree of trust which can safely be reposed in regulators, political authorities and the scientific advisory mechanisms on which they have come to depend.

As might be expected, such questions have overwhelmingly been asked from the perspective of communities or campaigning groups seeking to resist policies and developments which they perceive as damaging to the environment or to human health. The point has been to expose the institutionally framed and sometimes in the broadest sense 'interested' basis on which such developments have been presented by the relevant authorities as completely safe, only minimally risky or on-balance beneficial. As amply demonstrated in recent controversies over GM crops, for instance, our choice of scientific framework for analysis and prediction is always likely to be affected by the pressures driving those developments of which we are seeking to predict the environmental effects. Hence, for instance, 'test site' parameters which leave out such basic factors as the action of birds in distributing crop seeds, because these aren't amenable to the kind of measurement which will enable the test to deliver the clear results sought by the large-scale commercial interests involved, and by government departments concerned not to alienate them. Such institutional shaping of investigative processes is inevitable, and need not mean that anyone is engaging in deliberate deception – although campaigners are naturally on the lookout for this, since it is always a possibility where the profit motive lurks. Even without it, however, it is clear that democracy is ill-served if such results are presented to the public with all the authority of science and without acknowledgement of the contingent circumstances and pressures framing the findings.

But what is being relied on here is a very general feature of the use of scientific knowledge in policy contexts – the fact that our data and predictions are *always* underdetermined by the biophysical realities. And it is important to see that this cuts quite sharply in a number of different directions.

We can press this point further by considering a very revealing exchange recorded at a public meeting organized in 2001 by the late lamented Agriculture and Environment Biotechnology Commission (killed off, we may suspect, for asking too many awkward questions). The respondent was the then Chair of the Government's Advisory Commission for Releases to the Environment. The exchange is about the particular kind of techno-risk situation associated with genetic modification of crops, but it brings out beautifully the issues about science and its context which are so relevant to the general sustainable development picture:

> **AEBC member:** *Do you think people are* reasonable *to have concerns about possible 'unknown unknowns' where GM plants are concerned?*
>
> **ACRE Chair:** Which *unknowns?*
>
> **AEBC:** *That's precisely the point. They aren't possible to specify in advance. Possibly they could be surprises arising from unforeseen synergistic effects, or from unanticipated social interventions. All people have to go on is analogous experience with other technologies ...*
>
> **ACRE:** *I'm afraid it's impossible for me to respond unless you can give me a clear indication of the unknowns you are speaking about.*
>
> **AEBC:** *In that case don't you think you should add health warnings to the advice you're giving ministers, indicating that there may be 'unknown unknowns' which you can't address?*
>
> **ACRE:** *No, as scientists, we have to be specific. We can't proceed on the basis of imaginings from some fevered brow.*

At first glance this exchange seems merely to discredit a familiar kind of scientific hubris – or more accurately *scientistic* hubris, since it is scientism to assume that science can have all the answers that matter, whereas a properly scientific cast of mind will admit that science by itself can't answer a range of important questions about the scope and social uses of science. That the only alternatives in addressing profoundly significant human issues like genetic modification should be supposed to be accuracy within science or imaginings more or less fevered from without is just ludicrous. Those tempted to dismiss this view of the options as a straw man should recall that it came from a distinguished scientist entrusted by government with a crucial advisory role.

But the hubris shouldn't blind us to the fact that he also has a good point. Scientists *do* have to be specific. They are asked by the rest of us to provide us with a *quantified* grip on the various aspects of the world in which we are interested. The quanta which they offer in response are not necessarily precise figures calculated to several decimal places – they can be ranges or probabilities – but in whatever form, they do have to be specific *enough* to answer the questions being asked. The point of science is to describe and predict those features of the world which can be expressed and compared quantitatively. And it is of the essence of a quantum to be specifically that quantum and no other – something which is as true of an indicative range or a rough average as it is of a clear-cut, hard-edged integer.

It is then a matter for the rest of us what we make of the professional specificity of the scientists. (That is by no means to say that the scientists have no role in helping us to use it responsibly.) It is a matter for society how much *authority* it gives to differently relevant quanta when it is looking for guidance in policy- or decision-making. And the key to using quanta responsibly in any such practical context is to keep in mind that the numbers do not just drop out of nature when an appropriate measuring device is applied. They, and prior to them the measuring devices, always have a human history of production and shaping. Nor, once produced, can the numbers just be fed into mathematically organized models to yield predictions unproblematically backed by nature. The predictive models in their turn are always informed and charged with human purposes. In particular, they always involve generalizing from the past under various kinds of pressure to get a clear enough view of the future on which to base action. Hence the AEBC member's point: all such processes expose us in different ways to the risk of nasty surprises. We need to be as aware as possible of the specific pressures and purposes lying behind any particular figures, but we can't escape such influences. The appeal to quantification is never an appeal from a fallen world of vested interests and mixed motives to a realm of pure objectivity – the numbers are never merely innocent. Nor, of course, are they always guilty. They merely belong, like us, to the world where guilt and innocence are real possibilities.

All this is important to remember when science quoted out of its contingent context is being used to bounce us into a risky future. Crucially for sustainable development, however, *it is just as true when we are using quanta to support decisions intended to prevent ecological damage* as it is for proposals which might cause it.

Numbers, uncertainty and sustainability

A fascinating and readable account of the production o. ur quanta is given by the American historian of science Theodore Porter in his book *Trust in Numbers*.

Porter traces through many historical contexts the wide variety of ways in which different forms of quantification both express and construct social meanings. He illustrates, for example, how increasing availability of and attention to statistics in the nineteenth century constructed such entities as 'crime rates', helping to lift explanations of crime from the individual to the social level. Or again, how cost–benefit analysis as employed by the US Army Corps of Engineers early in the twentieth century initially offered an appearance of numerical objectivity intended mainly to get beyond political log-rolling in the allocation of state-funded waterways projects – and then took on a technical life of its own as its methods of pricing reified the value of intangibles such as landscape and recreational opportunity. He is at pains to stress that all this begs no questions about realism. To uncover the 'archaeology' of the various quantifications which we put in place is not to deny that they can yield truth about the world – rather it is to remind us that, if they do, they must do it through social processes, because there is no other way. Dependence on human organization and purpose holds even in the simplest cases of counting. How many people were at the committee meeting? Well, do you count those who came late or left early, or only those who sat there all through? Do you count observers or only voting members? The rules may be clear on this, but even clearly stated rules can require interpretation (if the rule is 'don't count observers', what happens if an observer is co-opted onto the committee halfway through the meeting?). That such possibilities lurk in so uncomplicated a situation only emphasizes the huge penumbral indeterminacy surrounding figures arrived at in more complex social contexts. Thus Porter notes how in a much more challenging count, the US census, it has been controversial whether to allow the Census Bureau's estimate of its own undercount to be used as a correction for the raw data. Since the undercount is assumed to arise disproportionately from difficulties in tracking the inner-city homeless, incorporating it will have politically sensitive effects on the directions in which Federal revenues flow. But so, of course, have any procedural rules for the enumeration of people with non-standard domiciliary arrangements – any census process must have such rules, and the objective validity with which we can credit census results will therefore be contingent on them.

This is, to repeat, a general truth about science for policy. Porter explores, among other applications, its consequences for the measurement of pollution. Accurately assessing waste discharges, for instance, requires not just appropriate instruments but a whole system of social organization. This system will inevitably be organized and disciplined by agreed *criteria* for such things as sample choice, sample manipulation, instrument calibration, methods of data recording, training of personnel and controls for inter-laboratory bias. The point about such criteria is not that they necessarily rob the resulting measurements of objectivity, which actually can be achieved by no other means, but that they mark the points where the business of being objective necessarily depends on human judgement.

Human judgement in turn depends on human practices of attention, selection and choice – all of them portals through which the social and broadly 'political' context of what we are doing, the human reality, can tacitly enter into and help configure the physical reality which we are seeking to characterize.

To say that this inevitable contingency makes the numerical upshots *indeterminate* is not to say that it makes them *imprecise*. We may come out with a very clear indication of percentage changes in pollution levels. But this precision can't then just be taken as reflecting how things stand with a nature which is as it is quite independently of what we think about it. Instead, it represents (and can only represent) an attempt to capture how things stand with nature, through social processes in which what particular groups and maybe even individuals think and feel about pollution may well have considerable tacit, and therefore untraceable, influence. The figure arrived at is precise, *given* its tacit framing by these processes of arriving at it.

The framing, as we have just seen, depends on a whole series of judgements and reactions which in principle could have gone somewhat differently, and we have no real way of estimating the probabilities of their having done so. This is one aspect of the indeterminacy flowing from social contingency. But there is also another, rather subtler kind. The way the judgements and reactions did go will at least partially express a range of institutional and even personal involvements with the issues raised by pollution: the figure which emerges, however precise, is thus to some extent an artefact of these involvements. If it is then set over against them as an objective measure of the reality which they confront – as its precision tempts us to do – then a crucial slippage is occurring. It is like the case where you take your own temperature, but don't leave the thermometer in place for long enough, perhaps because you are in a hurry and are sure it will be normal. The reading may then indeed be near enough normal – but if we use that to guide action ('See, I'm fine, no reason not to go to work ...'), we have introduced the order of indeterminacy in question. The figures in such cases are indeterminate in the sense that their apparent precision is not fully meaningful without their archaeology, the whole relevant human story of choice and impulsion, being taken into account – and if it is, they are seen to be partial artefacts of the concerns on which they are supposed to be providing us with a handle.

The implications for sustainable development of this perspective on social quantification should not need labouring. Consider, for instance, what must be involved in the construction of the official UK 'sustainable development indicators' published regularly by government. For an example almost at random, take CO_2 emissions from heavy goods vehicles, which the 2007 set of indicators tells us rose in line with gross domestic product (GDP) from 1990 to 1998, but have since stabilized while GDP has gone on increasing. To the extent that the indicator can be trusted, we might conclude that the environmental efficiency of overall production has been improving in at least this respect, even though HGV emissions are not yet declining in absolute terms. While a modest conclusion and not much to shout about, that seems so far clear. But now reflect on the archaeology of the relevant numbers. Imagine the ways in which those total annual emissions figures will actually have been assembled. Recollect that this process took place over a seventeen-year period during which public and official attitudes to sustainability (not traditionally a dominant priority among lorry drivers) have changed markedly. Think about how the demands for all that data regarding lorry numbers, engine sizes, trip mileages and so on will have been more or less enthusiastically met by the men and women in the cabs of the lorries – and in the offices of the haulage firms, with all their variations from the neat and orderly to the smoke-filled, *Daily Mail*-strewn and chaotic. This is not meant to poke fun at haulage industry workers particularly, so much as to give back to the whole process in imagination a bit of the colour which the bland numerical upshot bleaches out. If 'penumbral indeterminacy' sounds abstract and theoretical, this is the kind of concrete human reality in which it consists.

But realizing what lies behind a comparatively straightforward indicator of this kind is the merest preliminary rehearsal for imagining how a whole target-indicator regime for sustainable development gets constructed. Suppose, for the sake of argument, that an overall emissions reduction target has been agreed as robust, and picture what must be involved in working back from such a target for (say) 2050 to sector-by-sector targets for the here-and-now – in the calculation of emissions as divided up between sectors (public, industry and private consumption); in the way emissions-reduction consequences of particular technical developments, current and prospective, are estimated, validated and factored in; in the combining of all these estimates, which will not be just additive but will need to have regard to a whole range of possible systemic effects, knock-on consequences and feedback loops ... . The measurements which are relied on for these calculations and estimates at each stage, including the extent to which existing statistics designed for other purposes are drawn on and maybe reinterpreted, will depend at every turn on back-office histories and human realities not essentially different from those colouring the procedures of the haulage firms, but with a vastly more complex interactivity going on between them.

The point here is not to plunge into detailed sociology of science-for-policy, but simply to recognize the enormous scope that must be offered throughout such constructive processes for unacknowledged and frequently unrecognized *selection* of parameters and *interpretation* of criteria. Nor, again, need there necessarily be anything illegitimate about any of this selection and interpretation. Probing of specific cases may reveal judgements or choices made with a covert eye to the vested interest of the minister, the department, the commercial partner or even the research programme, but this will be the exception in a disciplined culture of bureaucratic objectivity. More to the point is that the construction of sustainability numbers goes on through processes which are fully involved in the human reality of tension between present expectations and a sense of future-oriented responsibility, which supplies the context for the whole sustainable development drive.

The possibilities of prediction

I will come back to that issue in the next section – it is crucial for the developing argument. But here it should also be emphasized how contingency and indeterminacy are affected by the dynamic complexity of the natural systems, the behaviour of which a sustainable development approach requires us to predict. If our measurements of what is going on now are contingent on the procedures, assumptions and judgements which enable us to make and use them, the associated indeterminacy is hugely multiplied by the need to feed them into scientific modelling of future trends and developments.

In understanding anything, we have to trade off the demands of perspicuity against those of faithfulness to the reality which is in front of us. All understanding involves some kind of simplification – all understanding thus in some sense models reality. Simplification, however, need not in itself mislead; sometimes it can yield insight, enabling us to organize what would otherwise be too manifold a series of phenomena into a surveyable, coherent whole. The trick is to get a model or picture perspicuous enough to make sense and also sensitive enough to the detailed reality for that sense to be reliable. But with scientific modelling of natural systems, especially living systems, for the purposes of longer-term prediction, this trick is peculiarly difficult to pull off. Real-world natural systems are complex, multivariant and emergent – that is, both interactive and open-ended. (Open systems are those where 'mass, energy and momentum can enter and be discharged through the system boundaries', so that future system change cannot be determined from any given system state.) Predictive scientific models, on the other hand, are necessarily selective, representative and finite. (A model must run in finite time and incorporate a set of rules specifying completely the allowable moves within the system. If you had to construct open models, the only model would turn out to be the whole world, which then couldn't be a model of *itself*.) Because these are radical differences, they entail that any predictive model of a real-world natural system starts off *just as such* with a strong inherent tendency to be misleading.

This tendency stems from the many points in framing a predictive model of this kind, at which long strides away from the actual texture of the reality in question need to be taken for any model at all to be constructed. These include the identification of parameters and of the interactions between them which the model will recognize (a closed and sequenced set on any model, as against an open and emergent one in reality); the extent of reliance on averages and other representative data (where the reality will often be almost inexhaustibly various); and, relatedly, how far the linearities of model evolution, with variables altering at uniform rates, can represent the non-linear relationships found in nature, where when one variable shifts another may change exponentially. Another important aspect is the extent of scaling-up from the observed tract of experience on which the model is based to the tract across which it is intended to predict (a very significant factor when we are trying to look across the globe, as understanding the biosphere requires, and also ahead over decades). A further such factor is the number of initial conditions, values for which have to be stipulated for the model to run – a rich source of modelling error, since extreme sensitivity to initial conditions is a characteristic of the highly complex and sometimes incipiently chaotic system relationships found in the living world.

In this light, it should be clear that the more specifically quantitative the upshot sought from a predictive model, the sharper the inevitable contingency of all these modelling decisions and judgements. Thus the more precise we are trying to be, the wider and deeper the associated indeterminacy runs, and the greater the uncertainty actually generated around any numerical value. Paradoxically, when we are looking to the longer-term future behaviour of natural systems, we *create* uncertainty by trying to be precise.

The extent of the necessary misrepresentation in prediction of this kind seems to be such, indeed, that only if a model is quantitatively modest is it likely to come anywhere near reliability. Modesty here means seeking to predict in terms of directions, trends, broad magnitudes and possible scenarios, rather than anything more numerically specific. This is an absolutely essential function, and one for which we rightly turn to science. And at a sufficiently low resolution, there are things looming about which we can be fairly confident. We know that world population will go on increasing, and (bar apocalyptic accident) will pass the 9 billion mark before stabilizing, though we don't know just when or by how much. We can be sure that global mobility and the pressures of techno-agriculture will produce more pandemics of the kind which avian flu was recently threatening to become, and also that each particular outbreak will take us as much by surprise as did that threat. And similarly, to come back to climate change, there is now a huge expert consensus behind the conviction that greenhouse gases generated by human activity are indeed warming up the world. In this context, broad-spectrum predictions of the kind that figure so prominently in the Stern Report, for instance, are perfectly in order. With the Fourth Assessment Report of the UN Intergovernmental Panel on Climate Change, the first volume of which became available in February 2007, it has been shown to the satisfaction of an overwhelming consensus of relevantly qualified experts that this warming, if left unaddressed, will have consequences for people living a few decades after us which will be somewhere on a range from the seriously uncomfortable to the catastrophic.

We should not have known this vitally important truth without the science. But there are so many interlocking ifs along the way – *if* the Arctic ice disappears, *if* the Gulf Stream alters direction, *if* the Amazonian tree-cover is reduced by vast forest fires, *if* the capacity of the oceans to pump down carbon dioxide collapses ... and so much unavoidable contingency in conditioning for them, that any prediction more precise than that will have the uncertainty of effective indeterminacy. But the point is that, on the mainstream sustainable development approach, our predictions have to be precise enough to be translated back into specific targets and standards for present action. And no scientific prediction across a policy arena extending that far out into the future can be anything like robust enough to warrant one specific target, standard or action *rather than another*. It follows that identifying any target cut in CO_2 emissions (say 80 per cent rather than 60 per cent by 2050) achieving which would enable us to avoid dangerous climate change is a kind of scientifically disguised whistling in the dark.

It is also important to acknowledge that with at least part of our minds we have known this to be the case all along. Everyone actually understands quite well the uncertainties inherent in this kind of science, whether or not scientists playing their official role have a language in which to admit to them. For instance, research on the GM issue has shown that 'lay' people take uncertainty about the long-term consequences of GMOs for granted. Representatively, focus group participants in a recent study took the view that nobody knows *and nobody can know* the full impacts of GMOs in the long term. Unintended effects (both harmful and beneficial) will necessarily occur, but these will only become apparent later, when consequences 'which had not been imagined' become apparent. These views were supported by numerous past experiences, such as with BSE, asbestos and pesticides. The situation was not seen as exceptional and was not interpreted by focus group participants as a *failure* of scientific knowledge: it was described and accepted as a fact of life in any society where science informs policy as it does in ours. The general public, whom scientists often patronize as ignorant about science, are no fools when it comes to these crucial deeper issues about how far science can reasonably be expected to take us and what guarantees it can plausibly give.

The question is, then: just how is this pervasive awareness of scientific uncertainty in a culture which depends on science actually playing out in the pursuit of sustainable development?

FLOATING STANDARDS

Nature doesn't give a damn about the present or the future. It cares nothing for the fact that we are deeply attached to the comforts and conveniences of our present phase of civilization. If our continuing to enjoy them means that global temperatures rise by 4°C, or 6°C, or soar away beyond that, the consequences will simply follow, as far as nature is concerned – it's our problem. And so indeed it is, because we, uniquely in nature, can foresee these consequences in broad terms, and see that they are utterly unacceptable. Meanwhile, we remain attached to present habits and patterns of life, and for good reasons. Life really is materially a lot better now, for a much larger proportion of the human race, than at any time in history. We are better fed, clothed, housed, educated and cared for, our lives have more variety and our deaths typically less pain than for any previous human generation. There are lots of real downsides, psychological and social as well as ecological, but the upsides are real too – and as we all like to point out, even those who rail against them rely on them.

Sustainable development is all about the balancing of these realities – of our obligation not to sacrifice present benefits wantonly against our obligation to ensure a continuingly habitable planet, of our consumption against our prudential preferences, of our immediate inclinations against our longer-term sympathies. But this balancing is no cool exercise in rational adjudication: it is an arena of struggle, both between people and groups and inside individuals. Reluctance to abandon present comforts grapples with guilt at that reluctance and resentment at the guilt, in a tangle with dismay at the environmental damage already done, gnawing apprehension about the future and scepticism about the motives of those who feed that apprehension ... . It is, necessarily, a complex and highly conflicted business. And like any other area where our motives are complex and conflicted, it is beset by the very deep human tendency to *bad faith* – that is, to having things both ways at once.

Carbon cycling: A cautionary tale

The most tactful way to broach this issue of bad faith and link it to the points about quantification just made, is probably through a personal example. When I first began environmentally related academic research, my circumstances meant that I had to go on living at a distance of some eighty miles from the university where I now had to spend part of each working week. But my wife needed the family car for her own work, and I was quite determined to avoid our becoming a two-car family. So I started off doing this journey routinely by bike and train. The main biking part involved thirteen miles in each direction, to and from the station in our local county town. They were miles down (and later, of course, back up) through hill-country in the sometimes bleak North Pennines, carrying panniers stuffed with books, papers, dry clothing, bike maintenance tools and emergency rations. I didn't have to do the double journey on a daily basis – luckily, since the days when I might have managed that were already a good many years in the past. Nevertheless, some of my happiest memories are of making this trip in the dark and driving sleet of a typical February morning. They are genuinely happy memories, because as well as the exhilaration of exercise and fresh air, every heave of the pedals bespoke self-reliance and environmental commitment. Although there were also occasions when the need to go through this each week felt like a nuisance, I could still be conscious of labouring hard to meet some of the costs of my sustainability obligations. The idea that each individual might actually be allocated his or her own personal carbon emissions quota had not then been widely canvassed, but insofar as I thought of myself as having a notional one, I could experience the real pressure of its limits.

There came a period, however, when I moved beyond my original research project to undertake wider managerial responsibilities within the Research Centre, including a leading role in moving it towards an institutional merger which would (we hoped) create a dynamic new focus of environmental and sustainability education within the university. The paperwork which I had to carry back and forth burgeoned alarmingly, and started to become too bulky for my panniers. There were also more and longer meetings, often having to be scheduled to suit diaries more important than mine, which made it increasingly difficult to allow the margin required for bike-and-train travel with its unpredictable frustrations and delays. Quite quickly I reached the point of having to choose between either abandoning this new work or accepting the resisted second car after all. But I remained strongly committed to making an environmental difference – which was also, of course, an important incentive driving the new task. How to decide?

In this dilemma, the idea behind the notional carbon quota came to my aid. This is, of course, the recognition that in-principle-quantifiable carbon consequences attach to all our actions. And yes, I should be adding to the CO_2 emissions for which I was directly responsible by starting to drive regularly to the office. But doing so would enable me to carry through the creation of the new institute, which (if successful – as naturally it was going to be) would result in alerting more people to the issues, and in due course shifting public policy in more sustainable directions. The ramifying longer-term consequences of this project would surely have the overall effect of significantly reducing carbon emissions, and at least a proportion of these reductions should then in fairness be set to the credit of my own 'carbon account', as a main instigator of the developments producing them. This could mean that, overall, *I actually cut emissions more by biking less*!

Or so I reassured myself, as I did indeed adopt driving rather than biking as my default option. Of course it is easier in retrospect to see the unadmitted or half-admitted motivations which were also in play – the surreptitious excitements of office politics, the discovery that with each passing year the sleet was less exhilarating ... . For all that, such a decision was by no means simple hypocrisy. If the notion of a sustainable personal carbon quantum made sense in principle, however difficult to calculate out in practice, then my keeping thus in bottom-line credit surely had to be a real possibility. And if it didn't make the sort of sense which permitted such an in-principle calculation – if it had all along been just symbolic – what on Earth had I been doing previously in striving quite so hard to keep within it? So I wasn't abandoning my standard, or merely pretending to maintain it. But it's clear enough that I was engaged in what we might call *floating* it.

Human beings characteristically crave both to *have* real standards of behaviour and to be able to escape from them sometimes at need, and we also need to avoid recognizing that escaping is what we are doing while we are doing it. A standard or criterion of behaviour, whether prudential or moral, is supposed to be a general rule. Its action guidance is supposed to apply indifferently both to those situations where it sits comfortably with our actual inclinations, and to those more exacting situations where it doesn't. It is essentially there to indicate how we should behave *like it or not*. It 'floats' when what we take it to mean in particular circumstances changes (rises or falls, to pursue the metaphor) in response to whether we *do* in fact, in those circumstances, like it or not. By floating it, we seem to keep it, avoiding the appearance and consciousness of giving it up; at the same time, though, we *are* in effect giving it up. It becomes both a standard and not a standard – still appealed to for guidance, but with what it actually constrains us to guided by the motives of the particular appeal. This is precisely what was happening to the standard constituted by reduction of the quantified carbon consequences of my transport arrangements. When I was thinking about biking to the train as providing me with the satisfactions of eco-heroism, the relevant calculation could include only the saved emissions directly ascribable to the journeys in question (those from a car trip as against my tiny proportion of those from the train). When that would-be heroic struggle needed to be suspended in favour of other objectives, the calculation was allowed to factor in plausible carbon savings from anticipated consequences further down the line. And crucially, the considerations bearing on the decision as between these two bases for the calculation weren't really independent of those bearing on the substantive decision between bike and car, which the upshot of the calculation was supposed to guide. The feeling that this work was more important than sticking to the bike, and the recognition that further consequences deserved to be counted in, were really different facets of the same motive. The standard by which I was affecting to justify my choice was floating in response to the pulls and pressures on that choice itself.

I should probably record, to complete the anecdote, that the hopeful new institute succumbed fairly rapidly to interdisciplinary misunderstandings and the perverse incentives of the lethally comic 'research assessment' process in universities. Nature may not give a damn, but life has a wry sense of humour.

Equivocation by numbers

Now the point of this tale is not just to show *me* being feeble (or, from another perspective, 'realistic'). What I was exemplifying, in a situation of conflicted motives, was a kind of doubleness which is actually a deep structure of agency, an abiding pathology of the human will. The classic account of it is still that of the French existentialist philosopher Jean-Paul Sartre. In *Being and Nothingness*, he glosses bad faith as 'a certain art of forming contradictory concepts which unite in themselves both an idea and the negation of that idea'. This formulation sums up a number of cogent and richly described examples of how we play false with ourselves and others. Typically we do so by finding ways to treat various of our actions as both ours, and as somehow happening independently of our will. Sartre goes on to build a philosophical psychology and indeed a theory of being around this insight, but we needn't follow him down this path. What matter here are the ways in which we manage to side-step underlying contradiction, in order to have our cake and eat it, or to float our standards so that we can both endorse and escape them.

One important resource for self-deception is the very generality of principles or standards, as against the immediate particularity of the actions in which either compliance or evasion must consist. A beautiful illustration of how this resource gets used is George Eliot's comment on Matthew Jermyn, the peculating attorney in *Felix Holt*: 'He had had to do many things in law and in daily life which in the abstract he would have condemned; and indeed he had never been tempted by them in the abstract.' Jermyn isn't a crude hypocrite, as the novel goes on to show. He doesn't present himself to others as something he fully realizes he isn't – rather, he refuses to recognize something he doesn't want to admit to himself that he is. With one part of his mind he believes in traditional general values like 'stealing is wrong'; but he has also cultivated skills of tactical inattention which enable him to avoid making uncomfortable connections between stealing in the abstract and this or that bit of sharp practice which currently solicits him. These are skills which we are all disposed to acquire. If you want to think it's OK to do A while conscious both that you shouldn't do X and that A is a case of X, practical contradiction looms. But when we are adept at the relevant shifts, general thoughts like 'never *steal*' can coexist with specific actions which, if we are forced to characterize them at all, we call looking after our legitimate interests, or not saying more than we strictly have to, or exploiting a loophole ... and so no disturbing contradiction arises.

A different but closely related version of this move is resorting to *equivocation* – taking a concept in one way in one context and another way in another, while still affecting to treat it, and in particular to reason with it, as the same concept. Thus Jermyn might have been disposed to think of himself as *honest*. When needing that description for his moral comfort, he could apply it in its full traditional sense, of having no sort of truck with underhand dealing. But when he was in need of a bit of latitude, the standard represented by the idea would have slid or floated, so that the term could apply to anything that kept just on the right side of the law.

Clearly, the process involves a kind of self-*deception*, and this notion has been found logically problematic, since it seems to require believing both a proposition and its negation at the same time – something which analytic philosophers, at any rate, want to define 'belief' so that you can't do. (Existentialist philosophers like Sartre tend to be more open to the phenomenological reality of our experience.)

Jermyn needs both latitude *and* the more traditional meaning of honesty, if both of his conflicting wants are to be gratified. He doesn't just want to be 'honest' in any old sense compatible with getting what he wants, he wants to be (or think of himself as being) honest in the robust, temptation-resistant sense that allows him to feel comfortable with himself. So there remains the need to hide from himself that he is trying to have it both ways. The idea of actively and consciously deceiving oneself does indeed seem self-defeating – if you try to hide something from yourself, you will know where you have put it, so you won't have hidden it. But, as just noted, one can usually avoid such open confrontation with what one is doing.

What is the bearing of all this on our argument about sustainable development?

The first thing to note is that equivocation of this order can now be recognized as what was happening when I was trying to decide about appropriate modes of transport to work. The quantifiable carbon consequences of my alternatives were being conceived of in different and (actually) incompatible ways, depending on what I wanted to justify. A quantum which, though notional, was sufficiently determinable to legitimate a real struggle to keep within it, was being invoked when I was thinking about that struggle as providing me with various kinds of satisfaction (not all of them self-regarding). But the standard was being floated to invoke a quantum that was in effect indeterminate – calculated on a basis that could include open-ended knock-on consequences – when that struggle became something which I needed to suspend in pursuit of other things.

The second, more general observation is that this potential slide between determinacy and indeterminacy is actually *inherent in the quantitative approach itself.* Any quantum that gets produced in the predictive scientific and economic modelling so central to sustainable development discourse inevitably exhibits the characteristic duality of being determinate, insofar as *any* quantum is determinate (that is, just by being *this* quantum rather than that), but also having all the essential open-endedness of the highly contingent kinds of 'archaeology' which we have been examining. Correspondingly – and this is the key point – such figures always *lend themselves* to being regarded as hard data under some circumstances and soft data under others. Sustainability standards so conceived are inherently liable to get floated under pressure, to constrain us only when and as far as it suits us to be constrained.

How green is green enough?

Environmentally concerned readers prepared to look at the matter in a suitably detached light will, I hope, recognize here some of the daily bread of would-be sustainable living. In trying to be ecologically responsible, one is faced constantly by decisions having the kind of liability to bad faith which I have illustrated, and time and time again our action in bad faith depends on the inherent ambivalence of the relevant quantification. Nor is this just a point about the difficulties of merely individual action as against broad socio-political change. It is a point which goes to the heart of how the whole sustainable development paradigm is constructed.

Given surrounding social and economic arrangements with which it is perpetually necessary to compromise, the practical challenge for concerned action by ecologically responsible people is inevitably 'How green is green enough?' How much forgoing of the car in favour of public transport is enough? How much more such abstention suffices to permit oneself an annual flight? Intercontinental, or only European? How much difference does it make if this flight is essential to attend a conference on sustainability issues? How effective is offsetting the carbon consequences of unavoidable flying? And at a less exalted level, if the recycled loo-roll makes one's backside itch, can one buy something gentler so long as one also puts all one's newspaper out for recycling and composts the kitchen waste? What proportion of one's vegetable consumption should one aim to grow oneself (if one has the space), and how does this proportion alter if one sources purchased vegetables from a local organic grower, or if one buys organic from the supermarket? (And then what about having to drive to the supermarket?)

All these questions reflect at a smaller scale the structure of the central sustainable development question. 'How green is green enough?' is glossed at the global level as 'How much adjustment to our present needs, or to ways of meeting them, is enough to avoid jeopardizing the capacities of future generations to meet their needs?' And it is of the essence of the approach that the question, asked at any level, can in principle be given a usable quantitative answer. 'Green enough', in this context, is already a rough quantitative concept: it only makes sense in terms of in-principle comparable *magnitudes* of whatever is in question. Hence the availability of some metric is implied in the idea of sufficiency which underpins sustainability. But to translate this sustainability criterion from the theoretical level into something which can provide practical guidance for economic and social policy, it is obviously necessary to cash it out in terms of 'enough *of what*' is actually to be transmitted, and this must mean expressing the relevant constraints and requirements as measurable target quanta of this and that physical manifestation.

These considerations yield the general idea of *natural capital* and its various component substances, systems and capacities. Whether we then think of what is to be handed on in terms of the calculable value of enumerable capital stocks, or conceive of natural capacities in other ways (for instance as range of diversity in ecosystems), still the central thought is that we can identify and measure a variety of quanta in the passing on into the future of *not less than* which (or, in some cases, not more than which) practical sustainability can be taken to consist. Thus the idea of one's own individual carbon footprint as providing a standard by which to make one's lifestyle decisions is an unavoidable derivation from, not just the conceptual structure but the whole practical purpose and real-world purchase of sustainable development.

Most people who now try to take some responsibility for their footprint do so by making some adaptations in their habits of usage of domestic consumables and energy, and less frequently in their patterns of personal mobility. But even limited change in these areas is a hard matter. Our kind of society, with its permanent consumerist clamour for gratification *now*, makes it especially hard. There is always the standing temptation to minimize present adjustments as far as possible. The tendency of standards (targets, criteria) to float in response to this temptation can be observed at work across the whole scene when practical sustainability questions come up. We all know what actually goes on here. One finds a personal *modus vivendi* in relation to all these decisions which responds to demands and expectations arising from one's work and family commitments, one's own self-image, and the various social groupings to which one belongs. But that's an admission to be resisted, since coming to rest at just that point seems gratuitous in relation to the genuine and urgent issues ultimately at stake. By the same token, it is more than likely to reflect the level of change with which we are personally comfortable, rather than that required for making the necessary objective difference. We resist this admission by appealing covertly to the background idea of there being somehow a quantitative warrant in our real natural resource impacts for whatever decisions in pursuit of green ends we find ourselves able to take. Meanwhile we retain our underlying awareness that, when it comes to any particular crunch, the terms of this warrant will allow us all the leeway we might need.

It is vitally important to recognize that we are not talking here about any of the various forms of *denial* which social psychologists have identified as operating in the environmental arena. The denier does not get as far as asking how green is green enough: his tactic is to question how important green is anyway, at least in terms of his own actions. This can be done simply by ignoring uncomfortable facts, but also at more sophisticated levels by challenging their status as facts ('there's no proof that climate change is really happening'), pleading powerlessness ('nothing I do can make a difference') or diverting onto the perennial issue of casting the first stone ('all these environmentalists use electricity and drive around'). Such denial can indeed be in bad faith if it is a refusal to acknowledge truths which, underneath, the denier really knows. (Al Gore in his film quotes H. L. Mencken on the difficulty of getting a man to understand something when his salary depends on his not understanding it.) But my point is that, well beyond these diversionary tactics of denial, bad faith is still always soliciting even those who are genuinely trying to confront the issues, because it is inherent in the sustainable development picture of *how* to confront them.

Equivocation on the status of the numbers is what is essential to acting in bad faith here. The trouble is that *any* answer we come up with to the question 'How green is green enough?' can be taken to be quantificationally warranted in one sense or another. Making the changes we find we can make is explicitly warranted by the in-principle-calculable beneficial consequences (the quanta as determinate).

Not making those we find beyond us is tacitly warranted by the recognition that any particular calculation will lack robustness (the quanta as inherently uncertain). That is to say that typically there will be various different possible bases for the relevant calculations, the decision between which will not be taken independently of the pressures which the calculation is supposed to be transcending. Moreover, as we have seen, calculation on any basis will be contingent on a raft of assumptions and estimations, all of which are in principle contestable. Lacking predictive robustness in these respects, a quantificational model of ecological responsibility can never substantiate the charge that to have gone only *thus* far, rather than somewhat further, wasn't responsible – and knowing this, we settle very naturally for more-or-less what we find we can manage.

Calculated moves?

It must surely be this structure of paradoxical reassurance, for instance, which explains the popularity of those 'carbon footprint calculators' now so readily to be found on the internet. When I last tried it, Googling the term threw up fifteen apparently different ones in the first couple of pages. They are variously produced by government agencies, campaign groups, wildlife charities, universities and big corporations like BT. Some of them talk about emissions in terms of carbon dioxide, others just refer to carbon. Equally, some of them merely work out from the data which you enter a figure for your annual weight of emissions compared to an average figure (typically for the UK). The 'footprint' label is of course strictly a misnomer applied to a calculation which goes only this far, since it leaves the normative basis unclear. (Is even being average acceptable? How far below average should one be? ...) The normative idea captured with such appealing simplicity in the original 'ecological footprint' concept is that of equal entitlement to limited ecological space: your footprint being the size of your foot, those of us with enormously big feet are bound to be treading on a lot of other toes given that there is only so much standing room for all of us on Earth. The better carbon calculators use the footprint notion properly, translating emitted tonnes *per capita* into this area-based measure by relying on the idea that the bio-capacity needed to absorb your personal CO_2 emissions, or that proportion of them not absorbed by the oceans, must be provided by a certain area of the Earth's surface. This is certainly preferable from the point of view of giving us guidance – though it does bring into view the hugely simplifying nature of the modelling relationships which are going to be needed to produce any figures at all on such an approach.

Suppose, then, that one enters one's data into one of these more sophisticated programs – that produced by WWF, for instance, is quick and clear. (It can be found at www.footprint.wwf.org.uk.) On the basis of some very simple information about my domestic arrangements, travelling habits, and food and energy consumption, this tells me that I am emitting 6.99 tonnes of carbon per annum, equating to an ecological footprint of 3.66 hectares – and, much more graphically, to 2.03 planets, pictured like two full moons and a gibbous sliver in a row on the results page. In other words, if everyone on Earth lived like me, that's how many planets we should all need for enough ecological space to support ourselves with no-one treading on anyone else's toes. I am then told, encouragingly, that my result in planets is below the UK average (of just over three, apparently), but am reminded, somewhat redundantly though with a jocular exclamation mark, that one planet is actually all we've got.

What does one make of, and do with, such information? It is human nature in all sorts of situations not just to prefer the good news but to find the good news better than we find the bad news is bad. So, typically, one will tend to find besting the UK average a good deal more of a reassurance that one is doing one's bit than one finds one's shortfall at the global level a shaming incentive to further downshifting. (And by the same token, if one had been shown to fall short of the UK average, that would have tended to become one's benchmark for improvement rather than the more daunting array of planets which it would have brought with it.) The standard upshot of resorting to such a calculator is, we might say, a structurally ungalvanizing model of our situation. This is not to say that one won't be incentivized at all, that one simply dismisses the adverse part of the message. For most people, to have tried calculating their carbon footprint at all means that they are at least prepared to be serious about their concerns. But it is no surprise that the tendency will be to hear the positive answer as louder, and to let it obscure more of the shortfall, than a purely objective attention to the whole would justify. Our motivation is hardly ever a straightforward or single-level business, and one needn't be *comfortable* with such a quantified result to be left fairly undiscomfited by one's discomfort.

But, to repeat – that is a kind of reaction which quantifying such results actively encourages. The website doesn't need to show us – in pictured pinches of salt, perhaps – how approximate all this is. Our inputs themselves either will have taken the form of averages or ranges (orders of magnitude for fuel bills and the like), or will have been quantified using crude averages where they are non-numerical (such as house type). Then there are all the assumptions necessary for processing this data to a unitary result in terms of carbon emissions. Some of the online calculators (www.carboncalculator.co.uk is an instance) even allow us a little way behind the scenes here, offering an outline explanation of how the figures are generated. Rough average usage and emission factors abound; assumptions about data compatibility over time, occupancy levels of planes and average food miles are all required. Beyond these calculations, of course, must come the fairly heroic simplifications involved in converting the approximate carbon weight of emissions totted up through them into a bio-capacity footprint expressed in hectares of land needed to absorb them … . But people don't have to explore these penetralia, or even be consciously aware of them, to sense the pervading contingency – even if they don't call it that. Just from entering one's own highly simplified data, one can't but recognize how very roughly estimated any output must be. So far, so normal in a culture where we meet rough quantification at every turn and in general know how to handle it. But in this particular conflicted area of sustainability, we can still use tacit differentiation to equivocate. The result on which we hesitate to act can happily be read as hesitant – provisional, hedged about with ifs and buts, *at best* a rough approximation. Meanwhile the result about which we can feel reasonably good gets taken as good enough for purpose: a rough-*and-ready*, sufficiently indicative approximation. Qualified optimism qualifies already-qualified dismay, and the ungalvanizing effect is warranted by the numbers. From the perspective of real ecological responsibility, it is like hurrying the wrong way along one of those moving walkways at airports – taking two steps forward, we are carried at least one step back.

Whatever their intention, in fact, the actual function of these carbon footprint calculators is, indeed, to reassure. That is why they have become so popular. Presenting themselves as guides to an urgently necessary transition, their effect is to encourage us in a consciousness of our own concern alongside a belief that by and large we're on track – without the need for real upheaval. In this function they are joined by a good many other nodes of scientifically managed bad faith, quantified hooks whose principal use is for letting us off them. These include carbon-neutrality aspirations as an advertising pitch for corporations making their money from increased consumption, eco-labelling of supermarket products which you have to buy from the supermarket, biofuels feeding cars before people and offsetting to encourage low-cost flying so that we can all keep travelling. I do not have space to pursue the analysis which would be needed to support each of these claims in detail, but I think enough might now have been done in this chapter for the general point to stand. In all these cases, a tool which in itself makes perfect technical sense on the sustainable development model is used to embed current patterns of behaviour in the very process of challenging them. And nestling at the hollow heart of each manoeuvre will be found a set of figures lending themselves to the kind of equivocal interpretation I have been illustrating.

The upshot of these considerations is disturbing. They drive us to conclude that a certain type-figure who has lately become rather more prominent in the advanced societies is also much more representative than one had thought – or hoped. This is the exponent of environmental-political correctness, the person characterized by a rather self-righteous complacency about their not-too-disruptive lifestyle shifts, for whom (one had supposed) all those colour-supplement pieces about gracious green living in your loft conversion were intended. But this person's mindset, it now appears, is not after all a travesty – rather it expresses something inherent in the way the mainstream model captures and tries to operationalize environmental concern. He or she stands not for a regrettable mutation of the sustainable development approach, but for a central strand in its DNA.

Shadow stewardship

By this point, some readers may be objecting to what will have struck them as an unduly cynical view of human nature. Yes, highly contingent numbers offer built-in opportunities for backsliding, but we surely aren't compelled to *take* those opportunities? The fact that we can choose to equivocate doesn't mean we have to – indeed, it has to mean that we can choose not to. For the evaluations to have any significance, a case where we can act in bad faith must be one where we could instead act in good faith; someone like Jermyn, morally alert enough to sense where the loopholes present themselves, has by the same token the option to recognize them as loopholes and plug them against himself. Standards susceptible of being floated can be pegged all the more firmly in place for that very reason.

Responding to the carbon calculator, for instance, someone may see a footprint of one-and-a-bit planets too many as inequitable enough to inspire really strenuous further efforts at lifestyle change. Someone else may see that result as uncertain enough to prompt, and justify, no more than those changes which they feel comfortably able to make. But isn't the difference between these reactions just that between genuinely trying to live up to a standard, and allowing oneself to fudge it for self-interested reasons? If so, while it may sometimes be hard to recognize or admit to doing the latter, there are also situations where we can see plainly enough the temptation to play false with ourselves, and simply resist it. And surely, so the objection might continue, the challenge of ecological responsibility presents us with just such a situation? In principle, however people may waver in practice, our strong obligation to behave responsibly towards the future entails an equally strong obligation to deal responsibly (that is, not self-servingly) with the inevitable conditions of predictive quantification mediating our relations with that future. It is clear enough in general terms that we now have the technological power to disadvantage future generations very seriously in respect of their global habitat. We have a correspondingly clear moral obligation not to do so, but rather to deal fairly and justly with them, by stewarding the Earth's resources and ecological capacities in our time, so that future people can rely on them as we have been able to do. By that standard of impartiality, it is also especially clear that we must be on guard against any kind of special pleading, quantificational or otherwise, on behalf of our own present comfort and convenience. To the extent that sustainability targets and benchmarks are recognized as contingently uncertain, therefore, that should if anything be spurring us all the more to *exceed* them, for safety's sake, rather than excusing failure to meet them.

But I want to argue that this whole idea, of an ethical standard of fairness or impartiality towards future people, is actually a central feature of the mirage. The best way to show this is to examine what happens to the requirement of responsible stewardship, just mentioned, when we try to pin it down to a clear meaning.

Making sense of stewardship

The picture of the present human generation as stewards of the planet has had a powerful presence in environmental thinking from its beginnings. It can be given a religious colouring, as by Prince Charles when he invokes 'the idea that there is a sacred trust between mankind and our Creator, under which we accept a duty of stewardship for the Earth'. More usually it is offered as an apparently secular form of the same thought, as by Jonathon Porritt:

> *The concept of 'stewardship', of taking responsibility in so far as we can for the whole of life on Earth, is a powerful source of moral inspiration for hundreds of millions of people.*

And there is indeed a sense in which this notion expresses something basic about the idea of ecological responsibility. Think back to the Apollo image of the Earth from space, which we summoned up to launch this whole chapter. An absolutely central recognition prompted by this viewpoint is that the planet where we live cannot be *at our disposal* – humanity's to do as we like with. It seems impossible that the life-processes which have produced *Homo sapiens*, as one species among others dependent on the intricate richness of the biosphere, could have delivered all this over to it, so that what twenty-first century humanity decided to do with it could be the proper culmination of the story. How could one particular kind of primate have that kind of relation to the whole? In another sense, however, the planet is now very much *in our hands*. How twenty-first century humanity decides to live will determine whether the biosphere across the whole face of the Earth is jeopardized or preserved, whether still-flourishing tracts become deserts and vast swathes of life survive or are extinguished. We are the species whose activities are now threatening the ecological integrity of the Earth-system, and we are also the first generation of that species which has really come to understand what it is doing in these respects. We also know, at least in principle, how to stop. From this conjunction, of something which is not ours to dispose of being nevertheless currently in our hands, the concept of stewardship seems to drop out very readily: for a steward is traditionally someone who is in charge for the time being of what doesn't ultimately belong to him. Our sense of ecological responsibility seems to resolve itself quite naturally into a felt obligation of this kind.

It is evident, too, how easily this notion can be taken to express the core principle of sustainable development – the idea of our managing a balancing act between using the Earth's resources for our needs and preserving them to meet the needs of the future. And it offers just the kind of compelling simplification which appeals to politicians. So it is entirely unsurprising that a *locus classicus* for the impact of the idea on mainstream political thinking should be the former UK government's 1990 White Paper *This Common Inheritance*. That document marked, if any single one did, the point at which environmentalism in Britain came in from the cold and the issues which it was raising began to be taken seriously by real decision-makers. In terms inspired by, and in places directly echoing, the then Prime Minister Margaret Thatcher's road-to-Damascus speech to the Royal Society a couple of years previously, it states that:

> ... *the ethical imperative of stewardship ... must underlie all environmental policies. ... It is mankind's duty to look after our world prudently and conscientiously ... we do not hold a freehold on our world, but only a full repairing lease. We have a moral duty to look after our planet and hand it on in good order to future generations. That is what experts mean when they talk of 'sustainable development'.*

But the idea of stewardship as mooted here simply will not make the kind of sense or do the kind of work for which it is being enlisted. The whole conception, despite the earnestness of the language and the evidently sincere intent, can only lead us into *shadow* stewardship. The key point here is that we cannot just treat future people unproblematically as *others*, existents standing independently over against us, in respect of our present actions. But the model of responsibility which we are drawn to employ here when we try to think of the present generation as stewards does involve our looking out for the welfare, or the rights, of others placed over against us. Any such model has two necessary linked dimensions, of consequences and of accountability: we are responsible, in this sense, whenever we are genuinely accountable for the consequences of what we do. And this is where the real problem for sustainable development lies.

Responsibility is in fact almost the whole of what this metaphorical language of stewardship entails. For we are evidently not *literally* 'stewards of the planet'. Few in the advanced world now believe that God or any other external agency has entrusted it to us, which removes a whole dimension of actual stewardship. In the full literal signification of the term, 'X is a steward' implies:

X is responsible for looking after something
... on behalf of someone else Y to whom it belongs, or who has a major stake in it
... and in respect of his care of which X can (at least in principle) be held to account by or on behalf of Y.

That is, we can only literally be stewards on behalf of someone who *owns* (or has an equivalent kind of right over) whatever it is we are taking care of on their behalf. But once God is out of the picture, if we try to think of any subsequent human generation as owning the planet, then it will seem wholly arbitrary why it should be them and not us who do so – the only relevant distinction being temporal position in the sequence of human generations, which can hardly make the necessary difference here. Equally, if we are to think of ourselves as stewards just because we recognize that we *don't* own the planet, then nor does any other generation. But if no generation owns the planet, the idea of literal intergenerational stewardship must simply drop out. Exactly the same point can be made about the old Green slogan which expressed this idea of stewardship long before it got into government white papers: 'We do not inherit the Earth from our parents, we borrow it from our children.' Unless our children actually own the Earth, which there is no more reason to think of their doing than of our already doing – in which case, inheritance is after all the appropriate relation – there isn't really any borrowing going on.

But just as evidently, there can be no literal 'holding to account' going on either. All that can happen, on any particular occasion of our making a decision with implications for futurity, is that we try to stand in for successor generations and hold ourselves to account on their behalf – try to govern our actions by some sense of what they could reasonably expect from us. This can certainly be done, and done in a serious attempt to take, as it were, a back-bearing from the future on present conduct. We can try to act responsibly towards future generations by making thoughtful judgements about, for instance, how much loss of the natural world they might be likely to see as a fair exchange for how much enhanced technological capacity. Nor need there be anything casual or perfunctory about this – we can really try to see such matters from their perspective. But we are, too, necessarily the only judges of how far we have succeeded. And holding oneself to account in this way isn't being held to account, any more than locking oneself in a room and pocketing the key is imprisoning oneself, however firmly one intends to stay put. There is no way in which the basic judgements of the human present can be challenged here, except by present humans – and that is, ultimately, a matter of having only our own best judgement to go on. But if that is the case, then there can be no genuinely constraining accountability in the frame. And what that means is that we can't actually deal *fairly* with the future at all.

Impartiality, accountability and the future

The issues become clearer if we consider by way of contrast a case of literal stewardship. Suppose I am house-sitting for someone while he's away – an ill-advised party gets out of hand and some of his good-quality furniture is damaged. He bought this stuff years ago, so the identical range is no longer available. Clearly I can't just replace the damaged items with flat-packs from IKEA. Hopefully I will replace them with what I sincerely judge to be reasonable substitutes – I will replace them, that is, in a way which I take to constitute fair dealing with the house owner. On his return, however, he may nevertheless object to my taste or to my level of expenditure – that is, to the criteria which I have used. And clearly, that's only fair – as it wouldn't be if the issue here were just down to me (or, for that matter, to him). We have to find criteria for fair dealing through a process which gives an appropriate voice to both of us if the replacement process is indeed to constitute fair dealing. It's the knowledge that my judgement as to what will constitute an adequate replacement can be challenged, and is both in principle and potentially in practice *defeasible*, which works to constrain my exercise of this judgement – I ask myself 'Would an impartial third party take this to be proper restitution?', rather than just 'Well, what seems OK to me?' (where there would be a real possibility of the answer's being tacitly influenced by what I think I can get away with). By the same token, he can't just ask 'What do I want out of this?', with an answer open to the influences of vengefulness or opportunism (he'd been meaning to go upmarket with the furniture for a while ...). Through thinking about and probably discussing the matter in this way, we have to reach unforced agreement on a standard which he can't expect me to more than meet, and I can't expect to get away with less than meeting. And if we remain in disagreement over this – over whether I have indeed restored him his house in as good a state as he left it – then a disinterested third party (in hard cases, perhaps, as part of a legal process) can be asked to arbitrate.

In the intergenerational case there is, necessarily, nothing like this. We can't enter into this (or any) kind of dialogue with future people, either now when we are deciding to act, since they aren't yet here, nor when they come to make a judgement about the adequacy of what we have left them, since we will no longer be around. And how in the nature of the case can there be any actually impartial third party in the frame? – since as between the present generation and future generations, there seems nowhere for such a third party to stand.

What is being exposed here is that the concept of fairness always works at two levels. At the *substantive* level, fairness means the kinds of thing we all recognize as exercises of impartiality, such as acting even-handedly and returning like for like. But there is also the *criterial* level, at which we decide what is going to count in the given circumstances as even-handed or as appropriately like (since usually, as just exemplified, 'like' won't mean 'identical'). In fact, when we cry 'That's not fair!', we most often mean not that there is conscious substantive doing-down going on, but that what is being taken as even-handedness isn't really – the protest is an invitation to reappraise the relevant criteria. And it is crucial to the possibility of fairness in practice that impartiality should rule at this criterial level too. An act of mine involving you can't be *fair* as between me and you if only I get to decide *what it is* for me to act fairly here, and you have no locus in that decision. (That just wouldn't be fair ... .)

Of course this doesn't mean that one cannot act fairly towards someone in particular cases without their knowledge and involvement. When, for example, I write a confidential reference on you, I can perfectly well give a fair report of your character and abilities without your having the chance to edit what I have said. But this is because there are generally agreed criteria of fair reportage in the offing here, by which I can if necessary be held accountable. (If someone is appointed whose skills I have seriously misrepresented or whose deviant tendencies I have glossed over, I will find myself at best discredited as a referee in that quarter, and at worst in trouble with the law.) The acknowledged standards of procedure in such situations bring into play an impartial judgement of what is fair here, to which I must conform my practice. They also act as your silent voice in the process, the assumption being that you will be signed up to them too. It is, however, only because such standards subsist in a public realm as between the parties involved that real fairness is possible. That status means that they can in principle be challenged and argued over by everyone with an interest in them – those supplying references, those relying on them and those being refereed. Should one, for instance, mention character defects that one knows about but which aren't strictly relevant to the job? That can't be argued over case-by-case, or the system would collapse; but there grows up around the business of requesting and supplying references what might be called an institution of mutual accountability, which keeps the operative standards in repair by ongoingly addressing and resolving such questions within the flow of the evolving social practice. Without such an institution, expressed in things like the current standard guidelines from Personnel – if, for example, each referee had simply to decide for himself or herself what constituted a fair report on someone else – there could be no genuine fairness in confidential refereeing.

The point is that generally, where the public existence of the standard, its status as both contestable and confirmable in principle as between all the parties, is dubious, so too must be the criterial impartiality of any judgement made – and so, consequently, must be the possibility that any action dependent on such judgement can be fair.

This is necessarily the situation with judgements about the fairness to futurity of our present resource-allocation decisions. As we noted, the sustainable development standard here is meant to be grounded in the fundamental requirement of fair play. We are being fair to future generations when we leave them like for like, or what the political philosopher John Locke called 'enough and as good' – that is, in the modern context, at least as much biospheric capacity to generate resources for human welfare as we ourselves inherited. But then, prevailing modes both of resource usage and of technological development mean that we shall certainly not be leaving them a planet in precisely the same physical and biological shape as we found it. So it becomes a further issue what is to *count* as handing on an 'equivalent level' of biospheric capacity. Does significantly reduced biodiversity together with significantly improved techniques for manipulating the residual gene pool so count, for instance? Or, less dramatically, what about an infrastructure increasingly dependent on electricity and all the hills covered with wind turbines? The answers to such questions are not simply a matter of 'doing the science right'; they involve *choices*, notably among available parameters for biodiversity and acceptable levels of future risk from genetic intervention, which help shape what we will take to be the right science. They also turn in part on what attitudes we are willing to adopt towards the whole human-natural context in which future people will have to meet their needs – in particular, on how far we think it will matter to them that ecological capacities will require complex technological means to realize them. And it should be clear that present humans can make collective judgements on such issues with more or less of an eye to their own immediate interests and convenience – that is, more or less *impartially*. How, then, are we to know that we are being fair to the future in this kind of criterial judgement?

There are, of course, higher-order criteria for fairness *in* judgement, which have to do with procedure rather than outcome. We judge fairly when we do not attach undue weight to our own concerns, are genuinely open to the perspective of others affected, give clear and honest grounds for our judgements, and so on. But then there are further, still higher-order judgements to be made about what weight *is* undue, what counts as genuine openness, which grounds are clearly honest. And how can we, present people, know whether we are making these judgements in the appropriate spirit of impartiality as between ourselves and our descendants? We can certainly, as already noted, try to judge carefully and scrupulously. More, we can seek to confirm our judgements through open debate across present society as a whole, rather than just in closed groups of 'experts'. We can use a wide variety of dialogical and imaginative means to increase our capacities for considering what future people are really likely to think about such matters. These various methods of projecting ourselves into future shoes are institutions of accountability in a sense, but not of mutual accountability in the full sense required for impartiality, and so for responsibility. Whether your shoes fit me depends on what size you take, not on what size I think you might take – but here it does, and must, all come down to what present people think. It needn't be a simple matter of what they think future people will think, but that is only because it has to be a more complicated matter: when we think we have done enough to reflect fully on what we are going to let ourselves think they will think, that in turn is going to be the bottom line. And that is just not enough for intergenerational fairness.

The intergenerational case, in fact, is flagging up something which is often missed or underplayed in considerations of the nature of fairness. That is that the underlying institutional framework of criterial impartiality can't in the last analysis exist merely *in our heads*. It is no good having a standard of impartial judgement, however well worked-out and rationally compelling in theory, if there is ultimately no actual mechanism by which the relevant parties to particular judgements can share (acceptably to each of them) in resolving (always provisionally and revisably) any disputes about how that standard is to be interpreted or applied. Absent such mechanisms, our standards of fairness can only depend on how fairly we apply our standards. Ethical practice is pervaded by the intricately networked institutions of mutual accountability which we have created to make real intersubjective judgement stick under these conditions. They range from the habit of unforced face-to-face discussion, through more-or-less informal procedures of appeal to the arbitration of third parties, all the way to infrastructures of decision and revision (ethics committees, tribunals, law courts and so on) formally embodied in 'institutions' of the sort that have corporate identities, addresses and meeting schedules. The point of all of them is to provide an appropriate practical closure to questions which would otherwise remain indeterminable in principle. If my (or your) judgement that something is fair depends on the further judgement that that judgement was reached impartially, and that in turn depends on an interpretation of impartiality which I judge to be fair, and that depends ... it is obvious that the issue of fairness at the substantive level will always remain open. It can only be closed by actual agreement, for the time being, between the parties to a relation of real mutual accountability. And, to repeat the obvious – as between present and not-yet-existing future people, that isn't possible.

A corollary which we should just note, and accept, is that there are relations with other kinds of necessarily voiceless being where it isn't possible either. These include not only other living species, but some kinds of human – infants and the grossly mentally deficient, for example. The notion of treating any of these kinds of being *fairly* or impartially also fails at the criterial level. This does not impair our ability to deal ethically with them, since there are other relations within the broad domain of the ethical in which we can stand to them – we can have naturally emergent responsibilities to care for them, protect them or cherish them. But none of these can be relevant in the intergenerational case. Impartiality is the *only* way in which we could ever hope to relate ethically to non-existent, wholly undifferentiated and merely potential people. And in the nature of the case, it cannot really obtain.

What we try to substitute for it, of course, are the numbers: the practice of counting going proxy for accountability. That is why *ethico-scientism*, which I called the spirit of sustainable development, needs both of the paired terms to characterize it. Our pseudo-ethical relation of impartiality towards the future seeks to represent itself as genuinely ethical by invoking a science which must scientistically over-reach its powers to do the job. If only we can accurately predict what quanta of what forms of natural capital will be available at what future dates as a result of what action taken or refrained from by us now, we can have in effect a mode of unforced, timeless agreement with the people who will be alive then. Any such quantum is, and will be, the one quantum it is – for them as for us. It thus provides a standard for fair dealing to which both we and they must subscribe, without the need to maintain it in being through all the collaborative dialogical processes which are here impossible. If less than 2°C of global temperature rise will enable the climate to go on providing for people after 2050, or 2100, more-or-less the quantified levels of service which it provides for us now, and we can determine with sufficient precision what reductions in CO_2 emissions that requires immediately, we can act fairly towards futurity by making those reductions. We can also govern that would-be-fair dealing impartially by ensuring we get the science right and don't fudge the figures ...

Except that, as we have seen, this proxy impartiality is unachievable. Through all the impingements of radical contingency which we have noted, the numbers in this whole domain depend on our present judgements, including our judgements of value in relation to future consequences. To take their objectivity as independently warranted (by 'scientific reality'), and then use it as a substitute standard for the impartiality of our value judgements, is really no more than to go in a circle. And once we acknowledge this, we can see that the sustainable development paradigm provides, at bottom, simply *no way of distinguishing* between impartiality and partiality in our posture towards the consequences of what we do. In other words, it offers no robust way to mark the difference between preparing to meet our obligations to the future and construing the future as putting us under obligations which we are prepared to meet.

Pseudo-standards and the mirage effect

I have been arguing that our relations with future people can't involve fairness or unfairness in the *full* sense – leaving it open that they might be understood as fair or unfair in *some* sense. And so indeed they can. The possibility of obligation doesn't fail entirely in the intergenerational case. We do indeed have what seems irresistibly like an obligation to prevent runaway global warming and the other forms of ecological catastrophe which now threaten. There are pretty clear criteria for what *couldn't* count under any reasonable interpretation as handing on undiminished natural capital value. It is not as if 'what will serve as the same' is entirely open, or something in respect of which our judgement is entirely unguided. If we hand on a planet with sea levels massively higher, huge unpredictable storm surges, widespread desertification and destabilized life-support systems worldwide, future people will have very little chance of living anything remotely corresponding to our present notion of a good human life. Just to neglect to do anything about this, once we can see it as a serious likelihood, would be to act in a way that thoroughly deserved to be called *unfair* to the future. Conditions which we would find unsupportable under any trans-formation of our attitudes and values that we can anticipate cannot be taken to be conditions which could count as acceptable to any future people. We have to assume that they and their situation will resemble us and ours to *that* extent. Correspondingly, we do find ourselves under a genuine obligation not to impose on them, for the sake merely of our own ease and comfort, what we should violently resent having imposed on us for the same kind of reason.

This gives us at any rate some baseline conditions for action here. In judging what to do when action affects the longer term, we shouldn't depart too far from what *we* would regard as materially 'the same'; we shouldn't make clearly self-serving assumptions ('There's bound to be a technological solution in time, so we can just go on behaving as we are'); we shouldn't assume that future people will differ much from us in their core values, whatever the socio-cultural shifts; and, without fetishizing the science, we shouldn't shirk giving the best scientific grounds that we can for our judgements. This is not an empty standard for judgements to meet. Considerations of impartiality will take us this far – but the problem is that they won't take us far *enough* into robust judgements about specific positive changes. The ethics of what we very clearly mustn't do is always much less than half the story, since action is necessarily a positive matter. We can't *just* refrain from entailing catastrophic changes on future people; we always have to do something specific which we judge will constitute avoiding this. And it is not with seeing that it would be grossly negligent for us not to change direction, but with supposing that we can decide what alternative directions would be fair, that the real crunch comes.

Consider, for example, the new debate over nuclear energy, with global warming now perceived as a serious threat in a way it wasn't during earlier phases of this long-running controversy. (And recall in this context the assessment of the consequences of warming, as something like a slow-motion nuclear holocaust, noted in the Preface.) We can see that acting fairly rules out consciously entailing climate catastrophe on our descendants – but can we see whether or not it rules in moving swiftly and seriously to reactivate the nuclear energy programme (as powerfully advocated by James Lovelock in his latest book *The Revenge of Gaia*)? Suppose we hand on to the people of the mid to late twenty-first century a climate and biosphere still on the hither side of catastrophic step changes, *but* we also hand on a new generation of reactors with their associated wastes and the dangers they pose to ecological capital and human health. Suppose also that by so doing we buy time for something like present technological society to continue for a while longer, so that there is at least a possibility of finding out how to manage these wastes, or perhaps of finding other kinds of new technological solution to the effects of warming. *Could* that count as handing on undiminished critical natural capital, and thus treating the future fairly?

On the sustainable development model, we always need to answer that sort of question before we can act positively in any direction against global warming or any other environmental threat. The point which I hope has now been established is that we can't know whether what we do now will result in any specific set of consequences that far into the future, so we can't be sure how to aim for this kind of balance, nor what specific combination of costs and benefits to future people would constitute its having been struck. Consequently, all we can do is to *invent* – as responsibly as we can. And that means that even if we address the question scrupulously, without making consciously self-serving assumptions or neglecting the best science, we can still encounter no firm distinction between finding an answer under pressure from our own present interests and finding one impartially as between ourselves and the future. The whole model of 'dealing fairly with the future', that is, although it can be seen to make sense in broad general terms of ruling out gross intergenerational negligence, can't support the following crucial kind of practical decision: we must do A, which is just outside our present-lifestyle comfort zone, rather than B, which is just within it. And that means, of course, that once we are contemplating B, it can't support either any robust distinction between doing *that* and doing something else C which would be even a bit less demanding ... . (So what will in fact almost certainly happen – is, indeed, already happening – in the energy case, is a recommitment to nuclear power, on the tacit basis that it offers the least uncomfortable solution in terms of changes to the present Western lifestyle.)

Again, what is going on here is motivated by something basic to ethics itself. We have already glanced at the fact that thinking ethically is fundamentally about putting oneself in other people's shoes. This is so whatever normative account of such thinking one adopts. Whether choosing morally is seen as a matter of deciding which course of action maximizes welfare or utility, or which one will without tacitly making a special case of oneself, or what would be the brave, honest or otherwise virtuous thing to do in the given circumstances, still the essential move is from considering these questions merely from the standpoint of one's own desires to assessing them also from the standpoints of others likely to be affected by what one does. The whole point of the shoe-hopping image is that other shoes pinch (or flop loose) if significantly different from your own, and this is what alerts you to the real differences in perspective and preferences that might go with being someone else. Where we are talking about situations which would be catastrophic for *anyone*, such difference of fit is not an issue: a world which would evidently be insupportable from any perspective, present or future, can be rejected on behalf of everyone while standing merely in my shoes. But when there are real questions about how things are going to seem to others, those others have to have a real possibility of contributing to the process of answering them for fairness to be genuinely at issue. Our sense of others' perspectives must be shaped dialogically, either directly or through the application of standards which they have had the chance of helping to shape. Putting oneself in someone else's shoes must ultimately involve more than just deciding how one *supposes* their shoes would feel. And that is just what the conditions of trying to be fair to the future rule out.

Hence bad faith can take its opportunities. Confronted with our own reluctance to do what we know we really ought to do, although doing it will be hard, we can often find the inner strength to press on. But reluctance to do what we know, tacitly, that our obligation to do is really no more robust than an obligation to do something else a good bit easier, is very much harder to overcome. The thematic inhibiting mechanism is always going to be triggered – as in those modern cars where the acceleration cuts out automatically when you try to go too fast in a lower gear. Or it is as if the ethico-scientist model of our relation to the future is so set up that it *has* to pull its punches, and so will always punch below its weight.

Or again, to put the matter back into the terms of our organizing image, the mirage effect: we can see how this deep structure of linked aspiration and

3

Mirage Politics

In Chapter 2 we saw some characteristic kinds of compromise which people strike with sustainability demands and expectations as these impinge on the business of daily living. The reason for our managing so easily to address these demands in a form of bad faith was traced back to a source in the conceptual structure of sustainable development itself. This ruling paradigm or rationale on which we understand action in pursuit of sustainability, it was suggested, actually licenses the floating of our standards. It does so because we all tacitly recognize that its picture of the motivation to such action is only pseudo-ethical. It must then rely, in the way we have explored, on scientific prediction which we all tacitly know to be radically indeterminate for pegging any relevant standards in place.

It would seem on this picture to be very plausible that we should find a close analogue to this pattern of reaction in the behaviour of relevant collective entities (communities, corporate institutions, political jurisdictions ...). If bad faith is indeed in the bloodstream of sustainable development as I have been suggesting, then it will surely manifest itself in one form or another at any level of collective activity for which sustainable development is the rationale. We might then naturally expect to see the political and institutional pursuit of sustainability exhibiting, under serious pressure, dealings with its standards and benchmarks essentially similar to those which we have been anatomizing.

But is this what we *do* see? Can the picture of sustainable development as permanently exposed to the ambush of bad faith really be extended in this way to corporate and collective entities? While all such groupings are ultimately constructions out of their component individuals, it does not automatically follow that the kinds of consideration which affect individual behaviour will be replicated at the level of collective organization. Specifically, it doesn't follow that there must be an analogue at that level of the kind of standard-floating which we have seen affecting the individual's commitment to sustainability. That possibility needs to be demonstrated. But even if the extension of the picture to collectivities does make sense, does it actually capture what is happening with the climate change and, more generally, the ecological sustainability agendas? And what are the implications if it does? With these questions we come to an important crux for the whole argument of this book.

Bad faith – Individual and collective

Bad faith is a pathology primarily of the individual will. As we saw from Sartre, its very possibility depends on the duality of consciousness, the permanent capacity of individual subjects to be both agents and observers of themselves as agents. We cannot think of collective entities as bearers of any kind of subjectivity in this sense. We do, though, readily think and speak of such entities as *acting*, and prior to action as considering their available options and making *decisions* about what to do. We seem naturally disposed to make sense of such collective action in terms of intention, purpose, commitment and so on. All organized human groupings have routines and procedures, the upshots of which answer more-or-less fully to these concepts borrowed from individual agency. Indeed, their having these procedures is largely what constitutes them as organized groupings, rather than mere agglomerations of individuals. The first issue is then whether enough for a plausible analogue of action in bad faith over sustainability requirements is transferable from individual to collective agency.

What happens, of course, is that within the national entity there will be people who are pushing for collective action in a particular direction, people who are preoccupied with the effects that such action would have on the various groups or institutions in which they are involved, people who are alert to none of this and just want to get on unhindered with the lives they are used to, and a wide range of intermediate variations. What we call the decisions and actions of a collectivity typically emerge from a hubbub of such claims and insistences, a whole force-field of interests and motivations operating at different levels and pulling in different directions. This force-field will be configured strongly by the motivations of people at large thinking of themselves and their concerns just as private individuals. It will also be shaped, however, by the often somewhat different motivations of the same people when they are thinking of themselves as citizens, members of a local or national community with a potential common purpose. Working across these will be the vested interests of institutions and corporations, both as perceived by their component individuals and as articulated by their various systems of management and governance. And a further crucial element will be the drives and desires, both the private ones and those oriented to the public interest, of a whole army of persons in leadership positions throughout society. The complexities of interconnection through which all these and other vectors in the common identity interact within the policy- and decision-making processes of a nation or a community are matters to be studied in detail by all the various relevant specialisms – sociology, social psychology, welfare economics, public choice theory … . All we need here is to remind ourselves of the enormous multiplicity lying behind anything which could be called the decision or action of such a collective entity.

It is in the way it relates such multiplicity internally to itself that collective action will be liable to whatever analogue of bad faith might be identified at that level. This, as we have seen, is its keynote in our behaviour as individuals: it is a tacit strategy for allowing seriously conflicting motivations to remain in play, without having to face up to resolving their conflict into a unified will to action. Within the force-field of any, even moderately, vigorous collectivity, there are always going to be conflicting motivations – and those to which its resolved collective action fails to answer are unlikely simply to disappear as a result. But for the collective action to be what we might call wholehearted, there will have to be standards, expectations and procedures to deal with this fact. These will allow collective intention and decision to be representatively voiced and implemented, through whatever appropriate structures are in place. (The idea of *representativeness* here begs no questions about the extent of democratic accountability and so on, which will differ as between different collectives and kinds of collective; it merely indicates that the decision-taking institutions, whatever they are, can deploy the community's actual powers and resources for getting things done.) There will also be means, ranging from authoritative force to the democratic acceptance of majority rule, for ensuring that those who disagree with decisions taken on behalf of the community do not carry their disagreement to the point of serious disruption or open revolt. In sum, these arrangements will enable a collective entity to act, issue by issue and always for the time being, with something resembling the single will achievable by an individual agent.

Correspondingly, for an analogue to bad faith, we can imagine a collectivity's processes of representative voicing and enactment being pursued *hollow-heartedly*, through a kind of representative equivocation disguising itself from itself. An example very pertinent to the sustainability context might be the development of such a plethora of targets and indicators that national policies can be presented as successful by *some* measure, more-or-less whatever their actual outcomes. It is clear that this is just the kind of equivocation to which the sustainable development model might be expected to lend itself, for the kinds of reason to do with its conceptual structure which we have been considering. The effect, and the tacit point, of this flexible benchmarking approach would, precisely, be to allow powerful motivation vectors in conflict with the supposedly agreed course of collective action to remain in active play – avoiding the discomfort of resolving their conflict at the price of structurally inhibiting action. Thus the scene would be set for what might aptly be called mirage politics: the collective erection and pursuit of sustainability targets which, although we seem to be taking them seriously, in effect recede as we try to advance towards them.

If that is a theoretical possibility, the next question is whether we can actually identify something like it going on in a particular society – focally, for this study, the UK – which is beginning to confront the demands of sustainability. Here there is an important methodological point to be made about this kind of enquiry. How we answer that question doesn't just depend on the available empirical evidence – it depends also on how we are prepared to *interpret* the evidence, which will be in part a matter of how convinced we are by the conceptual case which that evidence might be relevant to supporting. The empirical dimension remains of course a vital test bed, but there is no simple recourse to empirical confirmation or disconfirmation in such questions. What we conclude from what we can identify as happening is going to be a matter of the sense and structure we find in it, as much as of the mere facts of the case. That makes these considerations more difficult, but no less pressing.

The situation as regards evidence on the ground is further complicated in this case by the unprecedented speed with which sustainability has climbed the social and political agenda. As we have noted, the importance of sustainable development has only been seriously acknowledged in the political mainstream for some twenty years, and has only become a matter of urgency (at any rate in Britain and Europe) with the increasing attention recently being paid to climate change issues. It can now perhaps be said to have become part of the stock-in-trade of aspiring statesmanship, at the rhetorical level – but it would be only reasonable to expect action on the ground to have lagged somewhat behind such a very swift transition in the rhetoric. As we noted in Chapter 1, we have only just begun to tackle Tom Burke's 'hard politics of the environment'. Just by themselves, a time-lag, confusion in the various regimes and mechanics of governance, and the inadequacy of practical action to date might not count as very strong evidence of hollow-heartedness or bad faith.

Nevertheless, I shall try to show in this chapter that, given the kinds of doubt which I have been raising about the sustainable development concept, we already have enough evidence to identify a very real danger and an urgent issue. The danger is that the practical politics of climate change on a sustainable development model will indeed turn out to be mirage politics – the politics of never getting there. The issue is how we react to this possibility, given that our time is rapidly running short. Putting it starkly yet again, we have maybe fifteen years' grace to prevent runaway global warming. This will require efforts of concerted national leadership and of worldwide international cooperation well beyond anything that humans have yet managed. How much evidence of the inherent ineffectuality of our current ruling paradigm do we need in a situation where, if we wait until the evidence proves incontrovertible, we may very well find that we have left matters too late to act on it?

Sustainability, but ...

Before turning directly to what has been going on at the level of national sustainability politics, however, it may be illuminating to glance at something which has recently manifested itself at more local levels. This is the phenomenon of what we might call 'sustainability NIMBYism'.

NIMBYs – people whose reaction to proposed developments is to say 'Not in my back yard!' – used to be, on the whole, a pro-environmental force in the land. The term was used by people who were, by contrast, pro-development, to characterize the protests of individuals and communities who tried to resist various 'improvements' (from new housing in the green belt to bypasses cut through ancient woodland to nuclear waste depositories) which they found proposed for siting in their own immediate neighbourhoods. The trend of such resistance tended to be pro-environmental in practice, because it typically involved opposing developments which would be damaging to wildlife, ecosystems or landscape value wherever they were sited. For those who pinned the NIMBY label on it, however, resistance of this kind was always taken to be shirking a crucial connection. The NIMBY, it was alleged, was someone whose essentially parochial concerns extended *only* as far as the impact on his or her back yard. Willing to accept in general the benefits of nuclear electricity, rapid private transport, local economic regeneration or whatever, they merely didn't want the necessary infrastructure (which had to go somewhere) going anywhere near *them*. Some people involved in local protests were radicalized by this kind of critique into adopting a more consistent and generalized environmentalist position, moving from 'not in my back yard' to 'not in anyone's' and accepting the consequences for economic and lifestyle change. But this was by no means a universal response, and the pejorative force of the NIMBY label often had sufficient truth in it to help isolate and overcome a good deal of local community reluctance in the face of 'progress'.

Lately, however, with the mainstreaming of sustainable development objectives at least in principle, we have begun to see local resistance of the kind that used to get labelled 'NIMBY' being deployed against the technologies not of environmental damage but of sustainability – most especially, against the spread of onshore wind-turbine installations necessary for any serious attempt at renewable electricity generation. The file of cases where public opposition to such developments has been pursued through the local authority land-use planning process is now beginning to swell. The surprising strength of some of this opposition is already a significant factor in the prospects for renewable energy, since wind power is central to the UK Government's energy policy. The Energy Review of 2006 contains a target for 20 per cent of UK electricity supply to come from renewable sources by 2020, reducing both CO_2 emissions from fossil fuel generation and dependency on imports of natural gas. It is generally accepted that this will not be achieved without substantial increases in onshore wind power, even if a new round of nuclear power stations is commissioned (since on past performance none of them are likely to come on-stream in time), as other renewables such as offshore wind and solar power are less developed and considerably more expensive.

But the way opposition to wind farm developments has been mounted and rationalized is also potentially very significant for my argument about the nature and structure of the sustainable development model, and so for the prospects of sustainability policy across the board. This is because such opposition illustrates, in cases which can already be called in evidence, what happens when conflicting motivations push us into bad faith over these issues. The plea of the sustainability NIMBY seems to mirror the pattern of St Augustine's famous prayer as a troubled young man: 'Lord, make me chaste – but not yet.' The modern version is 'Yes, let's pursue sustainability – but not *here*, not with a dozen 300-foot turbines on my horizon and affecting house prices in my locality.' For many concerned people this is an equally classic case of feeling strongly that one ought in principle to want something, while being very reluctant to accept the consequences of wanting it in practice. The crucial move in this situation is 'sustainability, *but* ...'. There are, it must be admitted, cases where the move is arguably legitimate – where wind farm developments would dramatically change particular 'heritage' landscapes or impact seriously on patterns of bird migration, for example. Then the line of argument is 'There are good reasons for wind farms in environmental and sustainability terms, *but* equally good reasons in those same terms for not having one in some specific place.' Such frankly avowed clashes in the application of sustainability principles deserve to be respected and argued through. More frequently, though, the move reflects an illicit 'just-put-the-thing-somewhere-else' motivation, which has then to be made to *seem* licit by what overtly follows the qualifying '*but*'.

The point in the present context is that what frequently do follow it are claims which depend for their effect on the inherent softness of predictive quantification in these areas. So the argument might become: sustainability, *but* the value of a particular landscape, as captured by the costs which people are prepared to incur to visit it, is too great to be sacrificed to a particular proposal which if it goes ahead would henceforth deter them. In a more generalized form, this argument runs: sustainability, *but* the overall cost–benefit profile of onshore wind power over time shows that this is an uneconomic way of trying to achieve it. Sometimes technically quite sophisticated quantification is invoked to help make this case: thus it is argued that because of wind variability, backup fossil-fuel-powered generating capacity remains needed to ensure stability of supply, and such capacity operated in this stop–start fashion actually emits more CO_2 per kilowatt-hour than if operated continuously – hence, sustainability, *but* once all the hidden costs are added in, onshore wind looks less attractive. That all these numbers are tending to be used in essentially equivocatory mode (taken as hard or soft according to the needs of the argument) is strongly suggested by the way in which, alongside such reliance on detailed prediction, our ability to predict is frequently called into question. Thus the strategy of a prominent anti-wind-farm website was until quite recently to cast doubt on estimates of the shortness of supply of fossil fuels, pointing to the notoriously flawed forecasts of the 1972 Club of Rome report. Lately, this site has been flagging up scientific uncertainties over how much global warming we can anticipate, how much of it is anthropogenic and what the precise effects will be. 'Sustainability, *but* how much can we really know about future prospects ... ?' – whereas, of course, we know much more definitively what difference any particular wind farm development will make to the locality in question.

None of this is to imply that wind-farm protestors never have any right on their side. As with more conventional development, siting proposals can be crudely insensitive, reflecting the commercial priorities of developers rather than proper attention to local concerns and legitimate interests; people are often justifiably suspicious of the motives of the large firms now moving into this field. Moreover, the centralized electricity supply regime means that localities must stand any disruption and change involved, while the renewable energy generated disappears off into the national grid (and into an energy culture in which its responsible use is certainly not as strongly encouraged as it might be). All these are valid points which a too-ready resort to the 'NIMBY' label can obscure. But it should also be clear that the temptations to bad faith inherent in this kind of situation are very strong, and are by no means always resisted – and the ways in which non-resistance is glossed seem to bear out the claims about the sustainable development model and its encouragement of standard-floating which I have been advancing in the book so far.

The 'sustainability, *but* ...' pattern of reaction and argument, I therefore suggest, doesn't just help us to understand these contemporary local dramas. It can also sharpen our focus on the equivocations and rationalizations which this model brings in its train at the national level.

A case of hard politics?

While it is true that we are still in the twilight phase of the climate war, there have certainly been some brushes already with the 'hard politics' in the countries which are beginning to lead the campaign. We need to examine these in terms not just of what happened, but more significantly of the qualities of collective and political will exhibited in them. These qualities have to do with the spirit in which action seems to be undertaken, and the extent to which the relevant commitments are wholehearted, half-hearted – or something else. I make no apology for concentrating on the British situation for this purpose. Some of the analysis is a matter of reading signals and nuances, and one does that best in relation to one's own milieu. Moreover, the UK Government, as we noted in Chapter 1, has at least made one of the most serious attempts worldwide to devise and implement a sustainable development strategy: features of what is going on here are plausible portents for what will happen elsewhere as the real sustainability battle is joined.

Let us therefore examine an early test case. One of the most crucial issues on the environmental agenda of an advanced society like the UK is that of personal mobility. In an economy which depends very heavily on such mobility, the currently central role of the private car, with its implications for fossil fuel usage and hence for carbon emissions and for climate change, raises all the hard-political difficulties of pro-environmental adjustment in an acute form. Recently, in Britain, what must be recognized as a first real attempt to address these difficulties seriously was tried – and is pretty generally recognized to have failed. Personal mobility was an area in which the Labour Government coming to power in 1997 started with high hopes and exciting ambitions. The manifesto on which it had been elected looked forward to an integrated transport policy with an explicitly environmental dimension. Improved public transport, meaning not just more of it but better coordination among its various arms and increased flexibility in funding its provision, was deliberately linked to the aim of reducing environmentally damaging levels of private car usage. 'I will have failed', roundly declared John Prescott, the minister put in overall charge of this policy, 'if in five years' time there are not many more people using public transport and far fewer journeys by car.' As an earnest of this new passion for both joined-up thinking and accountability, the governmental machinery responsible for transport and environment respectively had been brought under unified direction for the first time in Prescott's enormous new super-ministry, the Department of the Environment, Transport and the Regions. Among the first fruits of this coordinated approach, unprecedented in the UK, was a medium-term transport strategy for the decade 2000–2010, key planks of which included significant rail improvements, with increases of 50 per cent in passenger usage and 80 per cent in freight; reductions in road congestion, especially in urban areas, with a 40 per cent reduction in numbers killed or seriously injured in road accidents; active support for cleaner vehicle technologies; a 10 per cent increase in bus passenger journeys, with extensive bus priority measures, more park-and-ride schemes and better rural services; and modern integrated transport information, booking and ticketing services.

Comparatively untrumpeted, but a vital factor in the background to these aspirations, was the so-called fuel price escalator. This was an innovation of the previous Conservative Government whereby the tax on petrol was to rise annually by a stipulated amount above the rate of inflation. The differential had been set at 3 per cent when the measure was introduced in 1993, and stood at 5 per cent five years later, contributing to a total tax burden on unleaded petrol of around 77 per cent of the cost at the pump. Although claimed from the outset as a green measure, and according to some studies actually having some effect in stimulating greater fuel-efficiency and slowing down the annual increase in traffic, this escalator was essentially intended by its originators as a revenue-raising device. In the context of a serious attempt to improve the availability and flexibility of public transport provision, however, it offered a real opportunity for fuel taxation to come into its own as part of a concerted pro-environmental strategy. Rather than just further targeting the poor motorist who, with nowhere else to go, was a classic fiscal sitting duck, it could be seen – and presented – as a responsible attempt to alter patterns of personal mobility by making the environmentally friendlier option increasingly the more eligible one.

Corresponding with this was the new government's equally ambitious undertaking to do even better that its international obligations in cutting carbon dioxide emissions. The Kyoto Protocol under the UN Convention on Climate Change (then advisory but in due course to become enforceable in international law) required the UK to reduce its greenhouse gas emissions to 12.5 per cent below 1990 levels by 2008–2012; the Labour Government, however, committed the country to a reduction of 20 per cent below 1990 levels by 2010. This represented, at a reduction rate of 1 per cent per annum, a much more plausible first step than the Kyoto agreement towards the (then) generally recognized necessity for 60 per cent cuts below 1990 levels by 2050 if the worst effects of human-induced climate change are to have any chance of being averted. Giving such a hostage to fortune was an attempt to demonstrate bold global leadership, but the strategic approach being taken on the key transport front could be held to lend this commitment some realistic warrant. Here was at least the beginnings of a real attempt to alter the gearing between economic growth and environmental degradation, and to confront environmentally damaging activities with their full social and ecological costs.

Then what happened?

The key symbolic moment in this history was undoubtedly the 'fuel tax rebellion' of September 2000. Although the government had actually suspended the escalator device as such in that year's budget, increases in crude oil prices worldwide combined with a still-growing tax take to push some of the more macho among British fuel users into direct action. Borrowing their example from similar action in France, and their methods of grass-roots coordination (by a nice irony) from the tactics of environmental protest groups, small bands of lorry drivers and farmers used their vehicles to blockade oil refineries and enforce go-slows on major roads as a protest against rising prices at the pump. Petrol stations could not be supplied, panic buying spread rapidly among ordinary motorists and for a brief while it looked as if the country might be brought to a standstill. At this juncture, however, the government gave in. Having refused at any point during the protests to mount a defence of fuel taxation on broad environmental and climate change grounds, it cravenly undertook to listen sympathetically to the protestors and review its policies in that spirit.

What that process of review meant swiftly became apparent. The crucial link at the heart of an integrated pro-environmental transport strategy was broken before it could be well established. The grand ten-year plan was quietly shelved. The coordinating super-ministry was unpicked, with an independent Department of Transport (traditional outpost of the motoring lobby) re-emerging. Joined-up policymaking was allowed to lapse in favour of a mixed bag of piecemeal measures for railway organization and road charging, none of which was dangerously premised on discouraging car usage. The cumulative effect of all this activity, in fact, was to leave private motoring a comparatively *more* attractive option: according to the Office for National Statistics, bus fares rose by 52.9 per cent over the decade to 2007, figures from the Office of Rail Regulation showed that train fares rose by 46.2 per cent over a similar period, but drivers of small family cars saw their motoring bills rise from 41.52 pence a mile in 1997 to 56.15 pence in 2005 – that is, by only 26 per cent.

By his own announced criteria, the super-minister had, indeed, dramatically failed. So far, perhaps, so familiar. That democratic politicians make high-sounding promises and then backtrack in the face of unforeseen difficulties and recalcitrant realities is hardly news. Equally, it is only to be expected that political commitment to measures intended to avert medium- to longer-term problems should rapidly have turned out to be negotiable when those measures threatened palpable electoral damage in the short term. This kind of sequence of events might indeed be reckoned entirely natural: fiscal and regulatory action in the early stages of any gradualist strategy will inevitably be experimental, ready to retreat and reconsider if particular lines of approach prove unworkable in practice. From this perspective, indeed, something paradoxically encouraging could even be found in the history just rehearsed – environmental issues brought in from the shrill, ineffectual purity of the sidelines and beginning to be normalized amidst the muddy compromises of mainstream politics.

That is certainly one way of looking at it. But here we must come back with a sharper focus to the quality of political will which was on display in these transactions. I noted earlier the way in which collective action can be wholehearted, resolving the variety of conflicting motivations lying behind it into something resembling for practical purposes a single unified will. This is pretty evidently *not* the quality manifested here. Had it been so, we could have expected at least a vigorous defence of increasing fuel taxation in an explicitly environmental context from one or more key figures, whatever the short-term costs in popularity. While it might still have been necessary to yield some tactical ground to the protestors, given the disruptive success of their intervention, this would have been accompanied by a re-emphasized commitment to the overall approach and to the swift improvement of the public transport alternative, including an active search for different ways of making this the more eligible option on price or performance or both. None of this was forthcoming – and one can be sure from what did in fact happen that nothing like it was even seriously contemplated.

Was political action then *half-hearted* in this case? This is also a condition of the individual will which we have all experienced – where one's commitment is for some reason qualified or provisional, or one simply isn't much concerned with the goal one is supposed to be pursuing, so that encountering obstacles and resistance is likely to stop one in one's tracks, or divert one onto another path altogether. This at any rate partially describes what actually happened. The trouble is that it by no means reflects the nature of the government's own *response* to what happened. Had the pursuit of an integrated pro-environmental transport strategy been half-hearted in this way, we might have expected a different and more resigned tenor to the whole business. We might have expected government to point to the difficulties of balancing short- and longer-term requirements, to stress the uncertainties involved in trying to predict environmental futures, and to resile somewhat from its earlier high ambitions – some overt ministerial shoulder-shrugging over emissions reduction targets might have been observed, and at the very least some toning down of the commitments made in subsequent statements about these matters.

In fact, however, precisely the reverse was the case. Along with the unravelling of a transport strategy which might have begun to make a real difference to our sustainability prospects went not a toning down but a marked intensification of the government's sustainable development rhetoric, culminating in what can only be described as the preening self-confidence of the 2005 Strategy document discussed in Chapter 1, with its language of 'decisive moves' and 'profound change'. What this actually suggests, of course, is not half-heartedness so much as *hollow-heartedness* – collective action in bad faith. This is characterized by progressively more vitiated action interacting with progressively more clamant avowals of commitment, because such a process of reinforcing feedback is an essential part of the condition: inadmissible doubts about the adequacy of our actions prompt us to assert our goals and principles all the more vehemently, tempting us still further to employ self-serving criteria for our success. The underlying pattern is 'sustainability, *but* ...' – yes, of course we are committed to a sustainable transport policy, *but* we have to be able to go on guaranteeing the electorate the kind of access to instant private transport to which it has become so attached. This position is under such obvious strain that it becomes: 'Sustainability, *but* don't worry, there are all these effectively painless ways of achieving it through emissions trading and more loft insulation and different kinds of light-bulb ...'. The same processes of unavowed burden-shifting and buck-passing will then be brought to bear on these demands in turn, in a continuing dialectic of hollow-heartedness and what is in effect a form of hysteria.

The politics of never getting there

That diagnosis might itself sound a bit over the top. But once the pattern has been spotted, I believe that it can be very plausibly identified across the whole field of national sustainability policy and target-setting. The crucially revealing feature, as one would expect, is what is being done with the various relevant figures.

Theodore Porter, whose work on the social use of statistics we have already drawn on in Chapter 2, offers at one point in his discussion this brilliant cameo case-study:

> *A congressional mandate permits the United States Forest Service to cut no more lumber than is renewed by annual growth. Since that law was put into effect, growth rates have been greatly enhanced, at least in the Forest Service accounts, by new herbicides, pesticides and tree varieties. Through such doubtful forecasts, it drew the teeth from the law.*

Here we can see very clearly in miniature just how the 'sustainability, *but* ...' move is made. The illicit real dilemma – 'Yes, we have to comply with the mandate, but we really do need the income from going on cutting the lumber' – becomes the licit qualification '*but* we can do both by boosting compensatory growth rates well above previous levels'. This in turn depends on finding ways to quantify the forecast effects of new interventions so that they show this to be what, over the longer term, we are actually doing. And this is exactly what is starting to happen on a national scale with climate change policies, as more stringent emissions targets start to be imposed in countries like Britain.

Consider, for instance, how the policy process was ebbing and flowing in the latter part of 2007 around the target of getting 20 per cent of energy from renewables by 2020. This was a European Union aspiration to which the previous Prime Minister, Tony Blair, had signed Britain up in the spring of that year. The prospect of contributing meaningfully to it clearly placed challenging expectations on a country where the proportion of such energy amounts at the moment to around 2 per cent, as compared to an EU average of 7 per cent (with Germany, currently leading the drive on this issue, on somewhere over 9 per cent) – but Mr Blair, of course, had his halo as the environmental conscience of the G8 to keep burnished. And in any case, evidence was busily accumulating that such an ambitious commitment represented no more than what was needed, if indeed it was enough. A report from the UN's Intergovernmental Panel on Climate Change had strongly implied at the beginning of the year that greenhouse gas emissions globally would have to peak by 2015 in order to avoid the danger of average temperatures rising by up to a disastrous 6°C before the end of the century. By the autumn had come a further major report, from the Global Carbon Project, demonstrating how reinforcing feedbacks – a combination of more coal than predicted being burnt by the Chinese and a faster decline than expected in the capacities of the world's oceans and forests to act as carbon sinks – were making the situation even more urgent than the IPCC had recognized.

It appeared, however, that government in the UK was far from speaking with one voice in response. A particularly influential whisper, that of the new Department of Business, Enterprise and Regulatory Reform, was in fact insisting (in leaked documents seen by *The Guardian* newspaper) that anything approaching the 20 per cent target would be just too ambitious for Britain. Meeting it would face severe practical and cost difficulties, ranging from funding the necessary increased R&D for wave and tidal power to persuading the MoD not to turn its fire on the necessary offshore wind farms. Instead of following through on Blair's brash agreement to this target, the government should now be working behind the scenes with other more sceptical or less progressive governments, such as that of Poland, to undermine the Germans and reduce the required overall percentage before it had to be consolidated into binding national commitments. This pragmatic approach was wholly in accord with the guidance of the recently retired Chief Scientific Advisor, Sir David King, who had famously argued for emissions reduction targets that were 'politically realistic'. Setting such targets because we think we might be able to meet them, rather than acknowledging what authoritative reports suggest is actually happening to the composition of the atmosphere, seems odd as a form of realism – but it is entirely characteristic (we can now recognize) as a form of the 'sustainability, *but ...*' reflex. The target, which after all will be a quantifiable earnest of seriousness, itself validates the reluctance ('but not if it hurts too much') disguised under the 'realism' ('but we have to be practical').

Voices from still elsewhere, meanwhile, were already suggesting how any renewables target would in practice be treated once it started to bite. Another leaked briefing paper originating in the former Department of Trade and Industry was found to have asked ministers to examine 'what options there are for statistical interpretation of the target that would make it easier to achieve'. Possible wiggle-room, for example, could come from including nuclear power as a form of renewable, or counting in solar farms being supported by UK investment in Africa.

There could be few clearer indications that the creative sustainability accounting spotlighted by Porter in the US Forest Service will be the favoured method of grappling with those serious challenges to current habits, expectations and vested interests which even a diluted target is likely to produce. Or, putting it in the terms of Paul Ekins's analysis from which I quoted in the Preface, we could very reasonably interpret these behaviours as outcroppings of an underlying and deeply embedded strategy for having one's cake and eating it. The goal to which the UK has actually committed itself at the end of the EU process is 15 per cent of energy from renewables by 2020. Glancing over this brief history, who can be confident that it will be vigorously pursued, still less reached? The target is surely going to function as a mirage, and we can see here into the precise tricks of political refraction by which it gets generated.

Like the shuffling over transport policy, none of these tricks should surprise anyone with experience of the UK policy process. Indeed, this is how all democratic governments behave in the ordinary business of negotiating international agreements which have to be sold to their own electorates as well as implemented and reported back on. What may still come as a surprise – though hopefully less of one, to the extent that my argument through this first part of the book has been found persuasive – is the recognition of how far such shifts and slides, on the face of it ways of evading the demands of sustainable development, are really *built into the conceptual apparatus of sustainable development itself*. It is just because that model of our responsible relation to the future deploys a pseudo-ethics loading far more weight onto labile scientific predictions than they can bear, that the temptation to use those same figures in the spirit of 'sustainability, *but ...*' is so difficult to resist. If sustainability is a matter of longer-term consequences, the grip of its obligations on present action can only be as firm as those consequences are determinate – that is, not very firm at all – and *we can't help but be aware of this*, even as we offer to rely on the model for stiffening our resolution in the present. The heart of the problem is that sustainable development configures our ecological responsibility unimpeachably at the level of theory. That is why it has proved such a good banner, under which the advocates of that responsibility have been able to march so rapidly from the margins to the centre ground. But for all its solemn impressiveness at that level, it can't be effectively operationalized. The danger is not really that as a society we will crudely elect to prefer present consumer satisfactions over avoiding the desertification of sub-Saharan Africa, the flooding of half Bangladesh and so forth. Put like that, in the sustainable development abstract, governments and public opinion could hardly refuse to endorse ecological responsibility. The far more insidious danger is that we will resort, tacitly but increasingly, to the multiple opportunities of equivocation between hard and soft quanta which the ethico-scientism of the model provides, so as to ensure that 'acting responsibly' – for which we will continue to claim credit – always stops short of any unduly painful changes. (The offset calculations will always allow us to keep flying ... .)

This, as I admitted at the beginning of the chapter, can still only be identified as a danger. We have been appraising straws in the wind. But they are some pretty representative straws – we have now called in evidence patterns of action at the individual, local community and national government levels. And if that is how the straws are travelling, they may very well be riding the early turbulence of a hugely destructive storm. Can we afford to sit tight and wait to see if it arrives?

With that question left hanging, let me summarize the case I have been making through Part I as a whole, in order to point forward into Part II of the book. That 'sustainability, *but* ...' is not a perversion of sustainable development, but a permanent active possibility within it, follows from the pseudo-ethical and scientistic shape in which sustainable development is conceptually framed. Given the conditions under which we have to act, that permanent possibility is bound to be actualized as the pattern underlying our operational pursuit of sustainability. It is in effect inevitable that it should become the way we think sustainable development into practice. But when we do so, what we will get is pursuit of the sustainability *mirage* – a horizon of targets which we will always be falling short of reaching, and which in fact are always presenting themselves to us in such a way as tacitly to *license* our falling short. Meanwhile the situation on the ground, and in the atmosphere, gets ever more pressing, the problems which the targets are supposed to address ever more serious and the demands of genuinely adequate solutions more exacting – the goal itself recedes as our advance towards it pulls back, so that we will have less and less prospect of ever overtaking it. This truly is the politics of never getting there.

We simply cannot afford to let such a politics establish itself. We must change the shape and impulse of our action in this whole arena, before it is too late. But to do so, we must rethink sustainability – and in particular, the kind of motivation which it involves. That is the job to which I now turn.

PART II

DEEP SUSTAINABILITY

To explore and affiliate with life is a deep and complicated process in mental development ... our existence depends on this propensity, our spirit is woven from it, hope rises on its currents. – Edward O. Wilson

Shifting the Focus

If ethical obligation to future people cannot provide enough impetus to make us change the ways of life that are causing climate change, what could? Suppose we accept the argument of the book up to this point: we are always liable, both as individuals and collectively, to be floating our standards for discharging difficult duties framed over such a long time-span. Consequently we will always tend to find ourselves slipping back from their more exacting demands. The sustainability goal, conceived like this, will always have that mirage-like quality of receding from us as we try to advance towards it. So what alternative understanding of what we are doing might help to prevent this?

Of course, there are already people who simply cannot bear being complicit in a way of life which they recognize as hazarding the biosphere, and who are prepared to make significant changes in their own lives in order to avoid that complicity. These people may well experience their motivation in ethical terms, as a feeling of obligation towards those who are to come after them. And in a way it is less important how such pioneers explain their motivation than that they are in fact motivated, and strongly (otherwise they wouldn't be out in front as they are). But the point is, as I stressed at the book's outset, that in countries like Britain we now have to build a *working majority* of people with that order of commitment to action. Unless we do so, and pretty rapidly too, there is no prospect of initiating the necessary changes worldwide before it is far too late. This means that (here in Britain, in the first place) very large numbers of people for whom carbon emissions and related environmental concerns are still little more than warm words, if that, need to be awakened to a full recognition of the kind and scale of devastating climate-shift which is actually in prospect. And much more: this recognition must somehow trigger in them a motivation to do more than worry spasmodically about these matters while letting things go on largely as before. Instead, they must be driven by it to call for, actually vote for and then help to implement, right across society, the large-scale changes in policy and practice which will be necessary to confront the problems. My claim is that to *generalize* pro-sustainability action as widely as is required for all this, we now urgently need a deeper shared understanding of what such motivation really involves.

No such understanding can motivate by itself. How we conceive of sustainability cannot ensure that we seek it, or do so in sufficient numbers to make a real difference. Certainly we have to *incline* towards pro-sustainability change to get started – and surveys do now show increasing numbers of people, newly aware of the issues, having an uneasy feeling that we must be collectively on a wrong track if these are the kinds of risk we are taking with the future. But motivation is a very complex matter, and how this feeling of wrongness operates can be highly dependent on the sense which we make of it. A particular paradigm will explain the feeling, and warrant and reinforce the move from feeling to action, in its particular way. Thus a future-oriented ethical model will explain the wrongness of our current track as its imposing unfairly stringent consequences on coming generations. It will warrant action to correct these consequences through the hold that matters of fairness and unfairness have on our minds, within a democratic culture of respect for the rights and autonomy of each individual. And thus tentative personal motivation will be reinforced by being caught up with a very familiar and respectable social momentum, the drive to rectify injustice. But when people whose feelings of unease have not already been strong enough to carry them on into action sense that this model is essentially *flaky* as applied to the long-term environmental future, and encounter it as tacitly offering a standing invitation to bad faith, then it is likely to carry very many of them only as far as action sufficient to placate their own feelings of unease – which, as we all know, can often be done fairly easily. And if the model is structurally deficient in the ways I have been arguing, then that is how the majority will indeed encounter it when it is paraded in full view on the main stage of public policy, as is now beginning to happen with sustainable development.

As long as people are encouraged to think that any grip which sustainability concern might have on us is fundamentally a matter of obligations to future people, to avoid and promote particular future situations, they will – I am suggesting – find certain other strands in their multiple motivation-set operating to subvert it. But that might not happen, or happen anything like so insidiously, if the urge to sustainable action could be made to offer another kind of public sense. It follows from all that has gone before that such an alternative sense would have to shift the operative focus onto the *present*. It would of course continue to be informed by grave concern over what might be going to happen in the future, but it would understand the present motivating force of that concern in a different way.

This is because the model about which I have been raising doubts is one which depends essentially on accurate prediction as well as a certain kind of evaluation. We look ahead to determine the likely consequences of our present habits and lifestyles, evaluate those consequences by a criterion of acting justly towards future people – 'fairness to futurity' – and read back to the present to suggest what we need to change in order to meet that standard. In the nature of the concern, this will involve handing on to the next generation enough resources for it both to meet its needs and to hand on in its turn enough resources for the same purposes, and so on indefinitely. The specific changes proposed for implementation in the present will be justified in turn by predictions of their consequences. Our conception of sustainability is then as a trajectory into the future mapped onto the long-term goal of a state of balance which can, once achieved, be maintained ongoingly.

If what I have been arguing about scientific uncertainty, floating standards and the longer term is correct, we need to break out of this mindset – since it is liable to send us in pursuit of a mirage. Instead, we need to remind ourselves that a goal involving the achievement of a certain relation between the present and the long-term future doesn't have to be a *long-term goal*. We need to see sustainability, not as something which depends on what might happen over decades, if the present takes a range of now-urgent actions for the sake of the future, but rather as something crucially involving our active stance towards the future which we urgently need to realize for our own sakes in the present.

Shifting the sustainability focus to the present in this way might simply be taken to mean recognizing that sustainable things, rather than unsustainable ones, can and should be done *now*, and not just aspired vaguely after for some future time. Thus, for a very straightforward instance, powering our lights from renewables is sustainable now – we can start virtually at once and go on doing it indefinitely – whereas powering them from fossil fuels is not. Similarly, trying from now on not to use our lights, or our electric space heating, in ways which demand a lot more electricity than renewables can plausibly supply, tends towards sustainability as using them profligately does not. (As I write this, very early in the morning at my mid-week lodgings, I can see a medium-sized tree entirely draped in Christmas lights flashing on and off, on and off – unwatched, almost certainly, by anyone except myself and the solitary urban fox trotting by.)

This emphasis on prompt action is of course important, but I want to mean something different by the shift of focus in question. I want to mean seeing the profligacy symbolized in that festive waste of energy as something which *damages* not future people potentially, but ourselves at a deep level in the here and now. It damages us because of what we know (in broad outline terms) that it is likely to mean for the future – but what should move us to change our ways, in all the respects which this small instance dramatizes, is a concern for what its meaning that kind of thing for the future means for present life. The orientation towards the future essential to all ecological thinking accordingly shifts, to provide us with the continuing *terms* of our concern, as it were, but no longer with its *object*.

These distinctions may be neither very persuasive nor even very clear at first blush. In this chapter, I try to clarify them by looking at three different accounts of what might motivate pro-sustainability change, all of which have already been canvassed in discussion of these issues. All three look for the spur to widespread policy and lifestyle changes in kinds of awareness focused on present rather than future objects of concern.

But I also argue that all three are inadequate to our needs. Either they are exposed to forms of the mirage effect, or they connect up motivation and its sustainability results in ways which are too accidental, too contingent for us to be able to afford to rely on them in the current crisis. These considerations and criticisms prepare the ground for the long following chapter, where I offer an alternative present-focused account which I believe could really meet the case.

Respecting nature

One very natural thought is that if we started to treat the rest of the living world much more respectfully than we are now in the habit of doing, we should find ourselves having to adjust our behaviour in ways that would promote our own chances of survival too. Current patterns of consumption and resource exploitation result in abuse of individual non-human animals through their use as food and the conditions under which they are far too often raised for that purpose, whereas wider use of non-animal food sources would be ecologically more benign in a variety of ways. Our greedy squandering of the Earth's remaining undeveloped land-surface puts whole habitats and thereby species under pressure, reduces biodiversity, and destroys ecosystem integrity. But these practices are also those which, directly or indirectly, pump CO_2 into the atmosphere, eliminate carbon sinks and drive the global warming which will in due course destroy humans in their turn. And – as advocates of this line of thinking often seem to feel, and sometimes actually say – if that's how we insist on going on, serve us right. If we don't like it, we know what to do about it. We have only to listen to our better instincts as sharers of the planet with – still – a diversity of fellow-creatures and a glorious profusion of wider life.

This approach has its heart in the right place. As I shall shortly argue, something like the claims of life must ultimately be what compel us to change, if anything is going to. But that picture of what is involved simply won't do.

For what does 'properly respecting the non-human natural world' come down to? On the one hand, it could simply mean not destroying it over the coming century through devastating climate change and the other consequences and accompaniments of unsustainable human living. Indeed, taken this way, the claim of nature to respect is often used as a strong additional recommendation for the sustainable development approach. In that case, however, the argument is trading on an account of the goal of long-term balance which we need to achieve to avoid such destruction; and that goal will inevitably be offered for pursuit on the planned-future-trajectory model. But even concern for the life-chances of future beings of our own species constitutes, as we have seen, a structurally inadequate motivation to present action on that model – an impetus which readily turns itself into mirage-pursuit and never getting there. There is no reason at all to suppose that concern for the long-term survival chances of other species and the integrity of ecosystems would impel us any more effectively in this regard.

Suppose, though, that we are trying to proceed in the spirit of shifting the focus away from a predicted goal-trajectory, as above. Then treating the natural world properly will mean meeting the rightful claims of other living things, here and now, to avoidance of suffering or respect for their autonomy – and trusting that this will involve sufficiently far-reaching changes in our habits to protect us also, in the longer run, from ourselves. But now we simply have a version of the problem of shadow stewardship already noted in Chapter 2. We stand towards the claims of present non-human others, however we describe those claims, in essentially the same position in which we stand towards the claims of future (that is, presently non-existent) humans. In either case, just how far any such claim rightfully extends and what actions can be regarded as satisfactorily meeting it are always matters for present humans to determine.

The utilitarian philosopher Peter Singer, for instance, suggests a general principle of inter-species impartiality: 'No matter what the nature of the being, the principle of equality requires that its suffering be counted equally with the like suffering – insofar as rough comparisons can be made – of any other being.' And of course, the suffering of non-humans is at issue not just in questions about eating them or keeping them in zoos, but when we think about the stress we cause them by narrowing their ranges, destroying their habitats and disrupting their life-worlds. But this is just where the complications of substantive and criterial impartiality must kick in. We are being substantively impartial when we give equal consideration to the like interests of every being capable of having interests. But to apply that criterion we have also to make a criterial judgement about what are to *count* as like interests. Such equivalences are by no means always simply a given. Singer half-acknowledges this with his parenthetical 'insofar as rough comparisons can be made'. The point is, however, not that the comparisons are only rough, but that which comparisons are not too rough to serve is very typically not something we discover but something we have to *decide*. It is maybe self-evident that the interest of any complex sentient being in avoiding excruciating pain is roughly comparable to that of any other complex sentient being. But excruciating pain comprises only a small proportion of possible suffering; and it is not self-evident at all that, for instance, being in a fair degree of chronic pain or distress would matter as much to a creature which lacked the capacity for self-pity, apprehension and regret as it would to a human being with those attributes. Whether this is so, and if it is, how *much* less it would matter, are things which humans must adjudicate – not of course casually, but after weighing up the evidence from physiology, biology and ethology and making a judgement.

No doubt we won't make this judgement in an explicitly self-interested ('speciesist') way, which would render the approach merely frivolous from the outset. But when it comes to the crunch and we find ourselves having to make significant changes in patterns of behaviour with which we are comfortable and expectations to which we have come to feel entitled – having to make do with less rapid private transit, for instance, because roads can no longer be driven so easily through fragile habitats – then the pressure for our standards to float will be just as strong as on the standard sustainable development model. Nor should this come as any surprise, since it arises, as on the sustainable development model, when essentially adjustable claims upon us meet a strong disposition to go only so far in meeting them. Once more, a version of the mirage effect comes into play.

There is no need to labour these points, since we have already sufficiently explored their basis. What they should tell us in this context is that trying to shift the focus away from humans *as well as* away from long-term future-orientation won't work. This brings us to the second of the more present-focused approaches which have already been canvassed.

Climate justice

It is very evident that the threats of global warming and dramatic climate change are building up for a world in which there are huge inequities in the distribution of wealth, opportunity and risk. Historically, much of this inequity has come about because the advanced Western nations have commandeered the rest of the world's resources, first imperially and then economically, and have used them to fuel patterns of industrialization and trade which are now putting the whole Earth under ecological pressure. A glaring consequence of this history is that those most responsible for oncoming climate change are not those who are likely to suffer its severest effects. In maps showing the changing coastlines which will result from sea-level rises as the Arctic ice melts, for instance, New York, Florida and much of The Netherlands are certainly under water. But the extent of inundation in such areas, rich and populous as they are, is small-scale compared with the vast tracts, inhabited by hundreds of millions, which will disappear from the Indian subcontinent and elsewhere in Asia.

These inequitable consequences are still in prospect. There are many ways, however, in which the dynamics and the early effects of climate change are impacting inequitably on the world already. Again, this involves more than the fact of hurricane damage hitting the poorest hardest in New Orleans, socio-economically significant and sadly typical as that outcome was. On a larger scale, it has been estimated by the World Health Organization that anthropogenic global temperature rise is now responsible annually for 150,000 additional deaths, and 5 million additional morbidity incidents, in the poorest nations. While Northern countries like Britain start to experience a run of unusually and sometimes uncomfortably hot summers, drought and crop failure stalk wide swathes of the African continent. And even our attempts to do something about it are caught up in this whole pattern of maldistribution – the increasingly eager crying-up of biofuels as a way of keeping private transport on the move in the West and North, for instance, means that cropland is pre-empted from growing food in a world where famine and malnutrition appear endemically across parts of the South. Meanwhile, continuing major causal factors in climate change – the oil extraction, the deforestation – reflect geopolitical arrangements and a global trade regime still systematically distorted in favour of the old, long-established polluters and exploiters. This is the point made so graphically by the 'ecological footprint' concept already noted in Chapter 2: in a world of limited ecological space, some of us have been trampling all over others for a long time, and matters are not visibly improving.

In the context of our discussion, these considerations clearly prompt the thought that rectifying such glaring present inequities might offer an independently compelling motive to action which could bring benign ecological and climate consequences in its train. Responding to the demands of justice, that is, should mean more than feeling obliged not to entail devastation on future people, and more indeed than not entailing more of such devastation on some future people than on others. It should even mean more than ensuring much better access to resources for adaptation and mitigation for those at most immediate present risk, such as the low-lying Pacific small island nations threatened imminently by rising sea levels. More radically and structurally, it should mean ceasing to act in all those *intra*-generationally unjust ways which permit the *drivers* of future devastation such continuing present scope. So, for instance, it should mean a global trade system which does not deprive poor countries of essential resources for ecological resilience – affecting not just their own economic and even subsistence chances, but the biosphere at large – in order to provide luxuries for the rich. It should mean an energy supply profile which does not depend on keeping whole regions compliant at (effectively) gunpoint, or subject to artificially maintained and grossly exploitative semi-feudal governments, in order that the oil can keep on flowing. And nearer to home, it should mean, for example, resisting a wholesale panic flight back to nuclear power as a carbon-neutral energy source – nuclear installations being so much easier to site in poor, remote and job-hungry communities – at the expense of properly developing renewables or seriously pursuing both energy efficiency and more responsible energy use. In all these and related ways, it might seem, a properly just and urgent concern for our present fellow-humans could motivate us actually to *do* things which a concern for future humans, or for other species, would tacitly license us to fudge or defer.

A good many Western people – in particular, idealistic young people – already feel this motive of justice, make these connections and try to live accordingly. It is not an approach which one happily criticizes, nor indeed in many contexts one which one ought to criticize. Motivation, as I noted, is a complex matter, and this kind of recoil from structural global inequity is likely to play an important if not a formative part in any strong sense that we simply cannot go on as we are. It is also the sort of motivation which makes one feel rather prouder of being human than the whole 671-page calculation of profit and loss contained in the published version of the Stern Report. But in the cold light of our specific present context – the need for a working majority in a country such as Britain within little more than a decade – a greyer realism has perforce to raise its head.

One clutch of reasons for this is akin, in some ways, to the floating of standards. A commitment to global equity is something fatally easy to adopt or pursue in various familiar kinds of bad faith. At simplest, it is notorious that the occasional small or even quite substantial contribution to Oxfam, or similar, can be made to go a very long way indeed in terms of one's conscience about these global disparities. And this is despite the fact that, unlike future people, the current victims of global injustice are frequently visible on our television screens – and sometimes, for travellers to various foreign destinations, visible directly. Indeed, it may be just because of these ways of encountering them, as one or another form of *scenery*, that we manage so effectively to keep the poverty and the ethical claims of distant people at a safe distance. Those comparatively few Westerners who actually take time out to go and really encounter them, live with them and try to serve and empower them, are the only ones with the moral authority to comment adversely on this widespread stance. But that it *is* widespread is a plain fact, and certainly germane to the issue we are now considering.

There is even the possibility that a certain gearing of global justice with ecological issues could work to *inhibit* rather that to incite action in the broader constituency about whose potential motivation we are talking. In all the ways which we have been exploring, it is subtly easier not to change things too dramatically when the claims of the future are in question than it is not to change them on behalf of the contemporary deprived. So people may be turning to pursue what they subliminally recognize to be the mirage-prospects of intergenerational fairness as a tacit distancing *strategy*, a preferable goal to confronting present world poverty and injustice because our ineffectuality, or our underlying disinclination, is not so liable to become apparent. This is speculation, but it does suggest how the mirage effect is not simply rendered irrelevant or inoperative by shifting the focus of our concerns towards climate justice.

There is also, however, a different and perhaps more forcible kind of reason why we should not let sustainable action depend on a concern for intragenerational equity. This is that such concern may be perfectly genuine, but qualified in ways which simply prevent it from doing enough to reverse the trend of carbon emissions and other ecological damage.

Equity is, after all, a legitimately contested concept. We might agree that the current global distribution of wealth, opportunity and risk is unfair, without by any means agreeing on the ways in which, or the extent to which, that is the case, or on what should be done about it. Ecological justice as between the present and future generations is identified by reference to a standard – the maintenance of a recognizably human form of life on the planet – to which we can all sign up very easily in principle, however this endorsement may play out in practice. But ecological justice as between societies and communities in the present requires to be identified by a standard on which there is no real agreement even in principle. Does rectifying global unfairness mean that everyone should (ideally) now have a roughly equal allocation of these various global goods and bads, despite all the manifold differences of history, geography and culture which distinguish them? Does it mean that the advanced nations, having hitherto enjoyed the lion's share of the benefits of resource exploitation, should now in compensation accept a disproportionately greater share of the downside? How much weight should we give in this connection to the argument that, if we look back far enough, the peoples of the world started in a state of roughly equivalent economic opportunity – so that it might be held to be the energy and enterprise of the West which have made it rich and dominant? Or how much of that should we ascribe to a kind of biogeopolitical luck which ought not to count? As within societies, in other words, so between them: we do not have to blame the poor for their poverty to question how far the rich are obliged to redistribute global goods, at any rate, on the basis of strict equality. And while the claims of justice should certainly take decent people far enough to counter the grosser forms of global bad – the logging that wipes out forest peoples' whole livelihood, the disposal of hazardous wastes that puts minority communities cynically at risk, the cash-cropping that starves whole regions – there is no guarantee that the associated changes will also go far enough to stall, still less to throw into reverse, the engines of global warming.

One aspect of this inherent contingency in particular should be noted. Even if equity is taken to require moves in the direction of rough material equality, there are obviously different ways in which this can be pursued. Those with a lot can try to take less, or those without much can be helped to acquire more. Overwhelmingly, of course, it is the latter, levelling-up approach to global inequity which is currently being favoured. We are on the way to remedying maldistribution, we suppose, when millions of Indian citizens have the chance to drive cheap cars, or when the carbon footprint of every Chinese begins to rival that of the average Westerner. That the planet simply can't accommodate this version of equality doesn't stop it being, precisely, a version of *equality* – and a politically attractive one (for short-sighted politicians) at that. What must intervene to prevent its increasingly damaging realization across the developing world are ecological and sustainability concerns independent of the claims of intragenerational justice. Thus the hope that motivation to act on these concerns can ride on the back of such claims for justice would seem to be rather forlorn.

Improving our quality of life

We might fall back, therefore, on the third kind of present-focused approach which has been on offer. This turns its attention from both non-human species and distant others, to concentrate, more pragmatically if less inspiringly, on *ourselves* – that is, on the affluent West. It says, in effect, that if we start trying to treat ourselves with a good deal more respect for our true nature and needs, we shall find ourselves led into planet-saving adjustments to our ways of life. For beyond a certain level of material satisfaction, it is argued, human beings are not made happier or healthier by the increasingly frenetic global consumerism which is now contributing to drive ecological disaster. In fact the reverse is true: lots of evidence now seems to show that we are less happy, more harassed and time-ridden, more prone to sickness and less able to love, the more such consumerism rules our lives. The levels of material welfare beyond which these ills kick in have already been reached, by and large, across the advanced Northern economies which are still causing most of the damage. We shall therefore be doing ourselves as well as the planet a huge favour by turning our aspirations from material consumption to the pursuit of a genuinely good life decoupled from ecologically destructive pressure on resources. This would seem to offer a potentially widespread motivation to which there is some real practical hope of appealing successfully.

This case has been advanced by a number of people on both the leftward and rightward sides of the mainstream political spectrum in recent years. It is perhaps put most crisply and cogently in a report from the Conservative Party's Quality of Life Policy Group, published in September 2007:

> *There seems to be a law of diminishing returns where the importance of income to wellbeing decreases as people get richer.*

> *This poses a simple question – could people increase their wellbeing with less, or a different kind of, growth. Up to now, the sustainable development debate has put a different question. Individuals are asked whether they will change behaviour now for the sake of future generations ... . What we ask here is whether a different way of living might bring a measurable improvement of wellbeing for this present generation – the people who made the change.*

> *If such a lifestyle change reduced our environmental impact and increased our sense of wellbeing at one and the same time, then that would move the whole discussion of sustainability from the remote into the measurable and immediate ... the prospect of wellbeing could become a powerful tool for motivating lighter, less resource-intensive lifestyles.*

What such lifestyle change might involve is, in turn, well summarized in another recent pamphlet from a different neck of the political woods, the Fabian Society:

> *'Richer choices' is a world in which more people substitute use of services for purchase of physical products; use energy- and material-intensive goods and services much more sparingly; have a lower turnover of consumer goods – which become seen truly as 'durables' rather than disposables – and have less waste to take for recycling and disposal; and in which more public space becomes enjoyable and usable in its own right, rather than being an arena to traverse as rapidly as possible between private spaces.*

In such a world more localized work and leisure arrangements would be complemented by more locally sourced (and therefore typically fresher and healthier) food. They would also make for more real satisfaction from face-to-face relationships and community engagement, in place of the quickly unfulfilling substitute satisfactions of automated movement and electronically mediated entertainment.

Again, there is a great deal in the spirit of this approach to welcome. It certainly encourages some vital life-truths about the kind of beings we really are to resurface from beneath the welter of consumerist distraction in which they have been sunk for too long. It tries to capture the wrongness of our current life-track in a way which puts human flourishing at the centre of the picture, rather than meeting obligations or maximizing beneficial consequences. The idea that by rediscovering ourselves as whole people in the present we can take the ecological pressure off the future is also a mind-shift in very much the right direction as regards sustainability.

But again, there are crucial flaws in the conceptual model within which these truths have so far been framed. This time, though, it is not a matter of looking for an understanding of our sustainability motivation in the wrong place – more a matter of not looking deeply enough for it in the right place.

That should make it plain that I am not relying, at this juncture, on one quite cogent practical objection to this approach – though it is one to which we shall need to return in due course. This is the point that it simply takes too little account of the world outside those Western societies which are, plausibly, already suffering from what has been nicely termed 'affluenza'. We in these societies may have passed beyond the optimum level of purely material welfare and into the area beyond, where more and more *stuff* is a gathering affliction; but in the emergent economies of Asia and South America, achieving that optimum level is still a dream being actively pursued, by many hundreds of millions of people. And, as we have already noted, although it is very awkward and embarrassing for the post-colonial West to have to say so, if all of these people reached even modest affluence on the current Western model it would wreck the planet's ecosystems irretrievably. Gearing the downshifting of the West and North to the legitimate expectations of the South within the actual possibilities offered by the Earth is a challenge which that downshifting purely in itself does not begin to address. But even if we set that problem aside for the moment, and concentrate just on how we ourselves might be motivated to get started, there are quite enough difficulties of a different order.

Could a concern for quality be enough?

The trouble is that the link between easing ecological pressures and improving our experienced quality of life will not bear the weight being placed on it. Its weakness, as with one aspect of the concern for global equity, is its contingency – its depending on too many factors of circumstance or opportunity.

The idea is that growing frustration at increasingly gridlocked traffic and fume-filled air (for example) might get enough of us out of our cars to make a real difference to CO_2 emissions, whereas just on its own the perceived need to reduce these emissions won't spur us to action in sufficient numbers. This is quite persuasive in principle. After all, we each of us personally suffer these disbenefits, in the form of wasted time, frayed temper and polluted lungs, and they are things which we could each do something about directly – while it is not actually *my* driving to work, as such, which is costing us all the Earth. The uneasy awareness that I am nevertheless contributing might well have inclined me to look for alternatives, more or less persistently depending on my situation. But it could be the real prospect of quicker, calmer and healthier commuting which tips me into actually making the change. And no doubt this could be how it worked for a good many people who were already environmentally conscious, if some serious effort had been put into making the public transport alternatives more eligible. But for a lot of others, the extent of the changes they made, or whether they changed at all, would depend on how they were placed, and also on their perception of the comparative benefits. And if what is at issue is principally the improvement of our present life-quality, there can be no objection purely on those grounds to everyone's going just as far in this direction as happens to suit them. Across the board, that might ease the ecological pressures sufficiently for sustainability – but equally, of course, it might not. And indeed there are good reasons for anticipating that it would not.

One such reason can be foregrounded by supposing, just as a thought-experiment, that we had found a technological super-fix to *break* the connection between Northern-style consumerism and ecological damage. Suppose we had discovered some entirely non-polluting fuel, yielding no greenhouse gases and commandeering no cropland for its production, with which to drive something like our existing energy-generation and transport systems. (Some hopeful folk think that this might actually turn out to be hydrogen released from seawater, but the point here is to consider the mere idea of such a resource, rather than the practical possibilities.) Would we still, with this new opportunity to continue broadly as we are, want to pursue the kind of fairly dramatic downshifting towards more localized living which would improve our quality of life in the ways now being advocated?

Well, some of us might. But history doesn't offer much encouragement to suppose that, disconnected in this way from ecological responsibility, it would be a very general phenomenon. After all, the points that consumption can't make a fully human life, that merely material wellbeing taken as an all-sufficient social goal entails serious human impoverishment, and that underneath people really know this, are far from being new. In Britain they go back at least to Carlyle, Dickens and Arnold confronting the industrial developments of the nineteenth century. The tradition of such social criticism then passes on through Ruskin and Morris into forms of guild socialism and communitarianism, which in turn were clear ancestors of the earlier green movement in what might be called its garden-city manifestations – its emphasis on locality, autonomy, beauty and human scale for their own sakes. If such critiques are as cogent as they are now being claimed to be, 'affluenza' must have been bad for us, at an experiential level, well before any carbon consequences started to become pressing. In that case, why were not many more people striving to escape from it then? The patent fact, of course, is that they weren't – no such tendency has been observable on any significant scale in the affluent societies. If anything it has been the reverse, with a long-intensifying trend towards preoccupation with material betterment and economic 'progress'. And while the social limits to growth, as in traffic congestion and rising crime rates, have also been apparent since at least the latter decades of the last century, they have not deflected the trend, still less halted it. In this light, the hope that a revulsion from affluenza might just by itself, and independently of ecological considerations, drive ecologically friendly change, seems, again, forlorn.

On the other hand, if it is the fact that our lifestyles are now seen to be threatening ecological damage for the future which constitutes a large part of what we ought to feel to be bad about them, we are simply back with the need to motivate pro-sustainability changes independently of their purely experiential benefits. Advocates of the quality-of-life approach are often to be heard fudging these alternatives – sliding back and forth between 'more satisfying for us, and also happily good for the planet' and 'more satisfying for us *because* good for the planet'. But when the issue is motivation, in the way we are concerned with it here, the distinction is of critical importance – because if we are back with pro-sustainability change for the sake of future people, we are back with all the problems of sustainable development, which have now been sufficiently rehearsed.

Another consideration has to be the heavily middle-class bias of the quality-of-life approach. As we have seen, implementation of 'richer choices' as an engine for sustainability would have to depend on significant shifts in self-image, aspirations and behaviour among a quite substantial majority of the population in a country like Britain. It therefore has to assume an individual freedom to make the relevant changes which very many people just don't have – even if they should come to recognize these changes as desirable. Many lower-income inner-city or urban estate dwellers lack the financial elbow-room and employment flexibility to adapt their lives in such directions. They also very often lack the kind of social and economic infrastructure – the transport systems, retail facilities and community networks – that could support any attempts which they might make. More unpromisingly still, they are likely to lack an enabling cultural infrastructure. It is not scorn or condescension but mere respect for the real situation of many of one's fellow-citizens to point out the extent of this deprivation. Religious traditions in touch with the relevant human realities are now largely a spent force. In many cases, too, the educational system will have failed to introduce pupils properly to the environmental and sustainability context, even where pupils have had any real chance of attending to what the schools have to offer. And it will be the rare exception for people in these kinds of circumstance to have gained any secure cultural or historical perspective on their own life-options, independently of what is proffered insistently and relentlessly through a mass-media nexus owned and operated by those with vested interests in consumerism.

Advocates of quality-of-life politics from either end of the left–right spectrum now tend to look to government and the public services to supply the needed infrastructure, at least in its socio-economic and educational aspects. And of course there have been some inspiring examples in education and community development – inner-city schools where sustainability education is taken seriously and local urban projects genuinely enabling 'a better choice of choice' in terms of lifestyle, transportation or energy usage. But, as part of an avowedly realistic approach, it is only realism to wonder how far these achievements can be generalized.

Even if they could be quite significantly extended, however, the real problem with the whole approach would remain. This is a difficulty which goes beyond its evident class and income bias, and down to the conceptual basis. The point is that, where the concern is for quality of life conceived in the dimension of experienced satisfaction from goods and services (private or public), however these are produced and distributed, the essential mechanism for pursuit of this concern is *trading off*. Suppose it is true, for instance, that I can increase my overall enjoyment and satisfaction by decreasing the amount of driving I do; this will remain true *up to a point*, as I trade off the personal gains from reduced car usage against the drawbacks of driving – the expense, the frustration, the unhealthy confinement and so on. But beyond that peak point, my overall enjoyment and satisfaction will begin to trend downwards again, as the additional gains from driving less are increasingly outweighed by the lost real advantages – of convenience, availability and autonomous access to anywhere with a road. The shape of this satisfaction curve demonstrates how the whole approach is fundamentally tied to the cost–benefit economics in which it is grounded. It also makes the essential weakness obvious. Different people will simply have very different optimum satisfaction points, even if the terms in which we are now talking about them are those of life-quality rather than the economist's more usual jargon of preference-function and utility-optimization.

In a context of growing awareness of climate and ecological issues, no doubt some people would reach their point of optimum satisfaction only after making a fair number of changes in their habits. This is likely to be the case as green concerns are increasingly widely recognized, though still not very widely or concertedly acted on. Clearly relevant here is the striking growth over just a few years in the phenomenon of green consumerism. High-street retailers and other leaders in the corporate world appear to have been falling over themselves recently to align both their marketing and their product sourcing to this stirring in public consciousness. It is certainly clear that, as part of the ongoing dialectic of consumer demand and supply, more and more people are taking an interest in eating and living more healthily and shopping more responsibly, if not a great deal more locally.

On the other hand, though, some other people would be likely to reach that optimal satisfaction point very much more swiftly, or even after no downshifting at all. I am reminded of the man who kept reading in the personal health pages of the colour supplements about how his high-cholesterol diet was bad for him. Eventually, though only after a considerable struggle, he succeeded in giving up reading colour supplements. The point in this connection is that, purely from a quality-of-life perspective, no-one could have anything to object to in his response. Some people will just find their life-quality optimized by retaining the more-or-less vitiated satisfactions they have got used to, even if continuing to indulge in them is, prudentially speaking, unwise. Similarly, many people may well find that the drawbacks of possible downshifting, as these affect their particular situation, kick in almost at once – they may simply prefer the accustomed stresses and frustrations of the standard Western lifestyle, or most of them, to bothering their heads unduly about change. And if that is the quality-of-life trade-off that works for them, then from the point of view of life-quality as a factor in motivation, that is all there is to be said.

If the 'richer choices' approach were to become widely recognized as an option, and seriously seconded and facilitated by government, therefore, it would probably produce some real movement in the right direction. What it would certainly produce much more of, however, would be the sort of compromise reflected already in so much of the public response to these issues. This is the pattern of behaviour in which, as Mark Lynas acidly puts it, 'we would deceive ourselves by driving to the supermarket in a hybrid 4×4 to buy organic carrots, somehow believing that we were part of the solution rather than part of the problem'. At that level, of course, failure to address the real problem would still be rather blatant. But people would be doing essentially the same *kind* of thing even with much more significant downshifting and localization of lifestyles, so long as these processes took them only as far as their individual points of optimal life-quality. If only present satisfactions are in question, whether or not we dignify them as a concern for life-quality, bad faith cannot really come into it. As in all economics-based modelling of human action (which is why economics is always, in the end, so inadequate to these issues), the motivation we have is finally just the motivation we have. Thinking about motivations that we *ought* to have requires a different kind of language.

Meanwhile, there could clearly be no guarantee at all that encouraging or otherwise promoting quality-of-life improvements in a society like Britain would get enough people to go far enough and quickly enough to make enough difference, in ecological terms. In this respect, the approach fares no better than the other two attempts to shift the focus from the future to the present which I have examined in this chapter. The question is then whether a deeper understanding of this shift can take us any further.

'Life Goes On'

For all the problems we have been noting, there is one huge strength in the approach to sustainability through a concern with quality of life. This is the way it makes the future uncomfortably present to us, rather than distant and hypothetical. The oncoming inhuman fierceness of an overheated globe can already be sensed in a lifestyle where the inhumanities of frustration and insecurity seem to have become endemic. We begin to feel on our own pulses the damage we are doing, and make a crucial connection. For if the world is on an overheating trend, clearly it has to be the case that something in our present activity is already intense enough to overheat the world in due course. If the pan on the slow-burning stove is to boil in twenty minutes, we have to have stoked up the stove sufficiently by now. The temperature of the water will then increase gradually over the period, which is how we proverbially boil the frog.* But if for any reason we find the heat from the stove too much for our comfort now, we may be motivated to bank it down – thus perhaps offering the frog only a long warm bath, instead of creeping death. In just this way, the aspects of the present which we are starting to find intolerable are effects of the same factors that are driving the global warming trend: the frustrations and delays caused by the superfluity of private cars pushing up the CO_2, the lurking fear of terrorism generated in response to the geopolitical drive for the oil, and so on across the board. Then the hope is that addressing the ways in which Western life is already getting metaphorically too hot for comfort will mean banking down the intensity of all those activities which, unaddressed, will eventually cook the planet for real.

As I argued in the last chapter, however, there is a built-in risk that if quality of life is our motivation, this banking-down response will not amount to nearly enough – for all the complex reasons of compromise, trade-off and mirage effect which we have been exploring. Downshifting à la carte from the option-menu

---

* This traditional environmentalists' parable of slow catastrophe has been made familiar by Al Gore's film *An Inconvenient Truth*. It is alleged that a frog dropped into a pan of boiling water hops straight out again unharmed, whereas a frog placed in cold water which is then gradually brought to the boil sits tight until it dies. Even if, as one hopes, nobody has ever actually tried this experiment, it still offers a memorable image for the insidiousness of incremental change.

available, even if it is done society-wide, may alleviate immediately uncomfortable symptoms to the point at which they are bearable, but leave the disease itself essentially unremedied. Of course, this is a classically unwise move, and especially so in this case even if one's focus is firmly fixed on present quality of life – since underlying causes powerful enough to threaten future ecological catastrophe are also very likely to be deep-seated and invasive enough to generate unexpected new symptomatic outbreaks at any short-term moment. (The wholly unforeseen emergence of Islamist terrorism on Western high streets is a recent case in point.) And it must always fail to suppress entirely our dismay at the longer-term prospects. But the short term is still where human beings, the only creatures with brains sophisticated enough to discount the future, do always tend to operate.

The core of the problem here is something we have already noted: the merely contingent connection between doing enough to improve present quality of life in the advanced societies and doing what will check the global warming trend. The one may go with the other, but it doesn't have to – the strength of the correlation depending on too many intervening factors in our present situation. The present could be made more habitable in many of the respects which contribute to a good quality of life – it could be experienced by a lot of people as sufficiently rich, varied, locally convenient and first-hand for their needs – without the drivers of climate change being radically inhibited.

On the other hand, the only kind of non-contingent connection we have yet thought about is the formally necessary connection made by an ethical framework. If we were now failing in genuine ethical obligations to the future, the remedy could *only* be ceasing to fail – ethics just has that kind of necessity. But we have seen that this kind of position, while logically unimpeachable, doesn't stick. Because the ethical model is being misapplied here, there are just too many ways in which, under pressure, contingency seeps back into our long-term moral accounting. So where else might we turn? Is there something less placable than a queasy intergenerational or inter-species conscience, and less circumstantial than our need for quality experience, which must require people who recognize it to do all in their power to save the Earth? Can we find a connection which is both motivationally compelling and *unevadable* between our present life-concerns and meeting the gathering threat to the planet? If we can, building it into our public understanding of the issues must surely offer the only way forward – for it seems very possible that nothing else will be enough, while of course we can't hope to do better than all that is in our power.

A Faustian bargain?

To find a viable answer here, I believe we must dig down below the strata of satisfaction and ethical obligation to the stratum of life-meaning. That might seem to promise only obscurity, though I shall try hard to avoid it. But what is involved can be presented quite sharply and clearly, at least as a starting-point, if we consider the differences between three kinds of *bargain* that we might picture ourselves as striking.

In the first place, there is the *Brundtland bargain* of sustainable development: we can meet our needs, but only up to the point beyond which we should be jeopardizing future people's resources for meeting theirs. In this sense, it is a bargain struck with the future, though we must also operate as their agents in the present. It means we have to make some changes in present patterns of life (substantial changes, where avoiding runaway climate change has become the issue) in exchange for going on meeting at least a lot of what we identify as our present needs. This, as we saw in Part I, is really only a pseudo-bargain. It is at best a parley with our consciences disguised as a deal with the future, and as such lies permanently open to the bad faith of unacknowledged trade-offs made in our own interests. Hence floating standards, slipping targets and the mirage effect of never getting there. Here is a sustainability bargain which (as the man said about verbal agreements) isn't really worth the paper it's written on.

In the second place, there is the *downshifter's bargain*, where we might seem to narrow our life-options from the vast, greedy menu of apparent possibilities offered by a techno-globalized economy, but we say to ourselves, in effect, 'Never mind the width, feel the quality.' This, as we have seen in the last chapter, is essentially a trade-off – so much deliberate localization in exchange for so much extra leisure time, better food, improved health and so forth. It is, however, a quite explicit trade-off. This means that while bad faith is not really an issue, neither is there any obligation to strike anything other than the deal one chooses individually to strike. And while the sum of all those deals might go far enough to save the planet, it quite possibly won't. Here is a bargain with at best a chance of sustainability thrown in.

But now, thirdly, consider the *Faustian bargain* which seems to be the basis of our current civilization. Faustus was the legendary medieval German scholar and philosopher who sold his soul to the Devil for twenty-four years of magical powers. According to Marlowe's play, he used these powers to lead himself a dance of increasingly trivial self-indulgence – at the end of which he thoroughly repented of the deal, though the Devil didn't. As George Monbiot has pointed out, this 'tragical history' precisely parallels what humans seem now to be doing: using fossil fuels to give ourselves a brief lease of quasi-magical technological near-omnipotence, at the price of a future world which (if global average temperatures do indeed rise by 6°C or more, as we are now seriously risking) will be a pretty passable imitation of Hell.

Or rather – this *looks* like the bargain we are currently making. But the point is that, openly and explicitly, it couldn't be. Faced with that deal, as a deal – invited to a deeply chancy gamble, in full, deliberate awareness, with the future of life on Earth for the sake of *any* present benefits – no-one sane could accept it. It will be at once objected that this gambling is just what the large majority of people actually are doing at the moment: hence a world in which we get the M25, 'reality' TV and Christmas breaks in Thailand in exchange for global warming. And if most people really knew and reflected on what was at stake, or hadn't readily available a whole range of shifts for denying what they half-suspect, one would have to agree (and despair). Most people, however, don't yet know, or (like Faustus in the story) won't yet admit to themselves, what we are doing, what anthropogenic climate change and other impending ecological threats really entail. But once one *does* appreciate the terms of engagement of the climate war, the real risks with life on Earth which humanity is now running, it becomes apparent that nothing whatsoever could warrant them. Here, then, is an *un*sustainability bargain from which we must necessarily recoil, one which we categorically cannot strike.

Crucially, though, the reason why we cannot strike it is not finally to do with ethical obligation to future people or to other species; nor is it even to do with prudential considerations about our own future or present life-quality. All these more-or-less contingent concerns can certainly play a part in our thinking. But ultimately, we cannot cut an explicitly Faustian deal because to do so would destroy the very roots of life-meaning, and so of any humanly habitable present. That relation to meaningfulness is where the categorical quality of the sustainability drive – the drive *away* from risking the biosphere, at any cost – finally comes from.

This claim obviously needs arguing for, and I try to do so – in outline, and at nothing like the length the argument really needs – in the two following sections. Even in outline, though, one can't treat these issues at the necessary depth without doing overt philosophical anthropology. That involves conceptual exploration of a more abstract kind than I have yet ventured to offer in this book. I can only ask for the reader's patience at this juncture. What may seem for a while like a digression in mist soon picks up the sustainability discussion again – and I hope will then be seen, in the sunshine of retrospect, as no digression at all but the main path. I will at least try to argue at first hand.* And actually the phenomenological realities here are not difficult to grasp. The challenge is to confront the real features deep in the human condition to which they lead us. But confronting them is essential to understanding the claims of ecological responsibility. And I would re-emphasize that the point of all this is to reorder the framework of sustainability concern, first conceptually but then decisively in practice. Then, as that concern begins to gain real ground in the advanced societies, it might also gain an impetus which cannot be inhibited, pacified or played false with – the impetus to do *whatever it takes* to win the climate war. And nothing less will answer.

---

* Correspondingly, some points on which philosophers have written whole books are here compressed into sentences, which will therefore seem je'une or dogmatic to any professional reading them. But I don't apologize, since this is a . . which goes with trying to say *anything* about these issues that makes an impact.

Again, we can at least start by putting the issue crisply. Recall Faustus. There is, of course, a crucial difference between the mythic doctor and ourselves. He paid for his triviality by being packed off to Hell in person, but we are preparing the flames for others – for people who aren't even alive yet. On the ethico-scientistic model, recognizing this is supposed to provide our motivation for stopping. Actually, as I have tried to show, it provides the gap through which denial, compromise and tacitly doing it anyway will always slip in. So what we need to think of ourselves as doing, when we consider personally or try to get others to appreciate the damage we are really causing to the biosphere, is setting up a kind of personal *Faustus test*. Think of whatever it is that really matters to you – matters regardless of anything else, matters if anything does, matters as the touchstone of anything's mattering at all. You will have identified thereby something which is a central, if not *the* central, meaning-giving element in your own life. Then ask: Could that still matter in that way if I had explicitly been party to the modern Faustian bargain? – if I had deliberately accepted complicity in a way of life which I knew risked the widespread wholesale impoverishment and, in the worst case, virtual elimination of life on Earth (including almost everything that humankind has so far made of human life) – but only after my own lifetime was over? Could you, in other words, buy a still-meaningful life for yourself at the price of willed unsustainability in the context of potentially runaway global warming?

I believe that the honest answer which anyone who really submits to this test must give is *no*. And this is not because everyone feels too strong an obligation to future generations, although some people might. Rather it has to be the case because meaningfulness on such conditions is impossible. You could no more buy a life with a liveable point to it on those terms than you could buy honesty with your ill-gotten gains or longevity by suicide. A conscious Faustian bargain with biospheric life necessarily defeats its aim. The very minimum you would have to ask in such a deal would be for your own life to go on mattering meaningfully to you whatever else was to follow, and that is just what willed complicity in what *was* to follow would here undermine.

It is important to see that this would be so, whatever it was that mattered. If what centrally counts for you is your children's happiness or prospects, for instance, risking the potential habitability of the planet after your own lifetime tends pretty evidently to undercut this. But the same is true of very different central life-values, even such comparatively abstract ones as beauty or complex intelligibility, as in mathematics or music. That whether or not humans stupidly annihilate themselves, there will still have been Beethoven, is true and in some moods a comfort. But it doesn't mean that you could buy a lifetime's listening by willing the serious hazarding of future life, and still find even Beethoven finally worth listening to. Nor, less exaltedly, could dedication to one's work survive the Faustus test, even if one's work paid little or no heed to the needs of others and none to those of the future – unless, indeed, one took such egocentricity to the full lengths of the psychopathic. A natural human delight in the creative exercise of one's skills in burglary or embezzlement would still be intolerably hollowed out by the awareness that this was all just a kind of life-charade.

If that is right, it must be because there is a *conceptual* connection between experienced life-meaning, however framed for the individual, and one's trust in the continuity of life at large. That is the connection which I am trying to elucidate in what follows. At its heart, I will suggest, is a recognition that the force which sustains meaning from within is also the basic condition of sustainability: *life goes on.*

Life-meaning and life-hope

We find life-meaning through activities and roles which give point, direction or simply a kind of vigorous sufficiency-in-itself to the daily business of living. This in turn requires that some things matter to us in a certain way which we can all recognize – that they have an *intrinsic* value for us. This is a value which depends just on their being what they are and not on their relation to something else which is supposed in turn to give them point. Of course, there are many things in our experience which have this second, instrumental kind of value, which matter because of where they take us or how we can use them, but this kind of mattering can't be all there is if anything is really to matter at all. Our capacity to find intrinsic value is the basic creative power on which life-meaningfulness rests. Creative, because although we encounter intrinsic value given as itself – and nothing we simply *invent* could be encountered as meaning – we have to work, often quite hard, at realizing and expressing what we thus encounter. Nevertheless, this kind of value need not be, and in fact rarely is, anything out of the ordinary. Meaningfulness does not have to come from heroic commitments or transformative spiritual revelations, which is just as well since most of us do not have these opportunities. (In any case, the scope which they offer for grandstanding self-delusion should be enough to make us wary of them in all but exceptional cases). Life-meaning comes typically not from something transcending normal, central human satisfactions – those of friendship, food, art, sex, parenthood, work, achievement, exercise ... – but from experiencing those satisfactions (or enough of them) from day to day as *not empty*. This means their mattering to us, having intrinsic value for us, robustly enough to stand up against the inevitable corrosive 'So what?' that comes out of our awareness of finitude and mortality. Life has enough meaning to go on with when, ambushed by the recollection that happiness is unreliable, nothing lasts and anyway I shall sooner or later die, I can turn back to my actual project, relationships or joys and say genuinely, rather than as a whistle in the dark, 'But that still stands, that still has point.'

The trouble is that this, which might sound facile enough to make us complacent, is actually a peculiarly difficult thing to do. Intrinsic value, which we have to create to live as the kind of creatures we are, is always tending to elude us because of the kind of creatures we are.

Everything that matters, matters to *someone* – that is, to some self. What has instrumental value to me is what matters to me because something else does, and what has intrinsic value is what matters to me because it just matters. It is inevitably as persons, as selves, that we shape out these different values which organize our experience. We almost always do this in dialogue with others, and we can't escape doing it in language which only subsists between ourselves and others. But finally, what matters to me does so because I am the person I am, with a particular perspective of attitudes, desires and constraints, which in turn stem from what is core to my being the person I am – my being an intellectual, say, or someone trying to pursue a particular project, or a husband and father. But always, at the same time, it carries with it the awareness of detachment from that core. This is because it belongs to *being* a self, that as soon as one *thinks* of oneself, one is thinking of something *apart* from oneself – one is standing back in the consciousness one *is* from the self *of* which one is conscious. So as soon as I think of myself encountering value as a husband and father, for instance, I am also simultaneously aware that I am contemplating that self-identity from another standpoint, which seems for the moment to be where I am *really* standing. And if I try to grasp this new perspective as that of the 'real me', perhaps that of someone who somehow surprisingly got himself into the situation of being a husband and father – then again, I am aware of contemplating *that* 'real' identity from another remove. It is evident too that the process can continue indefinitely. Even my being as merely physical – this unique inwardness, with its aches and intimate pressures, its familiar yearnings and delights – becomes (as here) an object for contemplation by my*self* as something other. Recognition of this pattern of permanent recession in consciousness is one of the really significant advances in understanding which we owe to the existentialist tradition.

The effect this has on our valuing is radical. It means that whenever we need to draw on life-meaning and turn to what stands firm for us, that value is always tending to recede, as it were, into quotes – to become 'what stands firm' for a particular characterization of myself, one which I am always aware that *I myself* can contemplate from elsewhere. And thus all such value tends to lose its intrinsic quality in the moment of our reaching for it. This it does by turning, not necessarily into instrumental value, but into *conditioned* value, of which the instrumental is only a more particular form. What matters conditionally, matters *given* such-and-such: this given can be the fact that my relevant end or purpose is something else, but it can also just be that I am the specific conditioned person to whom whatever it is does matter. Thus what we have turned to as intrinsically valuable will tend to be found mattering just because or to the extent that the particular understanding of 'myself' of which I am now focally aware is taken to matter. What should stand firm for the husband and father, mattering as and in itself – loyalty, say, or loving-kindness – only 'stands firm' for me as self-contemplated husband and father, because it is only insofar as I go on endorsing that understanding of myself, with its particular history, strengths and limitations, that those values retain their robustness for me. That is of course to say that they don't finally stand firm, because into this fissure in the self, the ever-insistent 'So what?' immediately presses. So what if that matters to me as *that* person? – I needn't have been just thus, and if I have turned out to be, so what? Everything that might matter in the intrinsic way which silences that question – everything whose value might be given, given *nothing* else – only 'matters' in quotes, when we come to recognize its mattering as related only to a conditioned self. And about what only matters in quotes, the question 'So what?' – does its 'mattering' really matter? – can always ask itself again.

This pattern of regress is built into the very structure of conscious self-awareness, the unique dual relation both to the world and to ourselves as aware of the world, which humans naturally have. It is where a substantive intuition of the endless or eternal, as an inescapable element in our being, intrudes into the experience of otherwise entirely bounded creatures. As such, potential loss of meaningfulness in the way I have described must also represent a permanent feature of the human situation.* But meaningfulness is, on any account, a profound human need: indeed, the neurologist, psychiatrist and death-camp survivor Viktor Frankl argued forcefully that it is *the* most profound, the primary human motivation. Certainly it runs so deep that if we had found no way of ensuring it for ourselves at least somewhere and sometimes in our lives, we should have died out as a species long ago. And in fact we all know, in principle, how to combat the threat. What is required to encounter value as intrinsic is to wipe the lens of our attending clear of self. This means still to attend as an individual focus of vision and will, but as *impersonally* as one can, from as near as one can get to a purely unconditioned standpoint of attention. At this point, where one cannot see oneself because one's self *is* only the seeing, conscious subjectivity has not yet begun to congeal into 'personal' selving. Such characterizations are necessarily elusive – if our adopting that standpoint could be brought clearly before consciousness, it would not be the standpoint in question. What we can characterize, though, is the view into value which it affords. From this perspective, it is not as *my* project that what I am undertaking matters to me, but simply as the project it is. What that is will reflect the particular conditioned history of the person, the me, who created it, but its mattering, as created thing – if it really does, which is an *if* that one must always risk – is seen to be independent of all that. In the same way, it is not as self-regardingly *mine* that the various enjoyments which I relish matter from this perspective, but simply as part of the texture of delight which life presents to *this* focus of experience. Even more demandingly, it will not be under the aspect of my desire or need or affection that I see the person I love, but as she is in herself: not so much in her own formed

---

* 'Despair is a qualification of spirit … related to the eternal in man. But the eternal he cannot get rid of, no, not to all eternity.' – Kierkegaard, *The Sickness unto Death*.

personhood, undue attention to which can reintroduce the conditioned with a vengeance, as in something like her unique specific vibration of life.

We might call this kind of attention *objectivity* – except that in connection with value this is very likely to mislead. What matters from the standpoint of impersonal attending matters intrinsically, but it doesn't have *objective value* in the sense that it displays a value somehow residing in itself and such that it must matter to anyone. The idea, regrettably prominent in some environmental (and some other) forms of ethics, that value could be objective and external in anything like this way is a confusion and a distraction. The 'in itself' of intrinsic value is not the 'in itself' of water's consisting of hydrogen and oxygen. Of course value must be realized in language-structured practice to have any reality, and thus has its reality in what is crucially a public realm – but that realm is sustained, unlike the realm in which atoms combine into molecules, by the collaborative creativity of individual human beings. We share our values in expressing them, either in words or in action, and so live in a permanent process of empowering others and learning from them which is the condition of all art and indeed all meaning, as well as of value. But, fundamentally, the intrinsic quality of what matters arises from its mattering not objectively to anyone who happens along, but impersonally to an individual subject. We miss this distinction and get into a thicket of difficulties around value-objectivity insofar as we lack a firm working grasp of what it might be to summon intrinsic value creatively into being from a standpoint of impersonality.

But what, then, *might* it be? How could I be both *me*, this particular person, and *impersonal*, in the way that confronting value as robustly intrinsic seems to require? We can say *how* value seems to present itself in that confrontation, but can we say what must be *going on* for it to do so? We can perhaps understand well enough the idea of being selfless in moral contexts, where it means getting what Iris Murdoch called the 'fat, relentless ego' out of the frame, so that we can see other people's real existence and legitimate claims. But what sense could metaphysical selflessness – my attending impersonally – possibly make?

We might get behind this question by asking another one, at first sight different (and rather odd). How do I know that I am *alive*? Not, clearly, by observing myself – noting that I display various organic features, that I breathe, eat and so forth. The question isn't something to be decided from *outside*, as I might ask it of some other creature (does it show any signs of life, is it dead or just shamming ... ?). But neither is it decided just by knowing that I am thinking, which yields only the thin Cartesian assurance that a thinking thing exists here. Existence must certainly be the condition of any knowing subject, but *being alive* is more substantial than mere conscious existence. My livingness is not something that I, as its subject, identify either empirically or logically: yet the identification is there, phenomenologically, at the core of my subjectivity. And, evidently, it is there in some sense as *the condition of itself*. For I am conscious as not just a locus of identity, but as essentially embodied and engaged in a world, and that is not something I could discover *not* to be the case. Such considerations push us towards reframing the question so as better to reflect these relations between its elements: how does *life know itself* in my subjectivity? Now, though, we can answer it in a way that casts light on the earlier problem. As the ground of any such living self-knowledge – which must always be that of a *me*, a particular subject – there manifests itself a projective energy, reaching outward as concern and forward as anticipation to its embodied circumstances and activities.

This energy, as essentially experienced, I call *life-hope*. Not hope *for* anything in particular, which arises only later as a feature of conditioned selfhood:* life-hope is the form taken by life-energy as bare subjectivity. It is how we might imagine that any manifestation of natural energy, from the outflowing power of the sun to 'the force that through the green fuse drives the flower', would experience itself if it contained also in its being just the pure *for-itself* of consciousness. Indeed, it is how such energy *does* present itself to itself, uniquely in the world (as far as we know), in the human reality. It is forward-pressing, spontaneous natural force as it manifests itself in primordial consciousness – prior, that is, to the series of specific engagements with a mattering world which creates each of us as individual persons. Life-hope is life within us looking impersonally forward towards the project it ongoingly informs, the self it is always working to shape, in each given life.

Because life-hope is deeply prior to conditioned personhood, it is essentially unchallengeable, unquestionable in any of the ways in which my formed self is liable to question or challenge. 'So what?' or 'What for?' can't intelligibly be asked of life-hope, since that kind of living telic energy is already presupposed in the possibility of any answer. Or, again, something can only be *pointless* by contrast with something else taken to have point, but life-hope is the precondition of anything's having point, and so cannot itself be pointless, however things may seem with my own, personally conditioned life. There can be no thought of *justifying* life-hope, since it must already stand as the basis for any justification. What is acknowledged in these terms is always being sensed from within as an active principle of energy, the necessary ground of my individual consciousness and will and the lived values they create as intrinsic.

Life-meaningfulness depends on my finding intrinsic value in enough of the central transactions of a lived life. Intrinsic value is value that stands firm for me, things mattering in a way I can't get behind, explain away or fall into seeing in a merely conditioned perspective. And my ordinary circumstances, projects and

---

* Hope that lacks an intentional object is not a contradiction, since hoping is not just wanting some future state of affairs to come about, but can also be a purely open stance towards the future. We can be simply *hopeful* – think of the spirit often to be heard in Beethoven's music – but not simply *wantful*. That is why despair is always a pathological condition, while mere absence of desires need not be: in despair, the conditioned self attacks the roots of its own being as life-hope.

relationships can confront me with that kind of value only when I engage with them out of life-hope. Doing that means feeling inwards and downwards in the way described by D. H. Lawrence: 'Resolve to abide by your own deepest prompting. ... Try to find your deepest issue, in every confusion, and abide by that.' This is an exacting and always dangerous commitment to discovering in oneself, as valuing agent, the ultimate spontaneous unquestionableness of a *subjective force of nature*.

With this way of putting it – linking the impersonal attention which creates meaning to the deep impersonality of life within us – we can return to the issues of sustainability and our relation to the wider natural world.

Life-hope and sustainability

Sustainability is really just a Latinate way of capturing the idea that *life goes on*. But we use the latter phrase in many contexts where we aren't thinking about future generations, long-term resource availability or species survival. 'Life goes on', we say, when finally facing up to some grief or disappointment, for instance; and this doesn't always mean just that one lives to fight another day – that one will oneself, in person, have further life-chances. It can also sometimes express the thought that whatever has happened, perhaps irretrievably, to one's own life and chances, that is somehow not the end of the matter. But this is not centrally a claim about the future, though it has future implications. The thought can't simply be that there will be more individual human lives after mine, continuing on indefinitely – for how could awareness of that brute biophysical fact speak to my present case? Rather, the force of 'life goes on' here is its appeal to the inexhaustible spontaneity of life sensed within life. Of course, I can also say it casually or flippantly, when it usually has the force of 'never mind' or 'Who cares?' – but when I genuinely turn to the recognition that life goes on, it is as a way of trying to reopen myself to the permanent energy or force within my own being, which I have called life-hope. In life-hope, I can see as still mattering intrinsically, and quite apart from their relation to me, the project or the person I may have lost.

The spirit we invoke with 'life goes on' said in this kind of testing circumstance is also, that is, the spirit in which we sustain life's working meaningfulness from day to day. Here the emphasis tends to be not so much on the continuity of life-energy as on the life-energy of what continues. *Life* goes on, is the point implicit in such phrases as 'that's life', 'it's a life' – and sometimes, wryly, 'What a life!' – but always with reference to the force that simply gets one out of bed morning after morning, that keeps one undefeated, that is always renewing one's appetites and reaching forward for new thoughts, chances and human connections. This is the force that makes one's luck, keeping the central values, the key project or relationship or delight, real and drawing one onward, even with no idea of where one is going.

It is the spirit, too, which fades and sometimes fails when the light of meaningfulness goes out – as it can do for all sorts of material, psychological or biological reasons. Each of us is always also a conditioned, circumstantially shaped being and self in these respects. Pain, illness, trauma, various kinds of deprivation, frustration or imposed purposelessness can all make us lose our deep grip on intrinsic value. Then the sense of life's having point absconds into the always-waiting quotes, or just disappears into emptiness. That experience of lost meaning is now very common in our kind of society, in a way that matters seriously for its ecological destructiveness – a point I shall come back to shortly. It can even latch onto an organic or psychological predisposition and come to need some kind of professional help (something which is also an increasingly worrying feature of Western society). But unless this happens, we can usually find ways of turning back to life's basic ongoingness. And significantly, we very often do this by turning outwards, to the wider natural context of the self.

Such outward-turning is a vitally important resource to complement the inward exploration back towards one's deepest promptings which Lawrence invokes. One can sometimes, with enough courage, find life's ongoingness in the experience of genuine passion, the being carried away by heart and guts, rather than merely tickled by idea and will. Equally, there are those moments in parenthood when a sense of unfathomable completeness supervenes on the ordinary round of worry, guilt and laboriousness. But the dynamics of our relations with lovers and children can also very easily be distorting projections of the will, inner shadows of the formed self, rather than intimations of spontaneous life-hope. As Lawrence himself also says in the same place, 'the deepest self is way down, and the conscious self is an obstinate monkey'. We need, paradoxically, to turn outward at least as much as inward to repossess our deepest selves.

We all know the kind of moment this brings – the relaxation, the deep breath, the standing-back, a brightening like the sun coming out across the whole scene of our concerns. Such a simile is inevitable and right, because very typically life-hope renews itself in what might be called epiphanies of the natural. These are encounters of various kinds in which we are opened to the flow of life-energy from beyond what has gone dead in the conditioned self, so that we see afresh into what matters. Such encounters can be with natural beauty (an old Romantic cliché, of course, but like so many of them a cliché because it captures a truth). Or they can be with a sudden grace transforming the merely commonplace – the breeze dancing in the battered little tree beside the garage. They can be with avatars of natural permanence, from snow-capped ranges to hidden streamlets – or rather, with what we had always assumed would be naturally permanent, which already indicates how the conventionally ecological dimension is coming back into the frame. Relatedly, such epiphanies can come through our awakening to (in Iris Murdoch's words) 'a self-forgetful pleasure in the sheer alien pointless independent existence of animals, birds, stones and trees'. They are not, however, restricted to the externally natural, nature in the wild, but can also arise from more homely encounters with the naturally given, met in the right spirit – unsentimental sensed kinship with the dog as 'ambassador from the kingdom of fun', or recognition of the cat in its soft malicious remoteness. The key common factor in all these manifestations is that as we turn away from ourselves to life's inexhaustible spontaneity, something vital for life-meaning speaks from the core of us in answer.

This has had to be a very compressed argument. But what I have been trying to show is how our ability to find ordinary present life meaningful is intimately bound up with – expressed, reflected, scaffolded and enabled by – our sensed deep kinship with natural life at large. And this is not just contingent on happening to feel that way about 'nature' – it does not depend on one's sharing either the passions of the high Romantic poets or those of the field naturalist evoked so lovingly by E. O. Wilson – though some sense of both the wonder and the intricacy of life seems indispensable. And that means *necessary*, as key to the very idea of life-meaning. It should be clearer now, therefore, where the overwhelming resistance to a Faustian bargain over unsustainability comes from. Sustainability – whether of particular activities, of our form of civilization or of the whole human presence on the planet – depends entirely on *life's going on*. It depends on the continuing capacity of life at large, across the biosphere, spontaneously to renew itself in all the infinitely various, intricate and ungovernable forms out of which ecological balance and stability are indefinitely recreated. Hazarding all this in wilful exchange for a present lifetime would not just be potentially robbing our descendants of a future, it would be robbing ourselves of the core of our own living by emptying out the present. Acting in a spirit of deliberate ecological irresponsibility to devalue and degrade life is travestying the fundamental sense we have of ourselves as valuers at all. It involves a radical contradiction in our primordial stance towards life, as if we said: Let life go on, in permanent inexhaustible spontaneity – until I've had my whack. In this way, it would be denying the deepest claim on ourselves that we encounter, the requirement to live hopefully in meaning. It would be to go directly against the grain of what in an older language (that which the original Faustus spoke) would have been called our souls.

In this light, it may be more apparent why I term what this conceptual link between the natural world and experienced life-meaningfulness commits us to, *deep sustainability*. The idea is emphatically not to be confused with 'deep ecology'. That position in environmental philosophy starts from a contentious denial of human exceptionalism, and has come to mean in environmental-political practice a particular style of decentralized communitarianism and would-be bioregional living. Deep sustainability, instead, is at heart just the categorical recoil from the Faustian bargain. It is *deep* because this recoil compels at the deepest human level, the level at which we are ourselves subjectively-given natural forces, vectors in the vast impersonal ongoingness of the life we are called on to respect. That note of commonality only sounds as if it chimes with deep ecology until we insist that humans are nevertheless unique and special – the only manifestation in the known universe of the impersonal in personal form. The deep sustainability imperative, moreover, in itself says nothing about trying to escape from the conditions of modern global civilization rather than trying to transform them from within, as we surely have to do.

For the business of doing so, the metaphor of depth, as against (horizontal) length, does serve to stress the associated focus on the roots of life-significance in the present. This is in contrast to the eye always on the longer-term future by which a sustainable development mindset is characterized and through which, I have argued, it enthrals itself to the sustainability mirage. There is, too, a further and related sense in which this alternative conception of sustainability concern should be called *deep*. Its direction of attention suggests that we should reject a scientistic and fairly simple-mindedly linear preoccupation with the longer-term – predict, evaluate, set goals, pursue them – in favour of thinking in a much more humanly profound way about our situation. How can we behave responsibly with a huge technological armoury, the impacts of which reach out across decades and centuries, when we combine that enormous reach with comparatively very little reliable foresight indeed? How can we hope for an answer to that question once we recognize that our limitedness is not a temporary embarrassment on the road to perfected scientific global management, but a necessary condition of the kinds of foreknowledge which the human condition permits? How, under categorical requirement, are we to shape policy on those terms? These are, in several senses, the *really* deep questions about sustainability.

What's the difference?

I will return to the implications of this depth metaphor throughout what follows. But it is time – well past time, some readers will no doubt be thinking – to start asking what immediate real difference all this could make. What do we actually *gain* from seeing things this way? Suppose this kind of life-impossibility, and not any form of ethical obligation, were indeed the source and tenor of the imperative acknowledged by people who say that we simply cannot go on treating the planet and the future as we are. How would that recognition help in the now very urgent task of ensuring that such people come to form a working majority in countries like Britain before the next decade is out?

In particular, we should ask: how does this alternative model of that imperative make it any more robust, any less capable of being endorsed in principle and shuffled around in practice, than the ethico-scientistic imperative of sustainable development? For, of course, we still confront it with all the motivations and reluctances and skills in equivocation that we have. And we are still going to need the science, with all its indeterminacies and openings for soft-quantified compromise, hollow-heartedness and double-mindedness, to tell us how and in what specific biophysical media and to what more-or-less dangerous extent we actually are risking the future of life. Have we done any more, in fact, than to turn through ninety degrees and spot the mirage on another quarter of the horizon?

It will take the rest of the book to answer this question properly. I want to use the remaining sections of this chapter to sketch out why I think it can be answered – why I believe that this alternative, deep-sustainability view does not delude and need not betray us (although it is, of course, still down to us whether it actually saves us).

Let us address the key issue of bad faith first. In his powerful and helpful book *Heat*, from which I gratefully acknowledge borrowing the idea for a Faustian comparison, George Monbiot presents us with this stark but realistic challenge: 'Curtailing climate change must ... become the project we put before all others. If we fail in this task, we fail in everything else.' That I take to be true, and Monbiot is admirable in the persistence with which he goes on saying it loud and clear. But although it certainly resonates with what I have been arguing in this chapter, it is apparent from the rest of his book that he means the challenge to be understood and met in the spirit of sustainable development. We will fail in everything else, because all our innovations and improvements – better education, more housing, lifting people out of poverty, rather-less-crumbling hospitals, shaving fifteen minutes off the train journey to Paris, and so on and on – will be rendered merely futile (after a while, and in retrospect) if the biosphere collapses, civilization implodes and the planet becomes uninhabitable. Agreed: but then the next question must obviously be, 'What are we going to have to do, what can't we any longer avoid doing, to prevent all this turning out in the longer run to have been futile?' Monbiot's book is full of hard-headed practical ideas in response. The overall picture it offers is that *if* we can do enough in the areas of energy usage, energy supply, transport policy and personal consumption patterns, we are in with a chance of cutting carbon emissions by the 90 per cent which he takes, plausibly enough, to be required by around 2030. This prospective possibility is meant to be encouraging. But out of it, on the sustainable development paradigm, also springs the mirage-danger, the wiggle-room which bad faith can always exploit – and will indeed tend to exploit, for the very persuasive reason that at the moment lots of these innovations and improvements seem not futile at all, and we want to carry on making them right up to what the ecological limits allow. So how can getting the balance right between present and future not be the name of the game? Yes, if we turn out to have failed in curtailing climate change we will ultimately have failed in everything – but we can still hope to strike a compromise deal to let us succeed in some things while keeping the climate broadly manageable for the longer term.

The radical difference on the deep sustainability account is that we have left the conceptual terrain of such compromises. Why can't we go on as we are? Not because doing so risks sacrificing future needs to present satisfactions in a way which leaves those satisfactions nevertheless *real*, so that there can be a real conflict between their grip on us and that of our obligations and responsibilities. Rather, we can't go on as we are because even as we risk the future, to the extent of consciously acting against life-hope, we find that the present satisfactions for which we do so have turned unreal and slipped through our fingers. The *can't* marks our fundamental resistance to that existential loss.

Helping us to recognize this is one great advantage of putting talk about life-meaning in the Faustus-context of talk about souls. 'What shall it profit a man if he gain the whole world and lose his own soul?' There is no response to this question along the lines of 'How much world might be on offer for *some* of my soul?' – and this is because the concept *soul* cannot be used like that. Try to weigh some of your soul against what you might get away with of the world's delights, and you have already imperilled all of it. Nor can the cognate idea of life-meaningfulness as I have been appealing to it be a negotiating subject. That is why our resistance to the Faustian bargain must be categorical. There is no trading a certain reduced level of risk to planetary life for enough present meaningfulness to be going on with. And by the same token, there is no fudging around in the wiggle-room provided by a long-term risk horizon and the complexities of probabilistic calculation. Again, the concept just doesn't work that way. While we have, here and now, a stance towards the future that can substantively hazard the biosphere at all – that can see even *some* risk of its runaway destruction as worth running, provided the present benefits are high enough – we are already falling into a radical triviality which is humanly uninhabitable. If we fail to rise to the spirit of the climate challenge, that is, we fail in everything else not *later* and *possibly*, but *already now*.

It is important to see that a categorical resistance to this failure does not mean reaching out convulsively for some unavailable pause-button. We are still going to need all the resources of knowledge and technology which Monbiot so usefully catalogues, and which others are increasingly developing and publicizing. We will still need at least some of the apparatus of targets, indicators, incentives, regulations, tax-breaks and penalties which sustainable development has started politicians around the world on creating. (We might need a fair bit less of all this if what I argue about the role of enterprise in Chapter 7 is well taken, but let us leave that matter aside for now.) And we are still going to need all the skills of the sciences which identify and quantify risks, and a policy process through which we make the best decisions we can in response. But the terms of our engagement with all this will have changed fundamentally. Simply put, instead of working towards doing *what we can't avoid*, if we are to avert climate catastrophe, we shall be working towards doing *whatever it takes*.

This looks a thin difference – wouldn't the same outcome fit either description? – but in the context it is all the difference in the world. For the following out of what we can't avoid, when actually lots of more-or-less canny ways of avoiding it are always soliciting us throughout the process, is the pursuit of a mirage. Doing whatever it takes, by contrast, is finally just a matter of making the break and having the guts. We can return to the war analogy to reinforce this point. In terms which have now settled into the British folk-memory, it is the difference between 1939 and 1940. A war entered into on the basis of doing what we can't avoid, honouring obligations which we couldn't quite, at last, once more slide out of, is a war on the way to being lost. But a war aiming, in that unforgettable rallying cry, for 'victory at all costs, victory in spite of all terrors, victory however long and hard the road may be' is quite another thing.

None of this means that people, and governments, will stop trying to shift, dodge and fudge, and sometimes getting away with it. People are people – people in government, often more so. It does, though, mean that in behaving thus they will no longer be subtly seconded by mirage-tendencies inherent in the ruling model of what we are trying collectively to do. And actually, as I try to show in Part III, the alternative, deep-sustainability account offers a working basis for strategies and tactics which might instead minimize the effects of these human failings, to the extent that they can be minimized – at least while the climate war is being fought out.

Losing meaning

The danger of bad faith may be lessened when we turn to recognize a meaning-imperative for sustainability. But what of that imperative itself?

The climate war was always against aspects of ourselves. On the sustainable development picture, it was against aspects of our behaviour as epistemic and moral agents – those human traits which are always leading us to ignore the predictable consequences of our actions when it suits us and to let greed, or at best the desire for comfort, triumph over our response to need. On the deep sustainability picture, however, it is against those aspects of ourselves and our situation, including our stance towards the future, which tend to drain even comfortable and well-provided present life of meaning. I have tried to suggest the central conceptual relationship here, the involvement of meaning and sustainability with one another in the idea of life's ongoingness. But the ways in which this relationship plays out practically, the actual lived interactions between our meaning-needs and our ecological impacts, responsibilities and motivations, are extremely complex. I need to sketch their outlines here, though an outline sketch is all there will be space for.

Loss of meaning is not just something which happens when we try to make the explicit Faustus-move. It is now, in fact, an extraordinarily pervasive aspect of life-experience in the advanced societies. A kind of half-resigned emptiness or quiet despair has become so much the underlying tenor of common experience that, when we really allow ourselves to acknowledge it, talk of improving our quality of life in the downshifting sense seems either bumptious or ironic. Usually, though, we shrink from acknowledgement. Neither the sun nor death, said La Rochefoucauld, can be looked at directly – and nor, it seems, can this chronic modern disposition to despair, which though eerily undramatic works at the depth of life and death. But that it is always there, if only in the background just out of sight, is surely indisputable whenever we can bring ourselves to reflect honestly on our situation. There are the statistics of suicide, depression, divorce and various forms of addiction to be adduced here, all with their eager chorus of commentators telling us that they don't mean what they so palpably say. But an appeal to common experience is the simplest and most direct proof. For the young, meaninglessness or low-level despair is the sense that whatever you throw yourself into, ordinary adult life when you get to it has little fundamentally real to offer. Natural energy and the optimism of sheer physical vitality will serve to overlay this awareness for a while, but can never entirely eliminate it. As one passes into middle life, the feeling becomes less avoidable: whatever you strive for will fail to answer, even if you can achieve it, indeed even as you celebrate achieving it. There are the immediacies of work, pleasure, love and maybe triumph to be enjoyed – but (except perhaps for those who can still genuinely persuade themselves of religious comforts and sanctions) the familiar worm waits in the core of all these activities. With increasing age its gnawing takes an even sharper edge, as one realizes that without real meaningfulness there is also going to be no *redemption*. Life comes only once, one has had one's chances and squandered them, more or less successfully in the world's eyes, and now there is no help for the cruelties, the betrayals, the worse paths taken and the better ignored. 'So what? ... what for?' is the now inescapable question.

Of course, much literature, and a lot of recorded non-fictional living, testifies that standing helpless before that oncoming question has always been among the more terrible possibilities of the human condition. Loss of meaningfulness always threatens conscious selfhood in the nature of our kind of being, as we saw from the earlier discussion. But in our present society, this threat, from being one which people normally handled readily enough, has become a lurking danger on an epidemic scale.

One reason for this is fairly obvious. The pervasive disposition towards finding life meaningless is such a feature of Western civilization because institutional religion has effectively died. That kind of understanding of the human condition is simply no longer the ordinary, unquestioned background of our lives. (Revivalist or fundamentalist attempts to galvanize the corpse merely underscore this point, since they so evidently depend on a willed refusal to accept it.) Finding the ordinary satisfactions of life *not empty* is very much harder under these conditions. For a very long time, and despite its manifold drawbacks, organized religion served our fundamental wellbeing by creating space for the tacit recognition of our underlying existential situation. At the heart of it, the believer's relating himself in various ritual ways to the believed-in God reoriented himself within himself, away from mere ego towards the standpoint where he felt most reduced to nothing personally, and at the same time most empowered spiritually ('our peace in His will'). Such practices, within an overarching narrative of creation, sin and redemption, fed a recognition of contrast between one's ordinary conditioned self and something unconditioned (a 'soul') which one also centrally was. It must have been access to the standpoint of the impersonal unconditioned, prompted by this dramatization of experience, which enabled people to connect with life-hope at the core of human being, even though they were using a different language to describe it – so as to validate the ordinary, non-mythic intrinsic meaningfulness which by and large actually got them through their lives.

I take it that something like this account of its existential reality is needed to explain why institutional religion was such a vigorous survivor for so long – a fact which neo-Darwinists like Richard Dawkins are surely bound by their own assumptions to account for, but never satisfactorily do. After all, a basically medieval faith like Christianity prospered, with ups and downs, through a good many recent centuries during which key thinkers and a lot of ordinary people with their wits about them must always have suspected that it was talking about something other than Someone who didn't exist. But notwithstanding that long and successful innings, and for a huge complication of historical, cultural and intellectual reasons which there is no space here to discuss, institutional religion is now no longer an existentially valid option. And what our civilization mainly offers to fill the gap are more-or-less nervous excitements of the conditioned, merely personal self.

This reflects the fact that we have not only lost the kind of access to life-hope which religion at its best made available, but we have also cut ourselves off from it in other important ways. (These developments have not, of course, merely accompanied one another accidentally, though their interconnections are far too intricate and problematic to pursue here.) Thus, the sense of the life at the core of us as spontaneous, inexhaustible, creative and unquestionable does not easily flourish in a form of living essentially alienated from the unfenced and unmanaged natural world, as are huge numbers of modern, thoroughly urban or megalopolitan lives. That cities typically offer a riot of manufactured stimuli in quasi-compensation doesn't alter this point, since all these appeal at the level of the conditioned self, the self that defines itself in terms of its relational, cultural and shopping opportunities. The buzz and crackle from a multiplicity of ego-selves sparking off each other is not life-spontaneity, though it can sometimes serve for a while as a substitute for it. And the same goes for merely vacational exposure to the non-urban (in increasingly exotic places), which is only a more demonstrative form of shopping.

We also (and again, in ways closely interwoven with our urbanization) live at a growing distance from the spontaneous and creative in ourselves. I can only glance at this point here, though only glancing at it runs an even more serious risk of being misunderstood. Do we not lead freed-up, flexible and autonomous personal lives, with far more scope for authenticity and self-actualization than under the older, traditional restraints which have fallen away? Is there not art and literature coming out of our ears? Can one turn on the television without encountering an excitingly creative personality? But actually, beneath all this runs the radically disabling conviction that human creativity isn't *real* – isn't fundamentally creative of reality. We are confronted at every turn with a *made* world, not just materially and institutionally in the infrastructures which always surround us, but existentially. We meet a world the essential nature of which we experience as set over against us, *there anyway* in its ultimately physical forms, not something of which life-as-human-being is an actively constitutive source, or fount. In such a world, the creativity that might otherwise keep us in touch with life-hope is very typically reduced to a kind of game, whether art materials, concepts or human relationships are the pieces with which we play. Meanwhile the genuinely creative artists who know otherwise, the technically gifted whose inspiration opens into a spontaneity beyond the conditioned self,* are drowned out by the babbling of manufactured instant celebrities, and cannot help us, except accidentally.

If deep alienation from life-hope leads to loss of meaning, that loss in turn is the most deep-rooted driver of ecological destruction, because it is what really spurs on the consumerist obsessions of the advanced societies which are now placing the Earth's systems under breaking strain. Meaninglessness is perpetually in motion. The disposition to quiet despair is a state of mind or spirit in which, routinely, any goals or purposes which we adopt to combat meaninglessness themselves drain very swiftly of meaning, leaving the inescapably compelled quest to begin over again. Hence the profoundly characteristic *restlessness* of a world in which this spirit is so pervasive – the constant attempts to escape emptiness on a treadmill of unfulfilling movement. Such restlessness can be that of the never-satisfied consumer, spinning from each new nearly identical product, unnecessary service or futile fashion to the next. It can be the addiction to ever-intensifying artificial stimuli, whether alcoholic, narcotic, pornographic or merely those of constantly mediated chatter. Or it can be a literal restlessness, the mad obsessive multiplication of road-miles and air-miles because transit is at least a simulacrum of purpose, and 'one is always nearer by not keeping still'.

These points relate explicitly to the advanced Northern world. In much of the South, especially in the Asian economies, the link between meaninglessness and ecological destructiveness in more indirect. But it is there nevertheless. That these economies are beginning to generate massive ecological pressures is not just down to the fact that many more of their very large populations are now demanding the basic material conditions that the North has taken for granted. It is down also to the way they have adopted in such full measure, and often against

---

* 'There is a moment when you realize that the energy you're using is not your energy. When you're in that moment of absolute concentration, you feel that it's not you anymore. … All creative people recognize this.' – the novelist Jeanette Winterson in an interview in *The Guardian*, 22 November 2005.

much traditional resistance from within, the Northern consumerist model for economic progress. Without their having bought into that lately globalized model, the requirements of the South would look much less daunting. That model dominates the world because the North is hooked on it.

And as to the results ... the Millennium Ecosystem Assessment confirms that over the past fifty years humans have changed ecosystems more rapidly and extensively than in any comparable period of human history, resulting in a substantial and largely irreversible loss in the diversity of life on Earth. Approximately 60 per cent of ecosystem services are being degraded or used unsustainably, including fresh water, fisheries, air and water purification, and the regulation of regional and local climate – and there is clear evidence that the changes being made in these ecosystems are increasing the likelihood of accelerating, abrupt and potentially irreversible non-linear shifts with potentially devastating consequences for human wellbeing as well as the rest of life on Earth. In particular, ice cores extracted from the Antarctic show that the levels of carbon dioxide and methane in the atmosphere are now higher than they have been for 650,000 years, while CO_2 levels have been rising over the past century faster than at any time over the past 20,000 years. Already sea ice in the Arctic has shrunk to the smallest area ever recorded. (So book that sustainable-tourist cruise to the polar regions quickly, while they are still there ... .)

In sum, faltering access to life-hope in ordinary living drains it of meaning, and loss of meaning drives the ecological destructiveness which removes us progressively further from encounter with the natural epiphanies where life-hope might be recaptured. And very many people know in their bones that this is the real nature of the problem, though the conventional discourse of sustainable development utterly fails them for expressing it. Mark Lynas has an image which is very telling in this connection:

> *If you doubt the scale of the enterprise that human society is currently involved in, go and stand by the side of a busy motorway, and then look up at the sky. Remember that the breathable atmosphere extends a mere 7000 metres above your head. Then think of how many other motorways there are criss-crossing the globe, from Bangkok to Berlin, each chock full of cars and trucks ... and remember that this situation goes on day and night, 24/7, across the whole of the globe.*

This is meant to emphasize how human creatures are by no means too small to impact on such a big thing as a planet. But one's recoil needn't be, and surely initially isn't, from the gathering atmospheric-chemical consequences in which that impact consists. It is, rather, directly and immediately from the travesty of human living, the insult to human embodiment and the ruining of human life-space represented by this roaring insanity, this poisoned, insect-like mechanical scurrying. But very many people now live on the edges of motorways, or overlooking similar man-made environments – indeed, that scurrying is a prominent part of the daily context for countless millions. How to bear such lives? How could people be blamed for ... getting in their cars, and escaping, temporarily, to some new electrically powered distraction?

A compelling purpose

But then, how do we break this deadly cycle? How do we tackle the self-feeding dual emergency of endemic meaninglessness and its restless destruction of the Earth? Only by being brought, at last and perhaps still just in time, to face the Faustian confrontation: by coming to recognize fully what is involved in the need to change those habits and patterns of damage. But for this to happen, the green imperative needs to be articulated in the language of deep sustainability.

Here it is very helpful to have an eminent contemporary to call in evidence:

> *The climate crisis ... offers us the chance to experience what very few generations in history have had the privilege of knowing: a* generational mission; *the exhilaration of a compelling* moral purpose; *a shared and unifying cause; the thrill of being forced by circumstances to put aside the pettiness and conflict that so often stifle the restless human need for transcendence;* the opportunity to rise. ... *When we do rise, it will fill our spirits and bind us together. Those who are now suffocating in cynicism and despair will be able to breathe freely. Those who are now suffering from a loss of meaning in their lives will find hope.*

That is Al Gore, in the book of the film – and a politician's, or perhaps a statesman's, rhetoric. It is a sufficiently clear and vigorous prescription: we find, in the unifying cause of saving the future from ourselves, a purpose which will help us escape from the meaninglessness now driving us to imperil it. One can too easily be cynical about the rather creaking uplift of this. There is truth and inspiration in it for all that, but we need the deep sustainability picture to help us see that the uplift creaks because of the model of purpose on which it is premised, rather than because of the underlying vision or intention.

We can give Gore the word *moral* – when he says, elsewhere, 'This is a moral issue. ... Put simply, it is wrong to destroy the habitability of our planet, and ruin the prospects of every generation that follows ours', the only decent response is to cheer. The moral is, broadly, the domain of what properly shapes and guides our settled practice, and meaning-claims are at the heart of it. But when he equates that recognition of wrongness, as he explicitly does in *An Inconvenient Truth*, with the claim that hazarding runaway global warming is 'deeply *unethical*', warning lights should flash. Meeting the demands of the ethical, in the sense clearly intended – respect for the needs, rights and welfare of others – cannot provide us with life-meaning even when those others are real and present. The sharpest insight that I know of into why not comes, again, from Lawrence:

> *Is there nothing beyond my fellow-man? If not, then there is nothing beyond myself, beyond my own throat, which may be cut, and my own purse, which may be slit: because* I *am the fellow-man of all the world, my neighbour is but myself in a mirror. So we toil in a circle of pure egoism.*

Lawrence doesn't mean to deny that my neighbour matters, perhaps even in ways which may call on me to sacrifice myself to the limits in order to help him. But he, or she, can't be why *I* matter. Making the service of another into a substitute for life-meaning is trying to make a conditioned self which might as well have been one's own into its own purpose – a thinly disguised egoism which is both unattractive and self-defeating. It can't be the case, as a matter of mere logic, that everyone borrows the meaning of his life from someone else by ethically serving them. This is not to deny that the genuine life-project of some (perhaps, some few) people might place a central intrinsic value on serving life in others. But even then, the meaningfulness has to come from within, from the inner stance of life towards its own project, not from the outward object. And this necessary failure of the other to provide a substitute for meaning is even plainer in the intergenerational case. If ensuring the fairness of the deal which future people get, or protecting their welfare, is supposed to provide purpose for our present lives, the actions of the now-future people, protecting whose situation allegedly gives us this purpose, will themselves have to be thought of as purposeless without reference to the prospective situation of then-future people, whose actions ... and so we go on, in what is evidently a spirally ascending version of Lawrence's circle.

This is just the same pernicious game, in fact, as is played by parents who try to pin the meaningfulness of their own lives onto their children. The upshot there is often a kind of tyranny, and here only pretence, but in the context it might prove even more destructive. Since we can intuitively see (even if we might lack a framework for saying) that life-meaning from serving future generations is ersatz, the intended uplift won't actually lift us up very far for all that long, and meanwhile planetary destruction may go on running out of reach. (The link with the mirage effect is no accident.) And there is always the real danger that reaction from a 'shared and unifying cause' which turns out *not* to save us from meaninglessness will go all the more violently into further rounds of ecologically damaging distraction.

But once we see the relation between ecological responsibility and life-meaning as deep sustainability pictures it, this pernicious cycle can be broken. We can escape from emptiness and cynicism by regaining the strength to create genuine meaningfulness. We renew that strength through hearing the deep call of life-hope in our response to a wider natural world recognized as now under categorically intolerable threat from human activity. From that call, we are re-alerted to the creative force – life's sheer ongoingness – that can re-establish central human values of ordinary living, of relationship, community, health and good work, as authentic and intrinsically satisfying. And in seeking to avert the ecological threats which we have already generated, we will then be strongly aided by a recovering ability to live in those satisfactions and no longer consume our resource base and ourselves in permanent destructive restlessness.

If that sounds far too blithely win–win, remember that it is only an outline sketch. The rest of the book will be needed even to begin suggesting how it could start to play out in practice. But I want to end this chapter on a note which Gore sounds strongly: the sense of a decisive coincidence of historical, ecological and spiritual forces, an unprecedented challenge and a unique opportunity. I think he is right in this, but again, we need the deep sustainability picture to see why and how.

Some people will, indeed, find disturbing rather than inspiring the kind of appeal made in the short passage which I have already quoted:

> The climate crisis ... offers us the chance to experience what very few generations in history have had the privilege of knowing: a generational mission; ... the opportunity to rise.

Even allowing for the need to accentuate the positive in a public presentation, there is an inescapable sense here of *welcoming* this generational opportunity. Gore himself doesn't use the war analogy explicitly in describing the climate crisis, but for my own part I can't help being reminded of some lines of Yeats, written at the end of the 1930s:

> You that Mitchel's prayer have heard,
> 'Send war in our time, O Lord!'
> Know that when all words are said
> And a man is fighting mad,
> Something drops from eyes long blind,
> He completes his partial mind,
> For an instant stands at ease,
> Laughs aloud, his heart at peace.

When an appeal in this spirit is combined with talk about the 'restless human need for transcendence' and the chance to recover lost meaning in our lives, we might seem to be getting uncomfortably near to a worked-up quasi-religious fanaticism. Worked-up, that is, because its unadmitted *purpose* is evidently more about restoring meaningfulness and the sense of belonging to a great community and movement, where these spiritual resources have otherwise failed, than about averting the climate crisis. Hasn't the world had quite enough of this kind of motivation? – a point only underlined by its recent ugly recrudescence. The climate war as substitute *jihad* for the secular West is surely not what we need. One can well appreciate why, instead, very many people would like to see the climate change issue, and the demands of ecological responsibility in general, as essentially technical problems. Those problems certainly pose us horrendous challenges, in science, technology, economics and social policy, but we must overcome them, if we can, through rational use of our best knowledge and the machinery of scientifically informed democracy and international cooperation. Missionary would-be transcendence can only muddle us in that enormously demanding task.

In this response, however, one has to see something now patently inadequate to the actual situation. The war metaphor is understandably distressing to many people of goodwill. But as I argued in the Preface, no other analogy comes close to capturing the scale of the emergency we face and the mobilization with which we have to meet it. Yet it is largely a hidden emergency – unprecedentedly invisible, because of its bearing down on us through cumulative consequences and concatenations of natural forces which the huge majority of people are only beginning to learn how to appreciate. And if the now rapidly gathering weight of scientific evidence and authority are to be credited, *we have a decade* – two at the outside – to turn that around. I have already made this point too, in the Preface and again in the last chapter, but it bears much repeating. Starkly, unless we can within that timeframe get a working majority for very significant changes to our economic, technological and lifestyle arrangements in Britain and other countries with world leadership roles in this crisis, it will very likely be too late. Worldwide ecological devastation, quite possibly leading to a global biospheric catastrophe, will be unstoppable. We will not have been attentive enough to see that we were being presented with a Faustian temptation, but the Faustian trap will close on us notwithstanding. This is not the sort of danger which we can encourage people to appreciate, still less act vigorously to avert, by presenting it as a cluster of essentially technical problems.

But yet again: recognizing this might well be felt to make Gore's kind of rhetoric even less attractive. Climate *jihad* as surreptitiously welcomed spiritual quest, an exhilaration of rediscovered transcendence, rings falsely enough. As a *tactic*, a deliberately chosen language for putting across the scale and nature of the emergency, must it not be quite illegitimate, and indeed dishonest?

The deep sustainability approach as I have so far sketched it can offer us a way out of this bind. On that picture of what is involved, the concern for ecological responsibility certainly works at what we should not flinch from calling a spiritual depth. That does not make it into any kind of synthetic religion-substitute. But it does make it into a religion-*successor* – for our time, in the given conditions of the advanced secular world. Something very different from any form of religion, but nevertheless serving some of its profounder existential purposes, moves onto a terrain left achingly vacant for too long. There is nothing here but humans and their radical terrestriality – no gods (not even Gaia), no myths, no eschatological drama. But in the full recognition of our terrestriality and its claims and responsibilities, we repossess an understanding of the way in which, uniquely, we are conditioned creatures with the unconditional at the core of us.

There is no other way to reach this deep understanding of our unconditionality which will serve in present circumstances. By that I mean not just the circumstances of ecological crisis, but the whole self-alienated life-situation out of which we have to confront them. There is no prospect of our addressing this inner void without confronting our ecological destructiveness directly, because doing so offers, though in a complex way, the only language and practice now really open to us for any sufficiently generalizable recovery of life-meaning. Modern post-religious living is full of attempts to tackle the void, from new forms of holistic spirituality all the way to football fanaticism. Some, like the latter, are merely sad surrogates. Retreat into personal relations isn't much better. Love as charity, love of neighbour, can't substitute for meaning. Love as Eros, the brief, hazardous impersonality of real desire, can indeed sometimes spring life-hope for us, but the restless grinding of formed individualities against one another which ordinarily characterizes modern sexuality can then go near to killing it. Other, more formal recourses, like the disciplines of body and attention to be found in the Eastern martial arts, seem (to an outsider) to offer the possibility of a practice of focused energy in touch with life-hope – but to limited numbers, and perhaps only in a kind of protected space. The more overtly quasi-religious options, the 'alternative' or 'New Age' rituals and therapies which try to sacralize various inner dynamics and relational experiences, are too evidently products of the conditioned self – too patently willed, and often wilful – to reach anywhere near the creative spontaneity of life. Space precludes these discriminations being other than dogmatic – I can only trust to the book as a whole to show that the green turn provides the only genuine practical hope here.

But this historic turn or mind-shift must be understood in a deep-sustainability perspective for its full significance to emerge. In that perspective we can make a different sense of what I have called the daily bread of ecological living – all the activities and commitments which are increasingly, and necessarily, becoming an accepted part of our lives: the cycling, the recycling, the energy saving, the concern for food-sourcing and species-conservation, maybe the domestic wind turbine or the solar panels … . Rationalized by sustainable development, these are mostly sincere if sometimes rather random attempts to do one's bit. But because on that model they are perpetually open to the ambush of bad faith, they are always liable to shift into the mode of tacit compromise and half-acknowledged self-congratulation – the mode of doing *something*, anyway, and at least a bit more than Jones over the road. Rationalized by deep sustainability, this ramifying framework of small-scale individual engagement has the feel of a pragmatic and secular set of 'spiritual practices'. They are in this respect, if in no other, a bit like the routine prayers and observances of institutional religion used to be. As noted, these were things that people went through, often just as a matter of habit or because they were expected to, and without thinking very much about them – but which put them regularly back into fleeting contact with their deeper selves. Similarly, we might see our own partial and often spasmodic practices of ecological responsibility – always reminders, potentially, of the broader life-context – as ways of more-or-less routinely touching base with life-hope. These changes at the individual level, whatever their direct carbon-reduction or other ecological consequences, are always helping us to orient ourselves back towards the unconditional, the claims of the underlyingly natural in our lives, and so to make and sustain ongoing meaning.

There is thus a real sense in which practices of green living, however trivial and undemanding, may be said to be defending the natural. They are defending and reclaiming the natural life-hope in ourselves, by acting out however token a defence of life at large in the biosphere. I suspect that its answering to this need is a very significant part of the reason why the green turn to ecological responsibility symbolized by the Apollo vision has swept through human affairs in the West with such epochal rapidity. But in the current of this very understanding of ourselves and our situation, it must be clear that we cannot now remain at that level. Doing so would be a refusal to face up to the basically Faustian issue which has begun to insist on itself. The climate crisis – and here, Gore is surely ungainsayable – is now upon us in a way which must force us to realize, and very urgently, the *whole* of what was always implicit in the green turn. We need not just to find our way back into the natural, but to find for the natural, ourselves included, a way back from the brink. There is still an enormous task of education, publicity and (frankly) exhortation here, as well as that of crafting policy and strategy. But if we can reach the depth of recognition, across society, to which I have been pointing, and take it as an opportunity to rise to the required level of understanding and action, we could yet find the resources to fight this unprecedented battle.

We will not do that in the spirit of sustainable development. In the spirit of deep sustainability, we might. The rest of the book turns to ways and means.

PART III

GREENING OUR LUCK

Without victory, there is no survival. – Winston Churchill

6
Making the Break: The Carbon Framework

In Part I, I traced the failures of the sustainable development model back to serious defects in its conceptual structure, in the way it articulates understanding, ecological responsibility and motivation together. In Part II we have been exploring an alternative conceptualization of the sustainability imperative which is meant to avoid those defects. But the whole point of such reconceptualizing must in the end be to liberate our practical imaginations – to empower a new vision of the real possibilities open to us. In that spirit, this third and concluding part of the book looks at a range of practical approaches across the fields of energy usage, planning and policymaking, education and enterprise. Some of these are already in place, others on the stocks or at any rate on the cards. What matters, if my overall argument is along the right lines, is to see what difference a deep sustainability rather than a sustainable development rationale might make to the way we see what we are doing in all these areas – especially with reference to climate change. From that difference can be expected to flow some very significant differences in how we follow these practical measures through, and thus in what in turn might emerge from them.

For this purpose, we need to be clear what a deep sustainability rationale must involve for practice. Hitherto I have considered it as a relation between life-meaning and the motives to ecological concern. Now I must describe the face it presents towards active engagement. How would our understanding and expectations of sustainability policy and ecologically responsible action change if we recognized the sources of our motivation, the real sense and direction of that responsibility, to be what Part II has been suggesting? I address that question first in general terms, drawing out criteria for practice from the alternative idea-complex itself. I then turn to the main, decisively break-making shift into a new paradigm which would match up to these criteria.

Perhaps the most general point of all here is that when sustainability goes deep rather than long, it becomes a matter of the path at least as much as the goal. On the sustainable development model, sustainability is essentially a state of economic balance – resource usage not diminishing critical natural capital – which we are trying to get ourselves into and then maintain indefinitely. The term describes a desirable objective relation between present action and its future consequences. Deep sustainability, by contrast, characterizes a kind of attention to the present and future in relation, such that when we act out of that attention, an open future can go on emerging indefinitely from a meaningful present.

One very characteristic mark of this altered perspective is that the fundamental consideration of *equity* becomes important at a different level. For sustainable development, equity as between generations, considered in material or resource terms, defines the goal, and at least greater material equality across the present generation is seen as vitally instrumental in achieving it. This is implicit in the Brundtland bargain: the commitment to meeting present needs entails recognizing that the material needs of many present people are currently not met, and have to be if those people are also reasonably to be called on to comply with requirements enabling future needs to be met. There remains the question how far material equality among present people is desirable in itself. This is a legitimately contested question, as we noted in Chapter 4, and the contest can cut across the process of trying to deal fairly with the future. For deep sustainability, however, what really matters is our all being equally in need of meaningful lives, as a condition of our common humanity whatever our cultural and material differences. With that recognition must come processes of attention and action in relation to the emergent future which respect that radical equality. Present action is where the fact of our all being in this together (and our being, in an older terminology, all equal in the sight of God) has to be reflected, since there are no genuinely equitable relations except within the present.

Sustainability as learning process

Another, closely related, mark of deep sustainability is that it is radically a *learning* process. But learning here means not some potentially one-off performance of mastering facts or acquiring dispositions, which may then change subsequent behaviour (either of individuals or of institutions). Instead, it means permanent adaptive responsiveness to a permanently changing, ever-emergent set of circumstances. The key relation to equity is that we are all more-or-less ignorant – the equality of our ignorance far outweighing the differences in our knowledge – in the face of anything but the immediately short-term future. With this understanding comes a conception of responsible attention to the consequences of our actions very different from that which informs the sustainable development strategy of 'predict and evaluate'. For it is an understanding not just that all longer-term prediction is irredeemably 'soft', but that the only kind of existence the future has is *its always being under construction* out of such soft data in the present. The crucial practical challenge is to get an institutional and political framework flexible and adaptive enough to be capable of the continuous exploratory social learning which this implies.

Of course, acting responsibly in any field always involves being prepared to learn. But the crucial factor in shaping appropriate learning is uncertainty. Acting responsibly when we are basically *not* uncertain – when we have every reason to suppose that our methods of predicting outcomes are robust and that our evaluative criteria are reliable – involves what has been aptly called *single-loop* learning. In such cases, we review our alternative possible actions and predict their respective outcomes, compare these predictions evaluatively, and then proceed on that basis. The learning element simply means looking out for minor divagations from trajectory and adjusting as we go along to keep on the predetermined track.

Whenever real uncertainty comes into the frame, what we need instead is *double-loop* learning. We make some assumptions, and act on them in the expectation that certain results will follow. In the event, almost invariably, rather different results follow – in the light of which, we don't just trim our course of action, but also revisit and maybe somewhat revise our assumptions – on the new basis of which we again act in the expectation that certain results will follow. And so on. Note that this is a short-term process – albeit iteratively so. It doesn't usually take very much time, if we are paying attention, before the upshots of our assumptions start differing visibly from our expectations – and if we do leave off noticing this for any length of time, there is progressively less chance of constructively fine-tuning our assumptions as we go on, rather than having to ditch them pretty well wholesale and start again.

Double-loop learning, however, can still be what I call *closed-loop* – in the sense that it is seen as attempting to get progressively closer to the position of predicting consequences and evaluating outcomes. This closed-double-loop, essentially defensive model of learning is the one which underlies precautionary behaviour. We acknowledge uncertainty, accept provisionality and explore forwards, but still with a notion of ourselves as pursuing a desired ideal state in which we *shall have learnt*. We are still hoping, eventually and if we don't commit ourselves too soon, to be clear what we are doing and where we are going. *Open-loop* learning, by contrast, is responsibility under uncertainty which tries to get the best out of our standardly, characteristically and permanently *not* really knowing what will happen. We do this not just by constant attention to how things are actually turning out, but by building in options – moves we will be able to make, but not required to make, when the appropriate time comes. Thus we maximize our room to *respond creatively to the emergent*. The aim of open-loop learning is not to minimize uncertainty, but to ride its advancing wave with as few tumbles as we can.

As that image suggests, such a framework involves the *positive* valuation and welcoming of endemic uncertainty – something which calls for a fairly dramatic mind-shift in policy contexts. Routinely in these contexts, uncertainty is modelled as a bad thing – its presence and effects working to accentuate whatever downside may be in question. But this assumption is widely contradicted by the attitudes and practices that actually inform ordinary life. The positive value of uncertainty is suggested by all the values associated not just with open-mindedness and a spirit of enquiry, but with a readiness to complicate speculatively (to mix it and see what emerges) rather than trying always to simplify – the courage to trust our intuition and follow our noses ... the key values, that is, associated with human creativity.

But it is clear enough, too, from the way we actually respond to certainty. The man who is certain of his facts, without realizing that they stand only on as firm a ground as his current set of working assumptions, is normally felt to be a dangerous as well as a rather uncongenial companion – the man who is certain of his values, preferences, tastes or habits, even more so.

Open-loop learning is a process which never tries to take itself as completed, because it is *in principle* uncompletable. It accepts as inevitable the production, indefinitely, of new opportunities of adjustment – a precondition of which, of course, is our still being there to adjust. Hence, in the sustainability context of ecological adjustment, comes the idea of *greening our luck*. That it can accommodate such an idea marks one of the vital differences between deep sustainability and sustainable development thinking: sustainable development, fixated on scientistic planning, has no room at all for the notion of our reliance on luck. But luck isn't something wholly random, that just happens to one out of the blue if it happens at all. It can of course be like that, but we also speak meaningfully of someone who is on the ball, quick on his feet, quick to spot developments, as *making his luck* – setting himself up to make the best of whatever, at least in part unforeseeably, his opportunities turn out to be. That is how we now need to take forward the impetus of the green turn. The kind of learning involved is more like life itself than it is like progress towards any envisaged end. It is the active principle of sustainability as life's ongoingness. (And if someone asked why we should call such a process *learning*, when all it does is bring forward new uncertainties at each point to which we have advanced from previous ones, one could well ask in return: why do we call *life* something which never finally *gets* us anywhere?)

Government as heuristic management

This is the context in which we need to work with the real grain of capitalism, as I argued in Chapter 1 that sustainable development is unlikely to be able to do. Capitalism at its best is open-loop learning applied to the ongoing production, distribution and exchange of goods and services. The clearest insight here comes from von Hayek, who is a much more important thinker in relation to these issues than his caricature as a mere free-market ideologue suggests. His argument, historically mounted against the bureaucratic ambitions of centralized socialist economies, draws on conceptual resources which make it powerfully relevant to the pursuit of a sustainability mirage:

> *If we are to advance, we must leave room for a continuous revision of our present conceptions and ideals which will be necessitated by further experience. ... Though we must always strive for the achievement of our present aims, we must also leave room for new experiences and future events to decide which of these aims will be achieved ... the advance*

*and even the preservation of civilization are dependent on a maximum
of opportunity for accidents to happen.*

The role of government in this advance is to make dispositions which free up a
society's capacity for creative mistakes and illuminating accidents, and to facilitate
(though not to organize or direct) the processes of ongoing learning from them,
and of adaptive accommodation to their upshots. Deep sustainability requires a
rich texture of *optionality* in its productive arrangements. We cannot be
proactively learning our way into the open future if there is nothing we can *do*
with what we ongoingly find out about the assumptions to which we had
provisionally committed ourselves – if we haven't left ourselves scope for our
learning to make a real difference. Capitalism, insofar as it is not hypertrophied
monopolism but flexible, light-footed and creatively entrepreneurial, represents
the condition of that optionality. As such, its activities (as the left now seems to
have recognized) can't be closely planned, though they can be broadly guided;
nor (as the left in power still tends to forget) does it flourish in a society where
too much else is planned in detail. We will return to this theme in the next
chapter.

This doesn't, however, mean the end of planning. A society operating on a
deep sustainability rationale will seek to configure policy and action within a
learning framework as an absolutely basic requirement, but they will still need to
be structured by plans and targets. In that learning spirit, however, it will take a
different attitude to the figures and the science which supplies them, essential as
these will remain. Quantified targets will be seen as heuristics, exploratory
approximations to be ongoingly revised, the more so the further ahead they are
cast. What we do with them will reflect both this recognition, and also the way
the deep sustainability perspective works against bad faith.

In this connection, think of drawing a line in the sand. 'If you cross that,
that's it!' When we do that metaphorically in some transaction or relationship,
we don't just do so because it represents some quantum or extent of whatever
is at stake, exceeding which will have unacceptably adverse consequences –
when the main issue might then be over whether that is objectively the right
place to have drawn the line. ('Yes, I know we said that was the level of sales at
which that product line would cease to be viable, but are there considerations
we haven't factored in here?') We also draw such lines in order to say, 'Thus far
and no further, *whatever*!' We generally do this because we know both that
there will be pressure to go further, and that without a clear marker we will
always have a tendency to accommodate to that pressure. Lines in the sand are
drawn to stop oneself fudging, as much as to stop whatever it is one wants to
stop fudging about. They must not, of course, be drawn in totally implausible
places; but once drawn, the issue is no longer only the plausibility of here rather
than there, but that we have committed ourselves in a way that was necessary
in order to get on.

The key application here is to sustainability targets – which of course we are going to go on needing. A quantified target on the sustainable development model – say for a 60 per cent carbon emissions cut on 1990 levels – is meant to be the figure it is, because it is meant to be the intergenerationally equitable balancing point. (Smaller cuts damage the future, larger ones penalize the present unnecessarily.) Bad faith then has its chance, because we know, tacitly, that if the target presses too hard on us, it needn't actually be the figure it is, but can slide or float – that is, be treated as just sufficiently imprecise to allow us the leeway we need. But such a quantified target set and treated heuristically is an acknowledged place-holder for *whatever amount of cut it takes* to do the job – here, the job of trying to ensure that climate change remains such as can be adaptively coped with, ongoingly. We can fully admit, on this understanding, that the figure is very unlikely to be a place-holder for itself (that is, to be the figure it is) – we can only hope to learn more about what it should be, or whether it is even the right quantum to be targeting, as we go on. But we can still set it, and insist on it – for the line-in-the-sand kind of reason – as a working target. And because its practical stringency comes from that source, against an heuristic background, rather than from an objective specificity which we must affect not to recognize as illusory, it is much harder to respond to it in bad faith.

Politics as existential leadership

Policies appropriate to doing whatever it takes in the climate war, while learning our way forward into an open, emergent future, using figures as working heuristics and not as comfort-blankets, will have to be argued for and justified at a different level from that to which our politics has become accustomed – or resigned. Whatever it takes will call for a real shift in the material configuration of our lives, involving and affecting everyone. This shift will have to be legally backed, and the grounds for the laws defended in a way which ensures them popular acceptance. But these grounds do not appeal to our aspirations for material betterment, or even to our desire to protect our present position. Nor do they really appeal to our sense of people's underlying rights, after the manner of sustainable development. Rather, they appeal to the categorical demand for life-meaning at the centre of the human condition.

We have got so used to a politics of ethicized material micro-management that this kind of grounding for law and policy will now sound very strange. So it is crucial to note that there are some other legal requirements and restraints which do actually, when scrutinized, derive their warrant from the sense we find humanly habitable. Historically, not all law has been made to enhance people's welfare or express their human rights – that is, not all law is a codification of essentially ethical relations. At the most basic level, for instance, laws enshrining the position of marriage and parenthood within society, and privileging these particular forms of interpersonal relation, are not finally grounded in the extent to which such arrangements are supposed to conduce to more happiness or autonomy than others that might be imagined. Indeed we're all familiar with critiques of these institutions which argue powerfully that various alternatives would make us either happier or more autonomous, or both – critiques which are often very well taken, and typically at the same time feel as if they simply miss the point. In fact, such a legal framework expresses and formalizes a deep *meaning-claim*, an awareness that, come what may, privileging these relations in one way or another (and clearly, the specific forms change and develop) is a fundamental part of making sense of our humanity. Except as subtending some such institutions of special commitment, our nature in its sexual, reproductive and affective aspects just wouldn't cohere for us.

Similarly, legal rights of children to be educated are not best thought of as reflecting some fundamental human birthright to education, which opens up all sorts of familiarly insoluble difficulties. (A right to the same universal standard of education, regardless of socio-cultural context? Or a right to a socio-culturally appropriate education? – and then, who decides?) They are, again, better taken as expressing the fundamental meaning-claim that if we neglect *this* basic process of ongoingly regenerating the human world, then our lives cease to make habitable sense. Come what may, society must take responsibility for ensuring that the whole rising generation is educated.

Notoriously, we haven't always thought like this. That we do so now is not at bottom because we have grown more ethically aware (though perhaps we have), but because the domain of meaning has reconfigured itself, as it always periodically will as long as human being remains a going concern. The same can be said for other fundamental shifts and developments in our feel for what makes human sense, such as those by which slavery and the disenfranchisement of women changed from being normal and accepted to being unthinkable. Ethical argument obviously played an important part in securing these shifts, but what finally happened in each case was that one kind of life-meaning shaped out in a broad constitution of law and practice became unliveable, and another came to express how, come what may, we had to understand ourselves.

It is change at that level – an emerging meaning-demand recasting a whole framework of constituted legality – that the deep sustainability recognition impels. For this we need political leaders who aren't concerned only to tell people what they superficially care to hear, or to legislate only in ways that it is 'politically realistic' to expect people to want. Instead we need leadership which can respond and act at the existential level. It must articulate the profound ache of meaninglessness which pervades modern experience and give the equally profound turn away from it towards ecological responsibility the kind of legal and institutional expression that speaks from this depth. But the situation also requires that the recasting of our practice be unprecedentedly urgent and rapid. So we need in our leaders the real courage to go out ahead on the strength of their existential intuitions, and if necessary act beyond their notional mandate to compel the real mandate which our life-need gives them. Of course there is always the danger that leaders with that kind of energy and confidence will go out ahead at the prompting of their own egos and ambitions rather than in the light of deep responsibility, and so mislead us. But that is a chance which we must accept with the territory when the stakes are this high. The greater danger is that we find no leadership prepared to risk it.

Setting the framework

I have been outlining broad positive criteria for the politics of deep sustainability. I now want to suggest a number of ways in which those criteria might be met by some actual policies, programmes and arrangements to be found on the sustainability agenda – or which might be found there, if this perspective were to be increasingly adopted. It should be clear from what has gone before that these suggestions are not meant to be any kind of specific blueprint for a deep-sustainable society. But I will say it anyway, so that there can be no mistaking my intention here. The rest of this chapter sketches an overarching framework, and the next chapter a variety of activities and approaches within that framework, which could start to be adequate to that sense of our sustainability needs and motives. It could all be implemented, given the political will, and naturally enough I think that it should be. But so could a fairly wide spectrum of variations on it, without losing the essential vision. And since, in the nature of the argument, any such programme must be implemented heuristically if at all, there is simply no point in offering fine-grained detail which would start changing immediately and unpredictably in any case. There is necessarily no blueprint for open-endedness. Its essence is that we have to make things work without guarantees, and that means not just conditioning for but actively welcoming the inevitability of chance and accident. What follows roughs out some key themes of deep sustainability in practice, to indicate the practical spirit in which we shall have to green our own luck in order to survive.

The move that must make the break here, and put in place the kind of institutional and legal framework within which a deep-sustainability understanding would begin to make working sense, is the introduction of carbon rationing.

Talk of rationing is no longer, as it was until fairly recently, the political equivalent of saying a very rude word on television. Mainstream British politicians from both opposition and government, including some senior figures, have seriously canvassed the idea. When he was still at DEFRA, for instance, the present Foreign Secretary floated the idea of a system of individual carbon allowances for emissions associated with consumers' use of energy for domestic and travel purposes (currently estimated at about 44 per cent of total UK emissions). The kind of scheme that he proposed is one which had already become standard in discussion of this possibility. The allowances would be based on national targets for cutting CO_2 emissions and would be the same for every citizen, although they would also be tradable. If you didn't need all your carbon points you could sell them on; if you needed more you could acquire them – at a cost. The scheme would thus build in a strong incentive as well as a regulatory limit – personal energy efficiency would become, if not the new road to riches, at least in everyone's immediate financial interest. Allowances would be 'spent' by simply swiping or debiting a card at the point of purchase, as is now the way with so much of our actual money.

This system would not just cap 'carbon spending', important departure though that would be. The real crunch would be that individual allowances would be progressively reduced to assist the country's required progress towards its reduction targets. This would, of course, only work – and would only stand any chance at all of being acceptable – if emissions from the public and business sectors of the economy were being reduced at the same kind of rate. (Rationing in these sectors, as their overall allocations reduced, would be reflected for the consumer in changing price structures and availability patterns of the goods and services provided.) But assuming this were the case, such a scheme does start to look like the kind of framework that is needed for not just talking about emissions reduction, but really meaning it.

Key to this, of course, is the way the approach builds in a recognition of global warming as the great leveller. Like the wartime rationing of food and other essentials which is its obvious precedent, carbon rationing is based on the need to respond vigorously to something threatening us all, and to pull decisively together in that response. The sort of measures currently being taken to respond to this threat (a mixture of exhortation, tax-rigging and minor regulation) effectively place the main burden on those who are willing to comply, while allowing huge loopholes for those who remain unwilling. A carbon-rationing approach, by contrast, faces the plain fact that, where a major collective effort is vitally necessary, people will make it much more readily when they see everyone else required to make it too. This requirement must be a matter not of supposed ethical obligation seconded by incentives, but of straightforward legal compulsion. In this respect, carbon rationing is the only policy framework really adequate to fighting the climate war.

Another such respect is its de facto acceptance that energy-dependent *activity* across the economy is likely to have to be reduced if emissions are really to be cut back. At the moment the emphasis is on energy supply and energy efficiency – a higher proportion from renewables, and more productivity per unit of energy consumed. Meanwhile, the main thrust of the continuing push for economic growth is to generate ever-rising energy consumption. Supply and efficiency are very important considerations, but an exclusive concentration on them at the expense of trying to reduce energy usage is rather like providing the army with better tanks and more ammunition but not minding much if it never manages to catch up with the enemy. A commitment to climate victory whatever it takes, however, is a commitment to fighting and winning each year's emissions reduction battle as the bottom line. A rigorously enforced and annually reducing cap on emissions affecting everyone directly is the only real way to do this, since it means that any reductions not delivered by more carbon-neutral supply and greater energy productivity will simply *have* to come, in-year, from reductions in usage.

There is, however, a glaringly obvious problem with the carbon-rationing approach sketched so far. It could be introduced in the UK tomorrow, accepted wholeheartedly by the entire population, enforced firmly and fairly, and effective in delivering substantial reductions to time – without thereby making enough difference to halt the global threat in its stride. Anthropogenic climate change is an irreducibly global problem. As we have noted before, the UK currently contributes something over 2 per cent of global CO_2 emissions, compared to the US's 23 per cent, Russia's 5.6 per cent, China's 18 per cent and rising, and India's 5 per cent ditto. Unless all the significant carbon-emitters in both the developed and the rapidly developing world are signed up to achieving victory in grand alliance, the climate war can't be won.

But that signing-up can't be expected to be to across-the-board targets, the same percentage cut in emissions required from every country to make a global percentage cut. Those national shares of the global total mark huge variations in emissions *per capita*. The average citizen of India emits about one tonne of CO_2 annually, of China getting on for four tonnes, of the UK ten tonnes, of the US twenty tonnes. It is clear that a global regime which simply consolidated these differences would run counter to the legitimate aspirations of the poorer and more populous countries for material development. It would also fail to reflect the historical fact that those countries with the highest per capita emissions are also, by and large, those whose industrial development to date has brought about the greenhouse problem in the first place. Such an approach would not only be widely perceived as inequitable, it would be for that very reason entirely impracticable. The Kyoto process and subsequent international negotiations make it overwhelmingly clear that no global emissions agreement is going to stick which is perceived by well over half the world as deeply unfair. The model of equity, of our all being in this together, which starts with everyone on the same footing and progressively reduces the carbon allowance, can't be simply exported from the national to the international stage.

The total framework within which a UK carbon-rationing regime must be established if the goal really is climate victory is pretty simple in outline for all that. It depends in fact on one of those solutions which is so simple that no-one could see it until it was formulated by a non-expert thinking outside the box. This is the framework known as contraction and convergence (C&C), first proposed by a tiny NGO called the Global Commons Institute in 1990. It is probably best explained in the words of Aubrey Meyer, the man behind it:

Global greenhouse emissions need to be reduced by 60 per cent in less than a hundred years.

When governments agree to be bound by such a target, the diminishing amount of carbon dioxide and the other greenhouse gases that the world could release while staying within the target can be calculated for each year in the coming century. This is the contraction part of the process.

The convergence part is that each year's tranche of this global emissions budget gets shared out among the nations of the world in a way that ensures that every country converges on the same allocation per inhabitant by, say, 2030. ... Countries unable to manage within their allocation would, within limits, be able to buy the unused parts of the allocations of other, more frugal countries.

This means, startlingly, just what it says. Over time, we converge on *an equal share for every human being* of the carbon dioxide and other greenhouse gases which it is judged safe for humanity as a whole to go on emitting. The global percentage reduction target and the date for reaching it are decided on the basis of our best scientifically informed estimate of what will give us the best chance of keeping now-inevitable global warming within survivable limits. We then work towards meeting that target on the understanding that well before we do so, every country will be operating within an equitable national emissions allocation. This allocation will be equitable because it will depend only on national population, multiplied by the personal carbon budget on which we shall have converged for each global citizen. As within the suggested UK rationing scheme, trading around these national allocations is permissible, but the overall global emissions quota is firmly capped.

A standard reaction among people encountering these proposals for the first time is to say, 'How hopelessly idealistic!' And such incredulity is perfectly understandable at first blush. Genuinely equal shares worldwide in a key resource – equality not just in theory (high-sounding declarations of universal human rights and so forth), but in hard practice, to which the hitherto globally rich and dominant must conform themselves – and to a fixed timescale! Whose leg does he think he's pulling?

But this response will not survive much careful reflection. For what, actually, is the alternative? We have to turn the global-warming supertanker around, if not quite on a sixpence then certainly within a very limited stretch of sea – and its currently lumbering momentum is powered increasingly by the burgeoning carbon emissions of hugely populous and ambitiously industrializing developing countries. Any chance which a C&C framework offers for halting this process will be greater than the chance of halting it within a global regime where the already developed nations continue trying to defend their own turf, their own historic claims to far more than their fair share of the planet's absorptive and regenerative capacities – because *that* chance is simply no chance. Whatever may have been the pros and cons, from all the possible perspectives, of real international equity in the past, the case for it now is irresistibly and urgently practical. It is with the climate war as Benjamin Franklin famously reminded the Continental Congress preparing to sign the US Declaration of Independence: we must hang together, or we shall assuredly all hang separately. That is now the hard unvarnished truth for global humanity. No doubt it explains why endorsement for the principle, at any rate, of C&C has in fact been forthcoming from a good many quarters where one would expect brisk intolerance of mere hopeless idealism. These include the World Bank, the European Parliament and the UK Royal Commission on Environmental Pollution. The UN's Intergovernmental Panel on Climate Change has explicitly recognized the logic, and the World Council of Churches has called for commitment to the framework. It would require impossibly high standards to regard *all* these bodies as lacking in seriousness. Together, the weight of their testimony suggests that it is maybe dismissing C&C as impracticable which is actually the unrealistic option.

What all this means for a country like Britain is that we must act, at last, to redress the historic balance, not through windy 'apologies' for this or that colonial atrocity, nor just through a much more generous development aid budget, but through making the break in this critical arena. That means setting ourselves a reducing carbon ration within assumptions compatible with global convergence, and then offering decisive leadership in the international process which will be required for choreographing the actual introduction of the C&C framework worldwide. This is a very demanding kind of engagement when compared with our current stance, but it is no less than a survival imperative.

There is still a huge job to be done in campaigning and preparing for C&C, never mind in implementing it. The question for this book and this chapter, however, is how all this relates to a deep-sustainability understanding of what we are about.

Deep sustainability in practice

So how does this overall carbon framework fit with the criteria for a practical deep-sustainability approach which I outlined in the earlier part of the chapter?

We have already considered the equity issue. It is, though, worth emphasizing that the fairness which the whole structure seeks to implement is no pretend-fairness to futurity. It has to obtain among the presently existing people of the world in all their various real geographic and economic circumstances, not as between ourselves and a future for which we must always stand in. This means that it can in principle be (and in practice most assuredly would have to be) genuine fairness, reached for through very hard discussion. It would need institutional mechanisms for genuine international and intercommunal impartiality in the establishment of commonly agreed targets and timescales. That it offers nowhere else than the present to look for equity is one of the conceptual strengths of a deep-sustainability focus, and the C&C carbon framework responds with a structurally embedded commitment to regarding each real human life as of fundamentally equal worth in this key respect.

This emphasis on present equity is not to deny that a viable carbon-rationing framework involves predictive quantification, looking decades into the future. Its basic requirement is rationing at a level which *as far as we can presently tell from the science* will give us a real chance of stabilizing atmospheric CO_2, over time, at a concentration with which global civilization can hope to live. This level then yields a determinate national carbon allocation towards which individuals must progressively adapt their current lifestyles and consumption habits. It might seem that all the problems of prediction for policy which we identified in Part I just come in again through the back door with this requirement. For evidently, we have to adopt measures which we reckon are *likely* to work across an envisaged timeframe of several decades to bring both public and private emissions within the agreed ration. Doesn't sustainability as a concern for the meaning-shape of our lives in the present still have to take a back-bearing from the future which depends on just the kind of scientific prediction that I have been impugning?

The key difference, however, is that from a deep-sustainability perspective the longer-term quantification actually driving C&C can be fully recognized as heuristic, while the quantification which needs to be comparatively precise is overwhelmingly short-term.

The figures we are going to need for carbon rationing, that is, can be represented on a spectrum. At one end are the principal framework figures which will need international agreement: the overall global emissions ceiling, in the first place, with the target date for achieving it in order to make runaway warming least likely, then the national allocations within this global total from which the process of contraction starts, the per capita allocation on which to converge and the agreed date for convergence. In the middle are figures for the individual carbon rations within the different national allocations, which will vary with the different proportions of emissions from public, corporate and private consumption sectors in different economies. At the other end of the spectrum comes quantification of the effects of particular consumption decisions in terms of the carbon currency – the measures relied on to determine how much an individual citizen's ration is to be debited for the purchase of a unit of petrol, gas, oil or electricity, and to establish the carbon efficiency of different vehicles, appliances and equipment in order to inform purchase and usage decisions.

The numbers at the global end of this spectrum certainly involve prediction over considerable time-spans. But from a deep-sustainability standpoint, identification of a longer-term safe ceiling of atmospheric CO_2 can represent an avowedly *broad-brush* prediction. As such, it is certainly no less secure than the now-established scientific consensus (of which it is just a corollary) that global temperature's rising beyond a certain broadly indicated range constitutes a serious danger. Thus we go for a figure for manageable CO_2 concentration (and hence, working back through permissible emissions and per capita allocations, for the individual carbon ration) which is scientifically respectable in terms of broad-brush prediction based on present knowledge. But crucially, it must also be sufficiently demanding to force us into real change. This is the 'line in the sand' kind of warrant for framework quantification, and it is unaffected by our knowing, all along, that these figures are heuristics as much as benchmarks. New and currently unforeseeable developments in the science, in relevant technologies, and in the interactions between technological possibilities, social attitudes and ethical commitments, will mean that we may well have to revise them as we go on – probably downwards, but in principle either way – and thus make continuous consequential changes, open-endedly, throughout the framework of policy and practice which depends on them. None of this, however, need detract from their robustness for policy purposes, since this derives at least as much from our commitment to action as from their objective validity.

At the other end of the spectrum, individual action and refraining are in question, with significant immediate effects on people's lives, and accurate figures are going to be needed to inform micro-decisions about personal 'carbon spending' if the process is to be genuinely equitable. Measures here, however, are all of the carbon intensities of *current* and immediately prospective technologies and lifestyle choices – that is, they don't depend on claiming inherently flaky precision for longer-term prediction.

They do, however, require the explicitly learning context which goes with deep sustainability. Indeed, not just at the level of individual action but across the whole spectrum, properly managed contraction has to mean continuously informed adaptation. Each of us as a consumer of energy would depend for this on smart technologies monitoring usage and updating us on its carbon consequences; and also on an unimpeded flow of genuine information about product performance (rather than the hyped-up disinformation currently supplied by so much advertising). At the same time, and at the other end of the scale, the global framework would need to be kept continuously responsive to developments, both in the best science of climate change and as regards the specific economic and social effects of rolling out C&C worldwide.

Importantly, the learning processes involved in all this are essentially open-loop, despite the fact that the whole framework is closed under an agreed global emissions ceiling and its subsidiary derivatives. Open-endedness characterizes not the target itself, but the ways in which it can be met. The new incentives which a rationing framework would create would ramify stimulatingly across the whole economy: technologies of energy production and supply, and of information gathering and provision; improved carbon efficiency in design, from buildings to white goods to small-scale appliances; a new emphasis on durability and reparability; and new educational and learning requirements across a huge range of trades and professions. No-one could hope to say much in advance about the patterns of relationship, advantage and opportunity which would rapidly start to reconfigure society – nor about the new, evolving forms of spontaneous order which would emerge. In such creative multiplicity, our best prospects of real sustainability – of making our own green luck – can be seen to lie.

The extra mile?

But there is a still more fundamental reason why such a carbon regime, surely the only one which is going to give us a serious chance of victory in the climate war, both requires and expresses a deep-sustainability perspective. This comes back to the central notion – rationing – and the very different faces which it wears within different conceptual framings. A ration gives a firm collective answer to the question 'How green is green enough?' But this question can be asked meaning 'green enough to get away with', or it can be asked meaning 'green enough to make sense of life'. A ration, of any relevant resource, on the sustainable development paradigm represents our best guess at *the most we can now have* while meeting our obligations to the future. From a deep-sustainability perspective, what might be numerically the same allocation represents *the least we can now do* to ensure that life goes on.

If we are concerned with the most we can have, a ration is a self-imposed limitation which seems automatically to bear a negative sign. It is a necessary restriction on something (the additional consumption which would generate emissions beyond our allocation) which we nevertheless want, and would still pursue if our obligation not to do so were for any reason to become less compelling. A global carbon ceiling worked back to an individual carbon ration reflects, ultimately, the ecological interconnectedness of the world experienced as natural limitation preventing us from doing everything we should ideally like to do. But most people still *do* want to do all these things – the flying, the driving, the consumption of exotic foods from far away ... and so much so, that the notion of *welcoming* constraint on these desires immediately smacks of asceticism or puritanical self-repression, attitudes which we find suspect if not perverse.

But no carbon rationing that isn't positively welcomed is going to work. It is of crucial practical importance to admit this and face up to it. Not only is the necessary practical machinery going to have to be complied with and incorporated across large tracts of life on a daily basis, but before that the rationing model is going to have to start making a powerful appeal to the public mind, and its introduction to win widespread support as a policy. Then politicians who pledge (credibly) to implement it must campaign successfully enough on that platform to be voted into government. The idea that all this will happen while people at large remain reluctant or resentful about the whole notion is simply implausible. A rationing regime can only hope to succeed if it comes pretty swiftly to carry a very strong positive sign.

What, we must ask, would make people actually welcome rationing? Maybe they would do so if they found that they wanted what it was bringing about a very great deal more than they wanted what it was restricting. An analogy here might be with the way the diet or exercise regime ceases to be struggle, self-division and temptation to cheat when we start to relish the benefits it brings much more than we still crave what it prohibits. The thought among the current proponents of carbon rationing seems to be that its corresponding conversion to a positive sign will come from our recognizing and welcoming an *ethical* constraint. Once they start to appreciate the sheer scale and the frighteningly unstable dynamics of the damage being done to the world, it is hoped, people will start to want the preservation of natural capital for future generations, as a matter of sheer justice, more than they will want to exceed their carbon allocations. They will do so, we must suppose, in essentially the same way that people wanted to defeat the evil of Hitlerism more than they wanted to evade the food rationing which was necessary to give us a chance of surviving through to victory.

But although widely recognized as evil and opposed for reasons of justice among others, Hitlerism was also a starkly imminent prudential threat in the Europe of the late 1930s. And once war broke out, it was perfectly clear to most people what defeat would mean not just for the cherished liberties but for the ordinary comfortable habits of everyone in Britain, and the spice of personal apprehension was always there to make rationing acceptable, if not palatable. There is really no compelling prudential analogue for climate change. It is indeed true that as part of appreciating what is now happening to threaten the long-term future, people are becoming aware of real prospects for climate instability and a degrading environment rather sooner. They are starting to be uneasy about the world awaiting their own children, and even, if they are in early adulthood, possibly themselves. But such degradation at its worst is likely to be slow and incremental over this shorter term, and can seem to call for similarly incremental measures of mitigation and adaptation rather than for a major gear-shift. Almost all the people in the developed world who would have to support decisive action to bring about such a shift are still doing quite comfortably enough as things are, and even on the most pessimistic scenarios for disrupted weather patterns, flooding, species loss and so on, this is likely to remain the case until well past the point when finally embarking on such action will be too late. In this context, it might seem, rationing of the necessary stringency, comprehensiveness and urgency could *only* be brought in on the back of an ethical imperative and actively welcomed for the sake of intergenerational justice – even if the generation to whom we are called on to be thus just might now be the next but one, rather than those a good deal further down the line.

Could a desire to recognize the claims of justice play this role? Could it hold our continuing desires for the benefits of carbon profligacy decisively in check? Could it make people go not just grudgingly and under protest, but in a positive and genuinely committed way, for a rationing regime?

That looks possible in principle. It seems to be built into our thought about justice that we *should* want it more than we want what it restricts. That is, desires for justice and for what it sometimes precludes us from having or doing are not simply competing on a level. The thief can't defend himself by saying that, actually, he found he wanted the money more than he wanted to be honest – this may often be the true explanation, but it is no kind of excuse. Considerations of justice, honesty and so forth are supposed to be *overriding*, and indeed most of us recognize them – in principle – as such. The trouble is that the moral life is riddled with ways of preserving their overridingness by adjusting what we take them to prohibit so that what we most want can still slip round behind it. That kind of shift is the characteristic move in bad faith, and we have examined some of its forms – the equivocation, the double-mindedness, the floating of standards – already in this book. We also saw how the intergenerational and scientific context of sustainability offers major opportunities for these moves, and removes the checks on them which operate in standardly ethical relations. When what is available to peg the standard in place and challenge the tendency to equivocate is not dialogue with, and scrutiny by, real others over against us, but only a set of numbers which are themselves fundamentally equivocal, the mere in-principle overridingness of justice is not going to be robust enough to make the necessary difference.

And so, it seems, with carbon rationing. We have been hesitantly probing this possibility, in fact, for a lot longer than the specific proposals outlined earlier in this chapter have been around. The whole sustainable development paradigm is basically a kind of rationing – the present rationing itself in respect of what would, unchecked, disadvantage the future. As the climate issue has moved centre-stage, that perspective has been used to warrant a set of constraints on doing what we should otherwise like, which has been creeping and thickening across both public and private life – from the renewables obligation, via congestion charging and the requirements for getting your car through its MoT, all the way to the right sort of light-bulb. In all of these domains, people in the UK are already on a form of ration. At the international level, correspondingly, we have the Kyoto treaty, with its binding emissions reduction targets in effect rationing the signatory nations – though only on the tacit principle of establishing targets which could be accepted without anyone feeling very rationed. And there, of course, is the rub. In that approach, the Kyoto negotiations were only reflecting the pervading spirit of sustainable development. If the argument of this book is well taken, it is only summing it up bluntly to say that this whole process of policy creep and personal accommodation, from top to bottom, is really one of doing just enough to avoid confronting the recognition that nothing like enough is being done.

Here too, I suggest, is the underlying explanation for the fact that C&C, so evidently the only global framework really fit for purpose, has been endorsed so enthusiastically at high levels, and measures compatible with it canvassed by an increasing number of serious politicians in key nations – while no steps whatever have been taken towards actually implementing it.

So how do we get people to go that vital extra mile? That needs a shift to the deep-sustainability vision. Justice won't cut it: we can give up on justice and still want what makes against it – indeed, we give up on it, tacitly, *because* of those persisting wants. This is the essential feature of the volitional structure which produces bad faith. While continuing to endorse explicitly, to others and to ourselves, the claims of justice, we allow them to be circumvented by wants which remain real and pressing despite being opposed to those claims, even when we can see (in some sense) that they are so opposed. On that basis, in the sustainability context, we will always remain too conflicted and equivocal to welcome rationing in the way it will require. *But we can't give up on life-hope and still want what makes against it.*

The reasons for this are those which I sought to open up in Chapter 5. I can only rehearse them briefly here. To want the meaningfulness which life-hope underpins is to want *whatever* – including whatever sacrifice of countervailing wants – may be necessary to reach it. This is not a contingent but a necessary matter. The intrinsic values, varying from person to person, which it takes life-hope to keep real in each of us, are at the generative, structural core of all our wanting. Not all our wants can be for what only helps us to pursue further wants: some centrally valued wants must be what it all depends on to make sense. If these central values fail, as in loss of meaningfulness they do, then the rest of what motivates us isn't simply left standing, but rapidly becomes incoherent and starts to disintegrate. Maintaining meaningfulness depends on being able to live in, rely on and routinely refresh and reconfirm life-hope. But the range of carbon-profligate activities and expectations which genuinely stringent rationing would preclude are now concertedly, and increasingly visibly, working to travesty life-hope in our ordinary daily lives as they work to risk imperilling life at large. On a sustainable development perspective, justice is why we shouldn't go on wanting these things. Under the aspect of deep sustainability, life-meaning is why we finally *cannot* go on wanting them, and can only welcome – perhaps with a complex kind of sigh, in which there will be relief as well as regret – the measures necessary to break free from them.

Natural limits, that is, do not have to be felt as privation. The need to make sense of our lives means that certain limitations on our possible actions, limitations which can be seen to flow from our natural situation, bear a necessarily positive sign. Our sexual interdependence and our relations with both our parents and our children are like this. They are meaning-issues because they are involved so intimately with life-hope – they are absolutely central arenas of life's necessary ongoingness. They seem to constrain us in ways which, though they do often mean that we can't do everything we want, are still recognized as central to our humanity. And experienced as such, their constraint can be actively welcomed, and embodied in social and legal forms of requirement. In the same way, the need for our living activity to be always moving into an open future which we are confident will extend indefinitely beyond our own span is a demand of life-hope which, once seen as such, we can't refuse and still live intelligibly – any more than we could refuse our need to understand things and express ourselves in language, though even that can in certain moods be felt as a burden. Here is the kind of light in which full realization of the rationing constraint always inherent in sustainability can be seen not as inhibition, but as liberation.

Presenting it vigorously and unapologetically in that light, finding the eloquence to link the new framework to people's deep meaning-concerns and courage to risk the real turbulence, uncertainty and open-endedness that will inevitably accompany implementation, is certainly going to call for a renewed politics. It will need precisely the politics of existential leadership to which I was appealing earlier. We can only hope that such leaders will emerge as the scene darkens.

Meanwhile, in that spirit, we can begin adjusting thought and practice in these broad directions within the existing framework. The next chapter looks at three areas where this is immediately practicable.

7
Widening Our Options

We can change by doing different things, but also by doing the same things differently. We can do the same things differently by using different materials, methods or tools, within the same broad understanding of what we are doing and why – but also, by coming to understand our purposes and rationale differently. Such a changed understanding can liberate us, in turn, into a new imagining of possibilities, of the prospects and opportunities really open to us.

Again, we can launch that re-imagination from our activities as we are already engaged in them – at least initially, although we may expect a changed conception to work through swiftly into practical changes. These changes will then tend to be deep-rooted, far-reaching and more enduringly transformative than simply doing things differently at the outset – since different things done within an unchanged conception of what we are doing usually turn out, sooner or later, to be the same things in disguise.

These reflections are the staple of many a guide to rescuing our personal lives from stasis or misdirection. They are to the point here, because the changed perspective on sustainability which we are considering will only be effective, and only worth pursuing, if it transforms what we actually do as a society in that fundamental kind of way. The difference between doing what we can't avoid and doing whatever it takes for sustainability will quite rapidly become huge, if we really go for it. But it may well start just with seeing differently what we were about to do, or indeed were already doing, anyway. I am going to look in this light at a little of what is now happening in business, governance and education. To repeat, this will be a broad and impressionistic view, offering no blueprint. But seeing even some of our plans and activities in these fields from a deep-sustainability perspective can help us realize, crucially, that we already have a lot of the creative capacity, the social intelligence and imaginative capital, needed to handle uncertainty and open-endedness. And recognizing this across a wide enough range of action might help us towards mastering the fear of real, decisive change which is now holding us back from going that extra mile.

ENTERPRISE

To handle open-endedness, we need a particular kind of security – the deepest kind. Security in an uncertain world requires the courage for both exploratory learning and diversity. In fact, these really presuppose one another. As we have already noted, genuine learning needs an active diversity of options, because learning is empty if, when you *do* find out that your provisional assumptions were misleading, you are by then committed to the single action-pathway which you chose on the basis of them. By the same token, for diversity to present us with continuing live options we need ongoing learning – we need always to be tracking how things are *actually* panning out, as against what we initially expected and acted on, so that informed pathway-shifting remains always a real possibility. A learning society is our best security, amidst huge uncertainties of environmental and other kinds. Security and sustainability, indeed, are closely cognate ideas – neither of them end-states to be reached and then preserved, but both ways of being, of finding our way indefinitely on. The question is, 'How does society condition for the heuristic diversity essential to its survival?'

One important answer is: by encouraging the entrepreneurial creativity of free enterprise.

I pointed out in the first chapter that this answer has until recently been somewhat awkward to advance, at least as regards environmental futures. Recognition that development must henceforth be sustainable has hitherto seemed to be a necessary *counter* to the driving forces of capitalism, rather than an incitement to encourage them. Even lately, when the potential compatibility of capitalism and sustainable development has started to be canvassed seriously, it has been a very heavily regulated and fiscally incentivized capitalism that has been in view, with sustainability as a limiting condition constraining enterprise to begin taking serious account of the longer term.

A deep-sustainability perspective changes these lights. It shows sustainability as in part *constituted by* society's acting most effectively to diversify its practical options in the present. One crucial way in which it can do this is by having a multiplicity of enterprises trying – with as little specific direction and constraint as possible – to make a wide range of activities profitable, and learning vigorously from the results in the iterative short term. Profitability and sustainability, that is, can more easily be seen from this perspective to go hand in hand. A profitable business which is using that position to create real options for its next phase and build management capacity for learning its way forward (rather than to overpay its executives, overcompensate its shareholders and generally make quick exploitative hay in the sunshine) is already itself an active node of deep sustainability.

Of course, this will only be the case if it also responds to the real ecological pressures under which enterprises will increasingly be operating. Businesses cannot be expected to identify these for themselves, nor to impose constraints on themselves unilaterally, any more than they can be expected to decide purely for themselves what sort of corporate accountability requirements they should be held to in other areas. Here, therefore, is the proper role of government. But it is a much more limited role than the sustainable development model has tended to encourage. Government sets the basic framework of social acceptability for business – it is rightly both stakeholder and regulator for things like the public safety, the public interest in a reliable social infrastructure (from healthcare to railways), the basic rights of employees and shareholders, and proper payment (through corporate taxation) for the use of public capital. That is, it keeps in place a basic legal structure for business activity grounded in the fundamental shared sense we make of our life (but not, at the hazard of liberty, incorporating more specific and contested ethical positions like the demand for material equality, positive discrimination or whatever, at least until these have achieved the status of a widely agreed common sense). This framework of shared meaningfulness now needs to extend to include a kind of Basic Law for Human Continuity – an excellent candidate for this being the statutory regime of carbon rationing for both individuals and corporations which we were outlining in the previous chapter. Government would have to establish and ongoingly review the parameters for such a carbon regime through the processes of continuous exploratory consultation and deliberation (reflecting the fact that the science on which any particular carbon rations would be based would always be provisional and revisable). It would also have to be responsible for policing it, as vigorously as it ought to enforce the laws against monopoly or corporate theft – or, indeed, blackmail or murder.

But within this framework, a deep-sustainability perspective sees enterprise being left, ideally, as free as possible to respond to the changing needs and priorities which a regime of carbon rationing would generate. The configuration of markets in energy-saving equipment, insulation, new kinds of construction, renewable energy, carbon-neutral travel and a wide range of other things would shift quickly and radically – as would those in lots of consumer items whose prices now don't reflect their full environmental costs. Competitive flexibility would be at a premium – and genuine competition, too, can be welcomed back on this new perspective, since it stimulates just the dynamic coupling of diversity (a multiplicity of firms) and learning (each trying to keep ahead of the curve) which enacts sustainability.

There are already good examples of new thinking and practice along these lines. Many of them are recorded in what seems to me the best recent book in this field, by Paul Hawken and the Lovinses. The authors claim boldly that making industry more energy- and resource-efficient is 'the next business frontier'. At this frontier:

> ... innovation ... can achieve large energy savings ... in most of the technical systems that use energy, in most applications, in all sectors.

Moreover, many of the changes that would help towards this don't require massive reinvestment or structural upheaval in production or distribution processes:

> Enabling America's half-million laboratory fume hoods to use 60–80 per cent less fanpower yet become even safer is largely a matter of

changing the position of one louver. In the mundane but very costly task of removing contaminated air from cleanrooms, a new mechanical flow controller, using a single moving part operated solely by gravity and airflow, can reduce energy use by around 50–80 per cent, reduce total construction cost, and improve safety and performance. ... Such simple but large opportunities abound in the heaviest industries too. Steel slabs are normally cast far from the rolling mills that make them thinner, so by the time they arrive to be rolled, they need to be reheated; moving the two processes closer together saves about 18 per cent of that reheat energy.

Often, all we need to push small, straightforward changes like these above the horizon of practicability are the new markets for eco-efficiency which current regulations, fiscal and other incentives are beginning to create – but which a responsible regime of carbon rationing would dramatically expand.

Individual innovation of this kind, that is, does not itself require a deep-sustainability perspective in order to start happening. Depending principally on the rapidly growing market value of energy saving, it can readily get under way on the sustainable development paradigm, and is increasingly doing so. Where the alternative picture becomes important is in relation to the broader economic context. Consider the vast armoury of taxes and incentives which all governments in the advanced world currently have at their disposal. The sustainable development case is that these must now be deployed to support 'sustainability capitalism' – that is, to ensure that capitalist enterprise now invests in restoring and maintaining irreplaceable natural capital, rather than going on taking it for granted and using it up. This means shifting the fiscal burden onto activities which are natural-capital-intensive. Even a partial list of these indicates the very broad scope of the required shift:

Nuclear power would be heavily taxed, as would all forms of electricity non-renewably generated. Diesel fuels, gasoline, motor oils, nitrogen oxides and chlorine would all pay their share. Air traffic of all kinds, from commercial to light aircraft ... all vehicular use and public roads ... Pesticides, synthetic fertilizers and phosphorus would join alcohol as heavily taxed commodities. Piped in water ... old-growth timber, harvests of free-run salmon and other wild fisheries ... irrigation water from public lands and depletion of topsoil and aquifers. From the ground, coal, silver, gold, chromium, molybdenum, bauxite, sulphur ... All waste sent to a landfill ...

This is the kind of intervention which governments are now beginning to use, or contemplate, to tilt the market towards sustainability. But, of course, each of them requires government to set a level of duty which balances the need to preserve the relevant aspect of natural capital against the need to allow the activity or process being taxed to continue, or at least give it enough breathing-space to adapt. Each therefore requires prediction of some quite specific likely consequences of intervention over longish time-spans in conditions of enormous socio-economic as well as ecological complexity. I won't repeat here the arguments which suggest that thinking we can really do this, across the whole economy, is a hubristic and dangerous delusion.

From the alternative, deep-sustainability perspective, it is surely clear that, in holding the ring, government should not only avoid as far as possible distorting the market by setting goals and imposing detailed sectoral targets – it should also put itself under a self-denying ordinance as regards incentives. The current arsenal of taxes, grants, offsets and other fiscal fiddling, indeed, might well be abandoned in favour of another Basic Law, which could be introduced even outwith the rationing framework which it would ideally complement. Firms might simply pay tax at a lower rate if they can show that they are replacing the social value on which they draw in production with real option value. This value is what is created by investment in a certain kind of capital – and such investment is of the essence of being deep-sustainable.*

Real options embody diversity and learning commitment in the actual form taken by a capital stock. A real option is a feature of the structure or organization of a capital asset which embodies the opportunity to make a future decision about how the asset is used, contingent on relevant circumstances at that time. The current value of such investments goes up under uncertainty, rather than down as on the conventional model where future returns are discounted to a net present value. This concept comes originally from financial markets, but recent thinking has applied it to physical as well as financial assets. Building such features into capital items usually costs extra, but buys future flexibility – being able to rely on which is a present benefit to offset at full rather than discounted value against the costs. (The techniques of actual valuation won a Nobel Prize for Economics.) A simple example here would be a power plant with burners that can run on either oil or gas, the switching capacity providing managerial flexibility to respond to future fuel price fluctuations. The 'real option' element is the set of material and organizational features allowing fuels to be switched, which are obviously going to be more complex and costly than for single-fuel burners. But their present value rises significantly with uncertainty about future conditions of operation. Importantly, this value doesn't depend on present predictions which managers make about these conditions, but is all about being able to cope with them as and when they arise, though of course such value is only going to be *realized* if managers keep on top of fuel price movements and switch in anticipation at the right moments – proactive management and learning capacity are vital to real option value.

---

* I owe this connection, the sort of insight that is suddenly revealing and decisive for one's whole thinking about a topic, originally to Steve Gough – see the notes to this chapter.

It will be evident how investment in real options by individual enterprises would be in the spirit of deep sustainability – where that means acting under a broad constraint of ecological responsibility without ever being able to know very far in advance just what that will require and entail. A topical example might be a budget airline which was responding to carbon rationing by investing not only in cleaner fuel and more efficient planes, but also in joint ventures with overseas rail and bus companies to keep the flight element of overseas travel down to short hops without sacrificing too much passenger convenience, and in setting up IT platforms for online conferencing, to be correlated with reduced essential business flying. This firm would not only be improving its own competitive flexibility and responsiveness, but expanding to that extent society's overall room for manoeuvre in learning its way forward.

Firms can thus invest in strategic real options for their own business. Those which supply capital goods can also invest in making such options available for their customers. In the construction industry, for example, the provision of houses incorporating 'smart' technologies represents a market opportunity which is already important in principle. As emissions limits tighten towards actual carbon rationing, it will become increasingly so in practice. These technologies, already being tried in various experiments round the world, include electricity and gas meters that not only monitor and report consumption levels (and, potentially, their carbon implications) but also audit and advise on consumption patterns. There are also intelligent controls for heating and lighting becoming available, with thermostats which adjust to room usage and occupancy as well as to ambient temperature, and switching which can be instructed remotely (say from a mobile phone) if you are going to be home unexpectedly late or early. Such features increase the capital cost of housing, but build in kinds of flexibility, enabling the adaptation of energy usage to changing life requirements and circumstances, which would rapidly become essential within a rationing framework. Again, fiscal help to reduce production costs and so costs passed on to the house-purchaser could already be energizing this market.

The total effect of diversity and option-richness achieved by many firms' acting in these and similar ways would represent a collective social investment in natural capital renewal, without the requirement for government or anyone else to second-guess the specific shape of the future. This pattern of capitalist enterprise represents the best humans have yet discovered by way of making their own luck.

GOVERNANCE

A constant challenge for institutions of social decision-making about the technological issues confronting modern societies is to find a proper accommodation between two different kinds of *authority*. On the one hand, there is the authority of professional expertise in the relevant sciences, and on the other, the political authority to make decisions on behalf of the community as a whole. These two kinds of authority have very different bases and may often be in tension with one another. Equally, neither kind is in itself unproblematic. Science is not univocal – without necessarily thereby failing as science, it can tell us different things depending on what questions are asked, what kinds of answer are required and (sometimes) who is doing the asking and answering. Political authority, meanwhile, is liable to be compromised by the sheer scope and complexity of these increasingly technical issues. It is not clear that decisions on such matters are best taken through the standard procedures of representative democracy, even were there no other grounds (such as their tendency to exclude minority voices and be captured by established power) for questioning the adequacy of those procedures.

Considerations of these kinds have led in recent years to much experimentation with more deliberative and inclusionary ways of making decisions, especially where environmental and technological risks are involved. Institutions working in the spheres of land-use planning, public policy formation and project assessment – the key areas where governance has to hold the ring for entrepreneurial creativity – have all been involved. So indeed have enlightened firms. They have all incorporated into their procedures a variety of methods including neighbourhood fora, citizens' juries and panels, consensus conferences, focus groups and online discussions, deliberative polling and multi-criteria mapping. Common to all these approaches is that issues for policy or decision are explored through moderated discussion and debate between participants who bring to the topics in question a wide diversity of views, experience and relevant standings (as local residents, consumers and other kinds of stakeholder, as well as simply citizens). Such discussion is informed but, as far as possible, not constrained by input from experts of various kinds. The assumption is that expertise has always to create its own authority within the dynamics of the particular deliberation. It can set the terms of discussion in the most general way, but not pre-empt its conclusions. Upshots from these processes can themselves constitute decisions, as with citizens' juries, (though almost invariably these are in fact shadow-decisions needing to be actioned by a body with actual statutory or administrative powers). More usually, they are advisory – fed back to such bodies with the clear expectation, and sometimes the formal requirement, that they will be influential.

It is fair to say that a powerful trend in the direction of such inclusionary institutional deliberation has already been established in complex democracies. So how might this changing profile of social decision-making bear on, and itself be affected by, the shift from a sustainable development to a deep-sustainability understanding?

Learning our way open-endedly into an emergent future depends *ultimately* on our collective judgement. How interpretation of 'what happens' (establishing what are to be taken as 'the facts') is accommodated to evaluation of the hypotheses yielding the predictions which get confronted by these facts, and to revision of the assumptions framing these hypotheses, can only be a matter of such judgement. There can be nothing by way either of data or rules generalized from the data to serve as guidance here, since all relevant data and rules are themselves candidates for heuristic revision. It is from the frightening implications of this that people tend to recoil into scientism, expecting from science an answer to *everything*. Surely we can turn in the last analysis to scientific truth about nature to guide our judgement? But no, behind even the last analysis we still find ourselves analysing – weighing, interpreting, judging.

This doesn't require that judgement be *unguided*, but it does mean that guidance can only come from criteria internal to the idea of judgement itself. Judgement must depend on all-round attention, as far as we can achieve it, both to our surroundings and situation now and to how those conditions are continually changing over time. Such attention requires the full range of our creaturely modes of alertness – sensibility and imagination (the rationality of feeling and intuition) as well as logical and analytical (the more conventionally 'rational') skills. But equally, the outward focus of this attention must not be distorted by inappropriately subjective factors – by seeing only what we want or need (still less, what the more powerful or articulate among us want or need) to see. Full attention demands disinterestedness. Taken together, these criteria define an always-provisional objectivity of judgement, which must be deployed in the sustainability context not just by individuals but collectively, as a learning *society*. The collaborative attention and overall, on-balance disinterestedness which has to inform the collective judgement taking us heuristically forward is what we might call *social intelligence*.

This is why leaving decisions up to bodies which have vested interests in the outcomes of those decisions is so palpably *un*intelligent. 'Vested interest' here, though, means a good deal more than just a financial stake: it includes also motives of the kind to which public choice theorists draw attention – preservation of familiar institutional structures, for instance, or compliance with ideologies strongly subscribed to. It is not just power groups and political elites which can have interests of this kind. In science, too, people can have interests vested in the preservation of established funding regimes, research and infrastructural investments, and also simply in the maintenance of dominant paradigms with which whole research cultures have become comfortable. Differential power and the potential abuse of expertise by power, but also the liability of expertise to certain forms of complicity with this abuse, are all problems for decision processes in technological societies.

Effective deliberative and inclusionary processes, therefore, aim to provide procedures for taking significant decisions, whether about particular projects and risks or about broader planning or social investment strategies, in a genuinely equitable way. That means fully involving and properly respecting all those liable to be affected by them, and on a basis of full information, including the widest possible and best-facilitated *accessibility* of that information even when it is complex and technical. Among the now many and varied examples of processes which have already tried to realize this ideal on the ground are citizens' juries assessing the value of contested environmental projects, such as the re-flooding of fenland areas to provide new bird habitats, or the siting and size of proposed wind farm developments; Planning for Real events associated with land-use planning; and visioning exercises used to inform the development of Local Agenda 21 strategies.

But failure of social intelligence is not just a matter of the distorting motivations arising from vested interests of all kinds. It is also, much more insidiously, a matter of the tendency towards what we might call mental monocultures. Decisions taken or unduly influenced from a single professional or disciplinary perspective of expertise are liable to be impoverished, even when this expertise is directly relevant to the issue in question and is made accessible to an equitably representative decision process. For expertise is too often (not, of course, invariably) the trained ability to know what you are going to see, and then duly to see it. Acquiring it is always a process of gaining theoretically informed insight, explicit knowledge, speed of response and explanatory power at the expense of the eye of innocence, first-hand tacit awareness of uncertainties, and an openness to expecting the more or less subtly unexpected. But these 'lay' capacities are vitally important to the maximal attentiveness – the unprejudiced attunement to the actually emergent – required for intelligent collective judgement.

If we are thinking about sustainability in terms of ongoing, open-loop learning, then the need for a rich, flourishing attentiveness will be as important as disinterestedness. In part it is a matter of ensuring that lay (non-expert) perspectives have the continuing right to question expertise – and to be answered, not merely placated. This is something that needs to be built firmly into the structure and procedural arrangements for any deliberative process. But, as importantly, tacit knowledge from a wide variety of individual loci of experience must always be able to confront the inevitable generalization involved in any explicitly theorized expertise. Criteria of inclusivity in the selection of participants must reflect this need. The issues for a sustainability grounded in life-meaning have to be seen whole: that is, not just in their biogeophysical, economic, sociological, legal and administrative dimensions, but also as they appear to the eyes of the historian, the philosopher, the poet, painter or musician. It is public deliberative fora informed by skilled contributions of these kinds which will be foci of the fullest, most sensitive all-round social intelligence that we can recruit for active sustainability. Examples of existing approaches which could be developed as templates for including these broader humane perspectives include the WWF's ACE (Act, Create, Experience) multimedia events for young people; Vision 21's guided visualizations for imaginary journeys into the future; and participatory theatre as used by an increasing number of community drama groups.

A deep-sustainability understanding will also tend to shift the emphasis from one-off or short-term decision-making to more longitudinal or cyclical processes. The value of such a shift is already beginning to be recognized in the context of public consultation over new scientific or technological developments. As a recent paper on this topic from Demos notes:

> *Upstream engagement – at a point where research trajectories are still open and undetermined – should be the start of a process of ongoing deliberation and social assessment, that embeds dialogue between scientists, stakeholders and lay publics within all stages of the R&D process.*

An example quoted in this paper is the Medical Research Council's Advisory Group on Public Involvement, which has been running in one form or another since 2000 and which plays an increasingly strategic and proactive role in the Council's decision-making. A sustainably learning society will generalize this sort of requirement, ensuring that deliberative panels of appropriate kinds become permanent structural features of governance and public policy across the board. They should not just operate at the stage of evaluating options and recommending decisions, but be still involved (and with significant continuity of actual personnel) when those decisions are being implemented, and when the results of implementation are being initially reviewed, and in subsequent reviews when the factors which no-one had fully appreciated begin to make themselves manifest, and in helping to identify the lessons thus needing to be learnt – and, still further on, at the stage of applying those lessons to the question whether alternative options should now be brought into play ... and so on indefinitely. Again, there are existing experiments in more longitudinal participatory processes which could be developed to inform good practice on a deep-sustainability model. A good example is the social auditing cycle used in the UK by a range of voluntary organizations, businesses and community enterprises (from Body Shop International to the Co-op), and in the South as part of participatory environmental appraisal.

All this comes properly under the rubric of widening our options – here, for acting with responsive social intelligence. The chances of making public choices which are wise, fully informed and humanly grounded are increased, the better these various forms of deliberation are understood and incorporated into the democratic process. They multiply the options for collective rationality by enriching the biodiversity of social attentiveness. This is more than metaphor. It means that governance decisions can emerge not from closed cabals of vested interest or assumption, but from the wide variety and spontaneity of experience in which life-hope springs. They can do so, however, in ways which remain focused and practical while still asserting the fundamental human claims of meaning. Our prospects depend increasingly on the hope of such governance.

EDUCATION FOR SUSTAINABILITY

It will be clear from the foregoing that we need a new understanding of the relationship between education and sustainability.

There is now a lot going on around 'education for sustainability' as currently understood. It has been recognized as a priority in the UK Strategy for Sustainable Development, there are national departmental strategies and policies in place (the Scottish Executive's Action Plan *Learning for our Future* being easily the best in the UK), and initiatives funded by the European Union abound. In the background, there is the United Nations Decade of Education for Sustainable Development (2005–2014). As the various labels suggest, this whole new set of demands on education systems and their hard-pressed workforces are generated very much within the sustainable development paradigm. The Scottish plan already mentioned demonstrates this clearly, identifying the principles underlying necessary action as:

> Interdependence: *understanding the connections ... between people, other living things and places ...*
>
> Diversity: *understanding the importance and value of diversity ...*
>
> Carrying capacity: *understanding that there are limits to the world's resources ...*
>
> Rights and responsibilities: *understanding the need to lead lives that consider the rights and needs of others [and] implications for what life might be like in the future;*
>
> Equity and justice: *understanding that for any development to be sustainable it must benefit people in an equitable way.*

What is envisaged here is really education *about* the sustainable development model and *in* the knowledge and skills needed for making a contribution, as worker, householder or citizen, towards the pursuit of sustainability conceived on that model. As the green educationalist Stephen Sterling notes, 'There is an assumption among curriculum writers that we know clearly what sustainability is about, that it is uncontested, and that this can be codified and transmitted.' None of these principles, nor the associated skills of joined-up thinking and participative practice, are in any way irrelevant – far from it. But from a deep-sustainability perspective, education for sustainability looks both more far-reaching and more straightforward to articulate: it is simply education into living intelligence for the contemporary world.

Why this should be so follows from the whole account given up to this point. Sustainability is not a specifiable target state, but the continuous exploratory pursuit, through open-ended learning, of ways to ensure that life goes on. That learning mode of living has ultimately nothing to depend on except our collective judgement, our social intelligence. But social institutions and procedures of whatever sort are finally only going to be as intelligent as the individual people who constitute and operate them. Deep sustainability really consists, therefore, in the life-effort of men and women whose education has equipped them with enough knowledge, sensitivity, emotional range and moral imagination to act together as a genuinely learning community in modern conditions.

Education seen (or recognized anew) in that light will be a matter of the whole curriculum, not of some corner – even quite a substantial corner – allocated to issues of ecology and the human environment. It will require us to reconceive the purpose of both schooling and tertiary studies as the empowering of integrated, flexible, creative and well-informed human beings, rather than the production of suitably skilled potential employees and consumers for the global economy – something which is presently quite a long way from the spirit and practice of the national curriculum in UK schools. This is matter for a book in itself. The point here, though, is that we can at least move in this direction by re-conceiving what is now happening in sustainability education as education in deep sustainability.

At the heart of such education must be developing the capacity for *critical* understanding. This at its fullest is complex and multilayered, and acquiring it is the work of an extended educative process. It involves recognizing that all the knowledge which any field of study can yield must be shaped by judgement. There is nothing *given*, by way of information, which does not have to be interpretively applied in making any kind of knowledge-claim, and these paradigms must then be recognized as themselves the upshot or precipitate of past judgements, and so as arising within and expressing the living activity of the culture. From this perspective, however, it is evident that none of them can be taken as definitive; the judgements underwriting any knowledge-claim can only be assessed from the standpoint of other judgements having only the same ultimate status, so our judgement as a whole comes to be understood as necessarily self-dependent and self-warranting.

It is a mistake to think of induction into such criticality as something which has to wait until sixth form or even the university. The study of history offers a very clear example of how critical understanding can be developed. Attention to mere events passes inevitably into attention to how varying accounts of them are recorded and transmitted, in ways which students could begin to appreciate from the early secondary years. Not all fields of study display their inherent criticality as readily as this – notably, study of the natural sciences doesn't. But we should now have no difficulty in seeing the analogy between scientific and historical paradigms, and their role in relation to the judgements which underpin 'normal-scientific' practice. Again, understanding this is something which could well be begun in the secondary school, and the study of environmental issues actually offers an excellent opportunity. Meanwhile, critical thinking skills – of reflectiveness, open dialogue and attention, as well as logical sharpness – can be practised from a surprisingly young age in the primary school, as various experiments in adapting philosophical enquiry for these age groups demonstrate.

As regards education in a specifically environmental connection, technical environmental studies take the human–environment relation as in an important sense given, treating the environment naturalistically as a set of biogeophysical parameters within which humankind has to operate, and concentrating on the knowledge and techniques (typically scientific) needed to manipulate those parameters in pursuit of human ends such as pollution control. However, environmental study becomes critical as soon as it attends to the ways in which human societies are responsible for shaping and changing not just the natural environment, but also the concepts and values in terms of which both this environment and our interactions with it are understood. Environmental actions always involve judgement – whether interpretive, as of scientific indications or relevant legal requirements, or evaluative, about what states of the environment are to be valued and to what extent. The frameworks for these interpretations and values, including not just ethical or legal systems but also our scientific models of human–environment interaction, are historically and culturally emergent, and often powerfully contested. Historical and sociological perspectives in environmental study can thus help students to understand how humans have both lived differently with nature, and constructed 'the natural' differently, in different cultures, societies and historical periods. The contribution of literature and art is crucial here – as illustrative of different cultural phases, but far more importantly as ways of initiating students into the absolutely fundamental role of human creativity in these transactions.

There are, of course, broad educational aspirations and ideals of cross-curricular practice implied here: an emphasis on educating the whole person, a transformative vision of how the presently fragmented curriculum could be re-integrated to that end, a recognition of the way education *creates* human possibility (rather than subserving it instrumentally), and a commitment to ecological responsibility as the inevitable contemporary context for developing citizenship. Sadly, as things are, that combination is not at the moment being explicitly pursued anywhere in formal education, at least in the UK.

An increasing number of initiatives in education for sustainability under the dominant sustainable development paradigm are, however, now being recorded. (Sterling gives a very useful list of contacts and websites – see the notes to this chapter.) Some of them are clearly cognate with education for deep sustainability as I have been arguing for it. An example to be going on with is Frijof Capra's Center for Ecoliteracy in California. The website for this identifies examples of what it calls 'effective schools'. These connect children with the natural world through programmes and projects outside the classroom, such as school gardens, habitat restoration, and communicating their experience in nature through painting and poetry. They teach students about the people, history, culture and natural features of their local community and region. And they address 'whole children', recognizing that children's ability to learn is affected by their health and wellbeing, and that these are in turn affected by such factors as nutrition, exercise and the health of the natural environment.

This is evidently the kind of template for effective education which needs to be used in building capacity for the open learning society. It can be applied at the university as well as the school level. Here and there, particular universities have brought faculty and students together with local communities to address sustainability issues in relation to local forest ecosystems, local transportation and urban development. These collaborations, releasing and revaluing subjugated but sharply relevant local knowledges, have in turn helped to begin the development of an institutional learning culture within the university. A university, in fact, uniquely combines the local and the global – it is essentially about *seeing the whole picture*, across both space and time, while also an institution with a place-specific identity and history, rooted in local habitats, neighbourhoods, cultures and resources, both rural and urban. Focusing on practical sustainability challenges arising at these local roots can stimulate it not just to become a learning institution in respect of its management and administrative structures, but also to cross departmental and disciplinary boundaries in bringing together historical, legal, sociological, cultural and scientific expertise and imagination. While such liberated imagination still very rarely informs the academic curriculum itself, there is no reason in principle why it should not spur on the necessary re-invention of a liberal education for our time.

The spirit of all this, as in the areas of enterprise and governance, is to see sustainability education as a matter of genuinely widening our options: not just options to reskill ourselves as required, but options to understand our situation, imagine possibilities and create the emergent future as we go on. This is surely the point about education in general which the humanist psychologist Carl Rogers was making when he wrote in the 1960s that:

> *The goal of education, if we are to survive, is the facilitation of change and learning. The only man who is educated is the man who has learned how to learn; the man who has learned how to adapt and change; the man who has realized that no knowledge is secure, that only the process of seeking knowledge gives a basis for security.*

Writing only a little later, he could equally have said, 'Only a society actively committed to fostering open-loop learning offers itself a basis for sustainability.'

8

The Politics of Reality

For there to be any chance that humanity as a whole might win the climate war, we in Britain are going to need before very long a political coalition around the key idea of carbon rationing. I have already said as much as I am going to say (between these covers, anyway) about the case for this. Here, by way of epilogue, I want briefly to anticipate the politics of it.

The necessary coalition, whether formally a government or operating as a working agreement on legislative action, will require the mainstream parties to come together at least on this issue, transcending any differences of substance which might characterize their approach to it. *But the coalition will be the stronger, and success the more likely, the more such differences there are to transcend.* I hope that assertion will sound less counter-intuitive than it otherwise might have done, in the light of what Part III has been arguing about the importance of widening and deepening our options. But it nevertheless represents a strikingly different kind of thought from the approach to these matters which has established itself in recent years.

Ever since the green turn betook itself to politics, Greens have claimed to offer a radical break from the traditional dialogue between left and right. Green parties defined themselves not in terms of, but in direct contrast to, this dialogue and the political spectrum over which it was conducted – 'Neither left nor right, but out in front!' Aspiring Green politicians, and in due course a small but vocal band of practising ones, were to be heard excoriating the 'grey' parties for continuing to debate and contest the old issues of equality versus incentive, planning and regulation versus individual and corporate freedom, capital versus labour, when what now really mattered was the swiftly worsening ecological state of the planet and the way it was threatening everyone's future. Only if this were firmly emphasized as the central organizing concern, and the remaining questions of class, culture and ideological habit dividing conventional politicians allowed to fall into place around it, could society find an adequate political response to its real predicament.

Green parties, as such, haven't been very successful so far. They have achieved at best a limited share of power in various local, and briefly a few national, jurisdictions. But this vision of what is needed has been significantly more successful than they have – a fact which their undeterred insistence on promoting one version of it tends, if anything, to disguise. It has succeeded, of course, as sustainable development; that is, as the acceptance of that paradigm into mainstream political debate, not just as a way to understand environmental problems, but as the only conceptual and practical basis for greening real political action which the mainstream recognizes. Environmental issues are not yet seen as the central, all-dominating problem framework – not even climate change, the most urgently pressing of them. But as the evidence accumulates and they begin to climb up the agenda, something like a reframing of the broader political landscape on that basis is starting to happen. If turn-of-the-century geopolitics has left global capitalism as the only game in town, we are quite rapidly coming to see sustainable development as the only strategy for continuing to play it.

I have argued throughout the book that this now-hegemonic model of sustainability based on the Brundtland bargain is conceptually and structurally flawed. I have also sought to show how, to the extent that we actually pursue and try to implement it rather than just more-or-less eagerly talking about it, these flaws are likely to set us off in pursuit of a mirage – the politics of never getting there. If I am right about this, and meanwhile sustainable development goes on being the only model which politicians understand for greening the only game in town, our prospects are frightening.

But it is not – let's be honest – by any means clear yet whether I am right. My critique began from the palpable ineffectuality of the model to date, moved into an attack on its ethico-scientistic conceptual core, and then used the weaknesses identified to interpret various practical manifestations which seemed significant in the light of the attack. As I freely acknowledged, however, this very approach means that the case is certainly not proven by the examples of purported mirage-pursuit which I have cited. There would need to be a much more long-established and indisputably characterized pattern of such manifestations before one could claim any very strong empirical warrant for my analysis. The trouble is, as I have also noted here and there, that in the nature of the case we can't simply wait on events to prove or disprove an argument about the operational inadequacy of sustainable development. By all serious accounts, the threshold beyond which self-reinforcing feedbacks will trigger unstoppable global warming is not now far ahead. In that situation, the chance of being vindicated by time is also the near-certainty of its by then being too late for vindication to matter any more.

The real problem is that sustainable development lacks at the moment its *necessary antagonist* – the counterforce against which any argument and any interpretation, as well as any practical strategy, must be pitted if its robustness is to be properly tested. The main nodes of political thought and action have always been broad requirements, like equality or freedom, which were essentially contested in this way (equality of opportunity or outcome, freedom *of* capitalist enterprise or *from* its consequences ... ?). At the moment, however, while there may be disagreement and argument as to best implementation within the sustainable development model of sustainability, that model itself rules uncontested. Absent any counterforce, it is likely to survive critique, and go on informing (or deforming) practice, by default. I have tried to describe an alternative conceptual framework and mindset. But, just as such, that offers only a different way of representing what we are doing and might do. The key question is how to put it to the proof of real debate, contest and experiment.

What we urgently need around sustainability, in other words, is some genuine political *differentiation*. The way that happens in Britain, through long tradition embedded in the structure of our institutions, is by the two main parties, left and right of centre (wherever the centre happens for the moment to be), offering genuinely different positions and policy choices on the key issues.* That means positions which are philosophically distinct in their grounding, as well as pragmatically different in terms of the social forces they seek to bring into play and the laws and practices which they see as required.

The reasons why this is not the case at present as regards sustainability have, of course, in part to do with the way the dominant sustainable development model expresses strong dispositions and tendencies in the contemporary frame of mind, some of which we have noted in this book – the recoil from human complexity into scientism, the ethicized surrogates for lapsed meaning. But they are also in part historical. Ecological responsibility as sustainable development, as a recognizably coherent, realistic green analysis and prescription, first emerged into the political mainstream under the most right-wing, neo-liberal government Britain had seen for long decades, that of Margaret Thatcher. A very great deal of the initial emphasis was thus on encouraging and supporting *individual* responsibility in these matters. Then, in the mid-1990s, at about the time when the 'hard-political' sustainability problems, and especially that of climate change, were becoming visibly more pressing, there came an electoral reaction from a fast-unravelling Thatcherism to the brightly vacuous would-be inclusiveness of New Labour. In this camp, the possibilities offered by sustainable development for moralizing afflatus combined with centralized tinkering posing no threat to anyone – for characteristic bad faith, in fact – were found irresistible. A mildly managerial, intervention-lite conception of sustainable development correspondingly became the decisive mainstream model, sealed officially with the establishment of a standing body, the Sustainable Development Commission. Subsequently, as reality started to force its way in from around the beginning of the new century and sustainability considerations began to graduate from the rhetorical to the practical agenda, this was the only available paradigm for planning and policy. At the same time, three election defeats had forced the right to move cautiously back onto this now central terrain of earnest concern, fiscal tweaking and

---

* I confine the immediate terms of my argument to Britain, simply as the only polity in which I am at home. Readers from elsewhere will readily translate these terms, *mutatis mutandis*, into those of their own political culture and arrangements.

restrained regulation, and thus to come up with policies in this arena varying only in minor emphases from those of the government. This is roughly where we are now.

But need things stay that way? What are the possibilities for real, rather than cosmetic, political differentiation on these issues?

In this context, it needs to be recognized that you can be drawn to the deep sustainability paradigm, as I have sketched it, from more than one direction. At the core of that paradigm we might put doing whatever it takes to deal with the most immediate threats – endorsement of carbon rationing within contraction and convergence seeming like a good criterion of sincerity here – and finding the necessary motivation in the fact that our current way of going on is humanly insupportable, rather than insufficiently careful in managing the future. You could find that attractive, as I do, because like me you started as a fairly radical Green, initially welcomed the sustainable development consensus as evidence that your concerns were being taken seriously, and then began to realize the structurally compromised and essentially equivocal nature of that model when we actually come to operationalizing it. But there are other and equally valid routes. You could, for instance, get to the same position just from a desire for a sustainability policy which is effective by giving as much freedom as possible to entrepreneurial creativity and reining back the regulatory state. I hope to have said enough in the last couple of chapters to show why these aspects of deep sustainability in practice would not be arbitrary or accidental. They would reflect the need for open learning and the exploratory creation of options, which go with turning from the attempted balancing of long-term future consequences to a focus on present meaningfulness. Thus, what seems to follow from the desirability of that turn, or re-turn, can also follow independently from a long-standing and classically respectable right-of-centre position on economic and political liberty.

Another pathway to deep sustainability leads from the desire to emphasize cultural continuity and a collective responsibility to the past as well as the future, rather than an exclusively forward-looking focus and a tacit ideal of human perfectibility. The questions of life-meaning with which sustainability issues must engage, on my alternative model, work at a human depth which the politics of 'things can only get better' has simply forgotten. In similar vein, some may be drawn by the thought that the fundamental framework of law which holds society together should be warranted by our evolving conception of human meaning, and not by an exclusively utilitarian emphasis on human welfare. The 'welfare state' created by the post-1945 settlement has never really broken down: on the contrary, it has eaten up all other aspects of the state, in a way which would have horrified its original proponents, though it has changed its own initially statist and centralist face somewhat in the process. The only real test of policy in almost any field has for long been its effects on the 'standard of living', considered in essentially material terms. We are left, con_ _uently, with a politics of mere welfare-administration across the board. Many will feel that a public discourse requiring of its leaders that they are at least able to speak coherently and wisely about the more profound human issues – a politics appropriate to creatures with souls – would be worth having back for its own sake. Here, too, deep sustainability should resonate with serious concerns which have traditionally been expressed from the rightward end of the political spectrum.

I am not suggesting anything so crude as a polarization which would simply place sustainable development on the left and deep sustainability on the right of this spectrum. Matters are far too complex for that. These demanding new issues are already shifting and recombining some central elements of the ideological packages which used to define political debate. A strong concern for equity has not hitherto been thought of as characterizing the right, for instance – any more than acceptance of human aspirations as needing to operate within naturally given limits has been typical of the left. Both these elements must now figure in any politics of sustainability, however it is to be imagined. But still on this new terrain, there will be recognizable the old, long-standing differences between an interventionist and directive cast of mind, on the one hand, and a more libertarian, open-ended spirit on the other. The tendency to see the state as a human invention which can be refashioned and recalibrated to match any human purposes will still run counter to the tendency to regard it as something more organic, with its own inner principles of growth and development. These differences will remain because they express deep and permanently countervailing dispositions in human affairs. Really to get the environmental agenda into the mainstream would not be to transcend them as outmoded, to be replaced with some now shared ideology of ecologism (even if we call it, less alarmingly, 'sustainable development'). Rather it would be to make the environmental problematic the inevitable ground on which these abiding differences of feeling and experience are deployed and contested.

This being so, there is no denying that the now-standard sustainable development model, with its inherent ethico-scientism, does tend to insist on a more directive and interventionist approach than deep sustainability, with its emphasis on exploratory creativity and open-endedness, would be likely to do. Suppose that deep difference came to be reflected in the terms of actual political argument and proposal on the new terrain of sustainability. That might mean the alternative government offering genuinely alternative policies across the fields considered in Chapter 7, for instance. These would include policies empowering a robustly deliberative localism in governance and a reintegrated humane education in schools and colleges. Crucially, too, they would support far-reaching business freedom to create real option value for all the multiple forms of materials and energy supply and usage throughout the economy. If the mainstream politics of sustainability were to be increasingly differentiated in these ways, we should not be losers but gainers. Or rather, losing the false security of an untested and possibly self-defeating consensus, we should be investing in a collective political and social capital enriched by much-increased option value – by a genuine diversity of understanding and potential response in the face of whatever practical difficulties emerge as we go on.

So this is one way, through the standard dialogue of parties, in which a deep-sustainability perspective should diversify and strengthen the political resources which we have available for dealing with our situation. But there is another key contribution which it could make, which may at this stage be even more important. That is to the wider politics, beyond parties, where movements of thought and action originate and where significant social change increasingly takes place. We shall certainly need a substantial and rapid mind-shift in this wider arena, as well as in the representative electoral politics of Westminster, if we are to face up to the demands of the climate war.

What that now surely requires, in fact, is a huge popular campaign for carbon rationing. This would probably need to be launched by some of the major organizations in the field working in collaboration. Equally, the collaboration would be stronger, the wider the diversity of such organizations: ideally they would include not just the wildlife and heritage NGOs, as well as the environmental campaigners, but also the churches, the physical and mental health groups, the teaching unions ... . A campaign launched nationally would, however, need to develop very rapidly a vigorous local life and presence, because its initial pitch would have to be public education, and it is in local events and activities that such work is best done. This is already familiar territory for campaigners. Screenings of *An Inconvenient Truth* with follow-up speakers are already being promoted by various environmental groups across the country. Events like these in every town and village, but supplemented by an effectively packaged introduction to the principles of rationing, demonstrations of computer software for managing a typical family carbon budget, and displays placing the whole business in its C&C context of international responsibility, would be a natural development. They would also be straightforward to organize if the will was there. Organizationally more demanding, but perfectly possible in technical terms, would be to build a national on-line community of people running their own shadow carbon allocations and comparing notes on the results – perhaps with some significant incentives at stake. The overall aim of all such education and consciousness-raising could be to ratchet up the pressure on constituency MPs and on government nationally to endorse a draft enabling bill in the course of the next Parliament.

And could such a popular campaign for *rationing* ever get off the ground? Would people in sufficient numbers actually sign up to practical proposals for restricting themselves in this kind of way? Not, we can be reasonably sure, while the appeal was still being mounted in the classic sustainable development terms: 'We must do this now for the sake of the future!' Interest, unease? – yes; endorsement in principle? – very possibly. But real, active, life-changing support? – let's shift channels, who's got the remote ... ?

But for an appeal at the level of deep sustainability – an appeal confronting people explicitly and unflinchingly with something like my Faustus test, the demand to challenge their own life-meaning directly on these issues – the outcome might be very much less predictable. Such an appeal would certainly have to have a distinctly revivalist and even missionary zeal to it, as opposed to the tones of earnest popular-scientific elucidation with which campaigning environmentalism has now got comfortable. But here I return to my often repeated point (it can't really be repeated too often): we must gain a working majority for far-reaching and irreversible change *within a decade*, or the cause is lost. In face of that stark urgency, it is surely clear that only something with the effect of a spiritual revival is going to do the job. Of course it must not be factitiously quasi-religious, which would be the kiss of death. But it must engage people at that kind of level – speaking to their passions, fears, self-doubt, recoil from emptiness and capacity for life-hope, as well as their reason and conscience – if it is really to move them to action. Only the release of such elemental forces has the chance of generating the moral energy we now need. And the deep-sustainability perspective offers a way of articulating all these issues at the level where such forces await release.

These, then, are the essential political components of an effective drive towards carbon rationing in Britain: differentiation and diversification around sustainability in mainstream electoral politics, and a wider movement speaking decisively from the human depths. The alternative vision developed in this book is central to both.

Political differentiation would mean that the actual legislative coalition, when the popular will compels it into being, would draw on the strengths of the sustainable development model as well as avoiding its weaknesses. Those strengths are all in its science-based pragmatism, while its weaknesses come down to the slipperiness of its alleged ethical grounding and its tendency to implausible prescriptivity. The corresponding strengths of a deep-sustainability understanding are its endorsement of creativity and open-endedness and its much more robust model of motivation. At the same time, the degree of turbulence and chanciness to which it must commit us, and the sheer demandingness of facing up to life-meaning rather than placating ourselves with gestures, will by many be found very daunting. We will need active alertness to all these faces of our predicament, and a handiness with our whole armoury of possible responses, if we are to master our fate.

The most successful coalition government in recent British history, and the one which we must surely therefore now set as our standard, was the Churchill coalition which fought and won World War II. This coalition was strong because it drew both on people who knew that Hitler had to be fought because a Nazi-dominated Europe would extinguish the prospects for socialism, and on people who detested the prospect of socialism and knew that Hitler had to be fought to preserve the traditional values which would resist its triumph. Politicians of these very different ideological persuasions were pulled together in response to a clear and uncompromising popular demand that victory be fought for anyway, at whatever cost. Their collaboration held such unchallenged sway for five

Notes

Preface: Sustainability, Mirage and Reality

pxiii *The scientific consensus is now telling us*: see, for instance, the Fourth Assessment Report of the UN's Intergovernmental Panel on Climate Change, published in November 2007; for details see www.ipcc.ch/.

pxiv *a slow-motion nuclear holocaust*: see the Strategic Survey 2007 from the International Institute for Strategic Studies – details at www.iiss.org/publications/strategic-survey-2007/.

pxv *the Brundtland Commission*: the World Commission on Environment and Development, chaired by Gro Harlem Brundtland. See its report *Our Common Future* (Oxford: Oxford University Press, 1987).

pxv *Paul Ekins*: Professor of Energy and Environment Policy at King's College, London. The article quoted appeared under the title 'Path of least resistance' in *The Guardian*, 13 February 2008.

pxviii *as Hegel claimed*: quoted in Karl Jaspers, *The Idea of the University* trans. Reide and Vanderschmidt (London: Peter Owen, 1965).

PART I: WHAT'S WRONG WITH SUSTAINABLE DEVELOPMENT?

p1 *Epigraph*: from *Nineteen Eighty-Four*, Part II, Section IX

Chapter 1: The Sustainability Horizon

p3 *the Stern Report*: originally produced as a report for the Cabinet Office and HM Treasury in October 2006, now available in book form as: Nicholas Stern, *The Economics of Climate Change* (Cambridge: Cambridge University Press, 2007).

p4 *Carson, Commoner and others*: see, for the key texts: Rachel Carson, *Silent Spring* (London: Hamilton, 1963); Barry Commoner, *The Closing Circle: Confronting the Environmental Crisis* (London: Cape, 1972); Edward Goldsmith and others, *A Blueprint for Survival* (Harmondsworth: Penguin, 1972); E. F. Schumacher, *Small is Beautiful: A Study of Economics as if People Mattered* (London: Abacus, 1974).

p6 *the Sustainable Development Strategy of the UK Government*: Department of Environment, Food and Rural Affairs, *Securing the Future* (London: The Stationery Office, 2005) – also downloadable from www.sustainable-development.gov.uk/publications/uk-strategy/index.htm.

p10 *the 'Ehrlich equation'*: see Paul and Anne Ehrlich, *The Population Explosion* (London: Hutchinson, 1990). Paul Ekins's discussion is in his chapter 'Making development sustainable' in *Global Ecology: A New Arena of Political Conflict*, edited by Wolfgang Sachs (London: Zed Books, 1993).

p10 *As the Sustainable Development Commission observed*: Sustainable Development Commission, *Redefining Prosperity: Resource Productivity, Economic Growth and Sustainable Development* (2003). The report is available to download from www.sd-commission.org.uk/publications.php?id=41.

p11 *survey in the early 1990s*: quoted in James Blake, 'Overcoming the value–action gap in environmental policy: Tensions between national policy and local experience', *Local Environment*, vol 4, no 3, pp257–278 (1999).

p11 *DEFRA's 2007 survey of public attitudes*: downloadable from www.defra.gov.uk/environment/statistics/pubatt/index.htm.

p11 *easy politics of the environment*: the distinction between the easy and hard politics of the environment was first made by Tom Burke in 'The buck stops everywhere', *New Statesman*, 20 June 1997.

p14 *Increasing recognition of these realities*: see Paul Hawken, Amory B. Lovins and L. Hunter Lovins, *Natural Capitalism: The Next Industrial Revolution* (London: Earthscan, 2000); Paul Ekins, *Economic Growth and Environmental Sustainability: The Prospects for Green Growth* (London: Routledge, 1999); Jonathon Porritt, *Capitalism as if the World Matters* (London: Earthscan, 2005).

Chapter 2: Pursuing the Mirage

p17 *the astronomer Fred Hoyle*: as quoted in Norman Myers, *The Gaia Atlas of Planet Management* (London: Good Books, 1985).

p19 *a recent report by the Sustainable Development Commission*: *The Role of Nuclear Power in a Low Carbon Economy* (March 2006), constituting part of the Commission's input to the 2006 Energy Review in the UK. Downloadable from www.sd-commission.org.uk/publications.php?id=344.

p21 *my Lancaster colleague John Urry*: see his paper 'The complexity turn', *Theory, Culture & Society*, vol 22, no 5, pp1–14 (2005).

p21 *Kuhn and his successors*: Thomas Kuhn, *The Structure of Scientific Revolutions* (Chicago: University of Chicago Press, 1962). See also, for example, Peter Medawar, *The Art of the Soluble* (London: Methuen, 1967); Brian Wynne, 'Uncertainty and environmental learning: Reconceiving science and policy in the preventive paradigm', *Global Environmental Change*, vol 2, no 2 (1992); Sheila Jasanoff, 'New modernities – Re-imagining science, technology and development', *Environmental Values*, vol 11, no 3 (2002).

p22 *A succession of science-related environmental controversies*: as well described by Robin Grove-White, 'Afterword: On "sound science", the environment and political authority', *Environmental Values*, vol 8, no 2 (1999).

p22 *'test site' parameters*: 'The end-points chosen for observation, which perforce represent all conceivable "environmental change", are limited by various artificial requirements, such as the exclusion of birds because they circulate wider than the single-farm "laboratory"' – Brian Wynne, *The Guardian*, 16 September 1999.

p23 *a very revealing exchange*: as quoted by Brian Wynne, 'GMO risk assessment under conditions of biological (and social) complexity', a paper given at an EU conference on GMOs and precautionary policies, Vienna, April 2006.

p24 *the American historian of science Theodore Porter*: Theodore M. Porter, *Trust in Numbers: The Pursuit of Objectivity in Science and Public Life* (Princeton, NJ: Princeton University Press, 1995).

p26 *the 2007 set of indicators*: *Sustainable Development Indicators in your Pocket 2007*, published by the Department of Environment, Food and Rural Affairs (www.defra.gov.uk).

p28 *Real-world natural systems*: for several of the points in these paragraphs, see Orrin Pilkey and Linda Pilkey-Jarvis, *Useless Arithmetic: Why Environmental Scientists Can't Predict the Future* (New York: Columbia University Press, 2007), especially Chapter 9.

p30 *research on the GM issue*: published as Claire Marris, Brian Wynne et al, *Public Perceptions of Agricultural Biotechnologies in Europe: Final Report of the PABE Research Project* (Lancaster University: CSEC, 2001).

p33 *Jean-Paul Sartre*: the key text is his *Being and Nothingness* (trans. Hazel Barnes, London: Methuen, 1958), especially Chapter 2.

p34 *George Eliot's comment on Matthew Jermyn*: in *Felix Holt, the Radical*, Chapter 9.

p37 *various forms of denial*: a piece of research on this topic rapidly acquiring classic status is Suzanne Stoll-Kleeman et al, 'The psychology of denial concerning climate mitigation measures', *Global Environmental Change*, vol 11, pp107–117 (2001).

p38 *the original 'ecological footprint' concept*: as set out by Mathis Wackernagel and William Rees in *Our Ecological Footprint* (Gabriola Island, BC: New Society Press, 1996).

p42 *Prince Charles ... Jonathon Porritt*: both quotations are from Porritt's *Capitalism as if the World Matters* (London: Earthscan, 2005), Chapter 16 ('Visions and values').

p42 *the former UK government's 1990 White Paper*: *This Common Inheritance: Britain's Environmental Strategy* (London: HMSO, 1990).

p46 *John Locke*: see his *Two Treatises of Government*, edited by Peter Laslett (Cambridge: Cambridge University Press, 1988).

p50 *James Lovelock in his latest book:* James Lovelock, *The Revenge of Gaia* (London: Allen Lane, 2006).

Chapter 3: Mirage Politics

p57 *The Energy Review of 2006*: the government's report on the Energy Review, 'The energy challenge', was released in July 2006, full text at www.berr.gov.uk/energy/review/page31995.html.

p58 *St Augustine*: *Confessions*, Book VIII, section 7.

p58 *a prominent anti-wind-farm website*: www.countryguardian.net, where the argument that intermittently operated capacity produces more CO_2 per kilowatt-hour than if operated continuously can also be found. The Club of Rome Report is available as Dennis L. Meadows et al., *The Limits To Growth* (New York: Universe Books, 1972).

p60 *The manifesto on which it had been elected*: 'We will safeguard our environment, and develop an integrated transport policy to fight congestion and pollution.' See www.bbc.co.uk/election97/background/parties/manlab/labman.html.

p60 *'I will have failed ...'* 'It's a tall order but I urge you to hold me to it.' *Hansard* (1998-10-20).

p60 *a medium-term transport strategy*: *Transport 2010*, published July 2000 by the (then) Department of the Environment, Transport and the Regions.

p61 *private motoring a comparatively more attractive option*: the figures quoted were cited by David Millward, Transport Correspondent, in *The Daily Telegraph*, 12 April 2007.

p63   *this brilliant cameo case-study*: at p44 of his book already cited.

p64   *A report from the UN's Intergovernmental Panel on Climate Change had strongly implied*: findings of Working Group I for the Fourth Assessment Report, released in February 2007 – again, see www.ipcc.ch/.

p64   *the Global Carbon Project*: see www.globalcarbonproject.org.

p64   *leaked documents seen by* The Guardian: 'Labour's plans to abandon renewable energy targets', *The Guardian*, 23 October 2007.

p64   *retired Chief Scientific Advisor, Sir David King*: in a speech to the 'Decarbonising the UK' Conference, London, September 2005, quoted by Monbiot in his book *Heat: How to Stop the Planet Burning* (London: Allen Lane, 2006), p41.

p65   *Another leaked briefing paper*: 'Revealed: Cover-up plan on energy target', *The Guardian*, 13 August 2007.

PART II: DEEP SUSTAINABILITY

p67   *Epigraph*: from Edward O. Wilson, 'Prologue' in *Biophilia: The Human Bond with Other Species* (Cambridge, MA: Harvard University Press, 1984).

Chapter 4: Shifting the Focus

p73   *Peter Singer*: see his own chapter 'All animals are equal' in his edited collection *Applied Ethics* (Oxford: Oxford University Press, 1986).

p74   *150,000 additional deaths*: see Jonathan A. Patz et al, 'Impact of regional climate change on human health', *Nature*, vol 438, pp310–317 (17 November 2005).

p78   *a report from the Conservative Party's Quality of Life Policy Group*: *Blueprint for a Green Economy: Submission to the Shadow Cabinet*, September 2007, downloadable from www.qualityoflifechallenge.com – see section 2.1.2.5.

p78   *pamphlet from ... the Fabian Society*: Roger Levett, with Ian Christie, Michael Jacobs and Riki Therivel, *A Better Choice of Choice: Quality of Life, Consumption and Economic Growth* (London: Fabian Society, 2003).

p79   'affluenza': a number of recent books have picked up on this neat term – see, for instance, John de Graaf et al, *Affluenza: The All-Consuming Epidemic* (San Francisco, CA: Berrett-Koehler, 2005).

p80   *consumption can't make a fully human life*: see Thomas Carlyle, *Past and Present* (1843); Charles Dickens, *Hard Times* (1854); John Ruskin, *Unto This Last* (1860); Matthew Arnold, *Culture and Anarchy* (1869); William Morris, *News from Nowhere* (1890).

p83   *as Mark Lynas acidly puts it*: in 'Can shopping save the planet?', *The Guardian*, 17 September 2007.

Chapter 5: 'Life Goes On'

p87   *Marlowe's play*: Christopher Marlowe, *Dr Faustus* (1604) – see any edition of the complete plays.

p87   *As George Monbiot has pointed out*: in Chapter 1 of *Heat* (already cited).

p92   *death-camp survivor Viktor Frankl*: his classic work on this theme is *Man's Search for Meaning: An Introduction to Logotherapy* (New York: Simon and Schuster, 1984).

p93 *the 'fat relentless ego'*: see Iris Murdoch, *The Sovereignty of Good* (London: Routledge and Kegan Paul, 1970).

p94 *'the force that through the green fuse drives the flower'*: the first line, and title, of a poem by Dylan Thomas.

p95 *D. H. Lawrence*: see his *Studies in Classic American Literature* (London: Heinemann, 1964), the chapter on Benjamin Franklin and also the Introduction.

p96 *in Iris Murdoch's words*: from her book already cited – the chapter on 'The idea of perfection'.

p97 *'ambassador from the kingdom of fun'*: as I remember, this lovely phrase comes from Milan Kundera's novel *The Unbearable Lightness of Being*.

p99 *this stark but realistic challenge*: p15 of Monbiot's book cited above.

p101 *La Rochefoucauld:* Francois, Duc de La Rochefoucauld, *Maximes* (Paris: Morgand, 1883).

p104 *'one is always nearer ...'*: from Thom Gunn's poem 'On the move' in *My Sad Captains* (London: Faber, 1961).

p105 *the Millennium Ecosystem Assessment*: see *Ecosystems and Human Wellbeing*, available at www.millenniumassessment.org.

p105 *Mark Lynas has an image which is very telling*: in his *Six Degrees: Our Future on a Hotter Planet* (London: Fourth Estate, 2007), p254.

p106 *Al Gore in the book of the film*: *An Inconvenient Truth: The Planetary Emergency of Global Warming and What We Can Do About It* (London: Bloomsbury, 2006), p11.

p10ᴜ *'This is a moral issue ...'*: see, for instance, his speech to the New York University School of Law, September 2006, available at www.nyu.edu/newscalendars/ 2006_2007/gore/index.html.

p107 *'Is there nothing beyond my fellow-man?'*: D. H. Lawrence, *Selected Letters* (Harmondsworth: Penguin Books, 1950), p105 – from a letter to Catherine Carswell about the First World War ('This is what the love of our neighbour has brought us to ... a madness of righteousness.')

p108 *some lines of Yeats*: from 'Under Ben Bulben', the last of his *Collected Poems* (London: Macmillan, 1967).

PART III: GREENING OUR LUCK

p113 *Epigraph*: from Churchill's first speech to the House of Commons as Prime Minister, 13 May 1940.

Chapter 6: Making the Break: The Carbon Framework

p116 *single-loop ... double-loop learning*: a distinction first identified in Argyris, C. and D. Schon, *Theory in Practice: Increasing Professional Effectiveness* (San Francisco, CA: Jossey-Bass, 1974).

p118 *von Hayek*: the quotation is from his *The Constitution of Liberty* (London: Routledge and Kegan Paul, 1960).

p122 *the present Foreign Secretary*: at the time of writing, David Miliband, MP. The talk in question was the Audit Commission Annual Lecture given on 19 July 2006 (see www.defra.gov.uk/corporate/ministers/speeches/david-miliband/dm060719. htm for the text).

p124 *the UK currently contributes something over 2 per cent*: according to data collected in 2004 for the UN by the Carbon Dioxide Information Analysis Centre (CDIAC) within the US Department of Energy.

p124 *The average citizen of India*: again, from CDIAC data.

p124 *Aubrey Meyer, the man behind it*: from his book *Contraction and Convergence: The Global Solution to Climate Change* (Totnes: Green Books, 2000).

p126 *endorsement for the principle ... of C&C*: these endorsements are listed variously in Meyer's book and in Mayer Hillman, *How We Can Save the Planet* (London: Penguin Books, 2004).

p130 *recognizing and welcoming an ethical constraint*: see, for instance, James Garvey's book *The Ethics of Climate Change* (London: Continuum, 2008), where this position is set out with admirable clarity.

Chapter 7: Widening our Options

p137 *the best recent book in this field*: Paul Hawken, Amory Lovins and Hunter Lovins, *Natural Capitalism: The Next Industrial Revolution* (London: Earthscan, 2000). The two longer quotations are from Chapters 4 and 8 respectively.

p139 *real option value*: see Steve Gough's paper 'Increasing the value of the environment: A "real options" metaphor for learning', *Environmental Education Research*, vol 8, no 1, pp61–71 (2002).

p139 *recent thinking has applied it to physical as well as financial assets*: see Martha Amram and Nalin Kulatilaka, *Real Options: Managing Strategic Investment in an Uncertain World* (Boston, MA, Harvard Business School Press, 1999). The Nobel Prize mentioned was awarded to Robert Merton and Myron Scholes in 1997.

p140 *houses incorporating 'smart' technologies*: see, for instance, the Green Alliance pamphlet by Faye Scott, *Teaching Homes to be Green: Smart Homes and the Environment* (Green Alliance, 2007) – downloadable from www.greenalliance.org.uk.

p141 *a variety of methods including*: for a good overview, see Tim Holmes and Ian Scoones, *Participatory Environmental Policy Processes: Experiences from North and South* (Institute of Development Studies, IDS Working Paper 113, 2000).

p143 *Examples of existing approaches*: these and an interesting range of other approaches are described in the New Economics Foundation's *Participation Works! – 21 Techniques of Community Participation for the 21st Century* (NEF, 1998).

p144 *a recent paper ... from* **Demos**: James Wilsdon et al, *The Public Value of Science* (London: Demos, 2005), Available at www.demos.co.uk.

p144 *part of participatory environmental appraisal*: see the NEF publication cited above.

p145 *the Scottish Executive's Action Plan*: Scottish Executive, *Learning for our Future: Scotland's First Action Plan for the UN Decade of Education for Sustainable Development* (Edinburgh: Scottish Executive, 2006). Available for download from www.scotland.gov.uk/Publications/2006/07/25143907/0.

p145 *the green educationalist Stephen Sterling*: in his *Sustainable Education: Revisioning Learning and Change* (Totnes: Green Books, 2001), p60.

p147 *experiments in adapting philosophical enquiry for these age groups*: for more details, see the website of SAPERE (the Society for the Advancement of Philosophical Enquiry and Reflection in Education), www.sapere.net.

p147 *Center for Ecoliteracy*: see www.ecoliteracy.org.

p148 *at the university as well as the school level*: see, in particular, Michael M'Gonigle and Justine Starke, *Planet U: Sustaining the World, Reinventing the University* (Gabriola Island, BC: New Society Publishers, 2006).

p148 *Carl Rogers*: in his *Freedom to Learn* (Columbus, OH: Merrill, 1969).

Chapter 8: The Politics of Reality

p150 *equality or freedom ... essentially contested in this way*: for this analogy, see Michael Jacobs, 'Sustainable development as a contested concept', in *Fairness and Futurity: Essays on Environmental Sustainability and Social Justice*, edited by Andrew Dobson (Oxford: Oxford University Press, 1999). Jacobs, however, discusses only such contestation *within* the sustainable development paradigm.

Index